# A Troubled Constitutional Future

Also by Mary C. Murphy and published by Agenda

*Europe and Northern Ireland's Future: Negotiating Brexit's Unique Case*

# A Troubled Constitutional Future

Northern Ireland after Brexit

**Mary C. Murphy and Jonathan Evershed**

**agenda**
publishing

First published in 2022 by Agenda Publishing

Agenda Publishing Limited
The Core
Bath Lane
Newcastle Helix
Newcastle upon Tyne
NE4 5TF
www.agendapub.com

ISBN 978-1-78821-411-7 (hardcover)
ISBN 978-1-78821-412-4 (paperback)

**British Library Cataloguing-in-Publication Data**
A catalogue record for this book is available from the British Library

Typeset by JS Typesetting Ltd, Porthcawl, Mid Glamorgan
Printed and bound in the UK by CPI Group (UK) Ltd, Croydon, CR0 4YY

# Contents

# Preface

Northern Ireland's politics are characterized, and in large part defined, by volatility, conflict and instability. This is what makes them simultaneously so fascinating and so frustrating. Long before Brexit, attempting to make any hard or fast predictions about the trajectory of these politics had been a difficult undertaking, and arguably something of a fool's errand. Brexit, and the rapid and radical political, cultural and constitutional destabilization that has flowed from it, has made this task all but impossible. The pace of the change and disruption that Brexit has brought in its wake has been exhausting to experience, let alone seek to make sense of. Already at saturation point, just as we were setting out to write this book, the global coronavirus pandemic became yet another source of uncertainty and anxiety and another moving target for us to seek to analyse.

Including as members of the "Between Two Unions" project team, we have been involved in charting the Brexit process in real time since 2016. As both citizens of "these islands" and scholars of their politics, we have watched, often in horror, at the way that events have accelerated since 2016. When the United Kingdom finally, and irrevocably, left the European Union at the end of January 2020, it was an occasion of great sadness for us. We have both worried, above all, about the impact of Brexit on politics and the people we care about in Northern Ireland. It is a place that we love and, frankly, wish that others – particularly (though not exclusively) in the corridors of Whitehall and Westminster – paid closer attention to. Peace and stability in Northern Ireland, and on the island of Ireland more widely, should not be an afterthought. For too many, it remains so.

We are also concerned for the impact of Brexit on the Republic of Ireland: the place we both call home. Brexit's shadow falls here too and its impact will reverberate for many years to come. Factoring Ireland's fate into discussions and decisions is something we believe is not just important, but imperative for the health of the relationship between Britain and Ireland.

This book represents our attempt to keep pace with the impact that Brexit has had in and on Northern Ireland. We have made our best attempt to assess where the different agents involved in shaping Northern Ireland's constitutional future stand after Brexit; the balance of forces shaping the relationships between them; and the implications for the debate about constitutional futures on the island of Ireland. We have no doubt that there are those who will disagree with our analysis, but it has been shaped by several years of close involvement with Brexit's ebb and flow, and we offer it as our considered view of the impact and consequences of this process, at this particular juncture.

For Northern Ireland, Brexit will arguably never be "done". Each time we have finished one draft of this book, something has happened to cause us to reopen the document and begin redrafting to account for how all of the perpetually moving parts have once again been rearranged. We've no doubt that when we finally put this book to bed, some new contingency will problematize one or more of our claims or observations, or even render them false or obsolete. Hopefully, we have more enduringly captured something of the broad thrust of Northern Ireland's "post"-Brexit constitutional politics, and ask forgiveness for anything that has become less relevant or, indeed, true, since we wrote it.

# Acknowledgements

This book is a product of our work on the ESRC-funded project, "Between Two Unions: The Constitutional Future of the Islands After Brexit" (ES/P009441/1). The project facilitated our sustained engagement with a wide community of stakeholders in the Brexit process within and across Great Britain and Ireland, including politicians, civil servants, political advisors, journalists and academics. We are immensely grateful to those who gave of their time and insight and we hope we have done justice to their contributions. Our considerable thanks are owed to our co-members of the "Between Two Unions" project team, whose support has been both inspiring and instrumental. We share this book with these colleagues, who played such an important role in honing our understanding of this Brexit era.

Our gratitude too to the team at Agenda Publishing, particularly Alison Howson for her guidance and encouragement, and to the anonymous reviewer who provided helpful and constructive feedback and advice.

Our thanks to academic colleagues and students at University College Cork for providing a space and opportunity for us to be able to dedicate ourselves to writing this book. Particular thanks are owed to the members of the "Ports, Past and Present" project team, as part of which Jonathan was supported to continue and develop his research on the impact of Brexit on relationships on and between "these islands".

A huge thank you to our friends and families who sustained and supported us during the writing process. This book was written at kitchen tables during a global pandemic, and we are acutely aware that those closest to us must feel like they wrote this book with us! Indeed, that we were able to write it at all owes as much to them as it does to us. So finally, our deepest thanks are owed to Paul and Maia for their unfailing support, their patience and their love.

Mary C. Murphy
Jonathan Evershed
Cork

# Abbreviations

| | |
|---|---|
| ALDE | Alliance of Liberals and Democrats for Europe |
| APNI | Alliance Party of Northern Ireland |
| ARINS | Analysing and Researching Ireland North and South |
| BIC | British–Irish Council |
| BIIGC | British–Irish Intergovernmental Conference |
| CBI | Confederation of British Industry |
| CUWGUR | Constitution Unit Working Group on Unification Referendums |
| DUP | Democratic Unionist Party |
| ERG | European Research Group |
| ESRI | Economic and Social Research Institute |
| IRA | Irish Republican Army |
| JMC(EN) | Joint Ministerial Committee (Europe Negotiations) |
| LCC | Loyalist Communities Council |
| MLA | Member of the Legislative Assembly (Northern Ireland) |
| NSMC | North-South Ministerial Council |
| PBP | People Before Profit |
| PPS | Public Prosecution Service |
| PSNI | Police Service of Northern Ireland |
| RHC | Red Hand Commando |
| SDLP | Social Democratic and Labour Party |
| SNP | Scottish National Party |
| TD | Teachta Dála (member of the Irish parliament) |
| TUV | Traditional Unionist Voice |
| UCUNF | Ulster Conservatives and Unionists – New Force |
| UDA | Ulster Defence Association |
| UFU | Ulster Farmers' Union |
| UKIP | UK Independence Party |
| UUP | Ulster Unionist Party |
| UVF | Ulster Volunteer Force |

# 1

# Introduction

Long before Brexit took shape, the UK's troubled relationship with the EU had left destructive and divisive marks on its internal politics. Deep-rooted and long-held anxieties about the EU's perceived assault on British sovereignty and identity had spawned Eurosceptic parties, had widened divisions within existing political parties and exerted increasing pressure for a referendum on the UK's membership of the EU. Countless column inches, extensive media coverage and hours of political debate about the merits and mistakes of the UK's relationship with the EU had punctuated British politics since its accession and long before the 2016 vote. In the days, months and years after the Brexit referendum, the volume of commentary and critique exploded. In one of the first and best-selling Brexit tomes, Tim Shipman (2016) recounted the extraordinary tale that is the Brexit referendum and its aftermath. It stands as a rigorous and engaging account of that early Brexit period. However, for all its detail, depth and rigour, it is an incomplete and skewed study of the Brexit story because there is little to no consideration of the "Irish question"[1] – the singular issue that would come to dog the UK's withdrawal from the EU. Shipman's omission (or oversight) is emblematic of how and why Brexit has led to a constitutional crisis for the UK and produced a constitutional watershed for the island of Ireland. The critical failure by successive British governments to acknowledge or to understand fully the myriad complexities of the UK's departure from the EU, and its far-reaching political and economic implications for Northern Ireland in particular, created conditions under which some (as of yet undetermined) form of political and constitutional change now seems inevitable.

---

1. The index contains no reference to Northern Ireland, Ireland or the Republic of Ireland.

The 2016 referendum result forced "the Irish question" back to the centre of British politics, heralding a renewed interest in Northern Ireland in "mainland" Britain. Barely discussed during the referendum campaign, Northern Ireland and its border with the Republic of Ireland became the most complex, contested and vexing component of the Brexit withdrawal process (de Mars *et al.* 2018; Murphy 2018a; Cochrane 2020; McCall 2021). With a majority in Northern Ireland having voted Remain, and facing the prospect of a potentially economically disastrous cliff-edge Brexit, Northern Ireland found itself caught between a British government resolved to leave the EU on the hardest possible terms, an Irish state committed to maintaining an open border on the island of Ireland, and an EU intent on protecting the integrity of its single market.

The Withdrawal Agreement reached in October 2019, and specifically its Protocol on Ireland/Northern Ireland, means that Northern Ireland is now subject to a legal and political infrastructure which will mark it as enduringly distinct: as all the more clearly a "place apart". Protracted and heated disagreement between the British government and the EU on the implementation of the Protocol has been keenly felt in Northern Ireland, where it has complicated (and challenged) East–West trading arrangements, intensified existing political tensions and led to street-level loyalist violence. This political agitation and violence is linked to intense unionist insecurity and base fears around how Brexit has "mainstream[ed] discussion on Irish reunification" (Harvey 2018). There are deep and enduring differences between unionism and nationalism as to what constitutional formula is appropriate and desirable for Northern Ireland in the long term. As Northern Ireland marks its one hundredth anniversary, the question of its constitutional future has perhaps never been more open ended, nor the debate about Irish unification more salient.

As a moment of deep economic and political uncertainty and instability, the UK's Brexit legacy has created conditions which may lead to potentially profound constitutional shifts across "these islands". Brexit has produced a "critical (constitutional) moment" for the UK and Ireland: a window of opportunity for the pursuit and achievement of either a new constitutional arrangement, or an altered constitutional settlement for Northern Ireland. This book documents the genesis and extent of the UK's Brexit-related constitutional crisis in terms of how it applies to and impacts on Northern Ireland.

Based on an intensive level of engagement over several years with key stakeholders in the Brexit process in the UK, Ireland and the EU, we identify, track and analyse how the perspectives of key political agents across "these islands" have shifted (and in some cases hardened) in relation to Northern Ireland's constitutional situation. The specific focus here is on how Irish nationalism, Ulster unionism, Northern Ireland's so-called middle- or centre-ground[2] and the British and Irish governments have all been impacted by the Brexit crisis; their role in and responses to the constitutional dynamics which Brexit has unleashed; how they have confronted (and will continue to confront) shifting constitutional foundations; what this means for Northern Ireland's fragile "negative peace"; and how it impacts on relationships on the island of Ireland, and those between Ireland and the UK. By examining the impact and influence of key actors in events during, and perspectives on, Northern Ireland's "constitutional moment", this book seeks to document the relationship between choice and consequence: how the decisions and actions of those actors will be causally decisive in shaping Northern Ireland's future constitutional trajectory.

There is a particular emphasis here on how Brexit has disturbed key elements of Northern Ireland's post-1998 political settlement, which, prior to 2016, had come to be viewed as largely stable. We explore in detail how the UK's exit from the EU has challenged the wider constitutional framework within which the 1998 Belfast/Good Friday Agreement is situated. With the question of Irish unity gaining renewed and sustained traction, this book analyses and unpacks the factors and dynamics that are most likely to be influential and potentially transformative in determining Northern Ireland's constitutional future. Throughout, there is an important cautionary warning about how Brexit, and the existential crisis it has unleashed in and for the UK, produces conditions which, if

---

2.   Throughout, we have used "middle-" or "centre-ground" to refer to those parties, groups and voters who do not define themselves as either nationalist or unionist: as very broadly synonymous, therefore with the designation of "Other" as provided for by the Belfast/Good Friday Agreement and Northern Ireland Act 1998. This is in part because this is how many who designate as such – particularly in the APNI – define their own politics. However, we are aware that it does not capture the full complexity of this particular political space, which also includes those who define as "socialist" or "environmentalist", for example. We use "middle" and "centre" as indicating neutrality on the constitutional question, rather than to imply any judgement that this is necessarily a more "conciliatory" political position.

not timed and managed sensitively, are conducive to upheaval and insta-bility on the island of Ireland. In a situation where substantive (consti-tutional) change is possible, a range of outcomes exist. Nonetheless, in such moments, the possibility of unintended consequences cannot be discounted, and whatever constitutional path transpires, it is one that will inevitably be contested and will ultimately be irreversible.

## "An apparently stable consociational democracy"

Defined by the violence of British colonialism and its legacies, the his-tory of relations between Ireland and Britain is riddled with bloody con-flict (O'Leary 2019a, 2019b, 2019c). For centuries, politics on the island of Ireland were defined by unrest, rebellions and uprisings, and marked by hostility between natives and settlers, Protestants and Catholics, unionists and nationalists. In the early twentieth century, a new phase of anti-colonial struggle and instability marked by war, violence and polit-ical and constitutional upheaval ended with the partition of Ireland. In the south, what was founded as the Irish Free State eventually became the independent Republic of Ireland. In the six north-eastern counties of Protestant majority, Northern Ireland was founded as a "Protestant state for a Protestant people" within the Union. This devolved "Orange State" (Farrell 1980) entrenched patterns of unionist power and anti-Catholic discrimination which, in the late 1960s, catalysed a prolonged period of political violence known euphemistically as "the Troubles".

This conflict would endure for more than a quarter of a century, and it hinged, ultimately, on differing unionist and nationalist interpreta-tions as to the legitimacy of the Northern Irish state and its border(s) with the Republic of Ireland: that is, on the foundational question of sovereignty, and of Northern Ireland's constitutional status. The end of paramilitary violence in Northern Ireland in 1994 changed the politi-cal dynamic and facilitated multi-party talks on a new settlement and a new set of institutions and governance arrangements. Those talks produced the 1998 Belfast/Good Friday Agreement, which signalled a route towards a permanent political realignment, underpinned by a series of interdependent and interlocking institutions. The Agreement forms the basis for devolved power-sharing governance in Northern

Ireland, within North–South and East–West institutional frameworks (see Table 1.1).

The interlocking strands of the Belfast/Good Friday Agreement do not make for a conventional system of governance based on majoritarian democracy. Rather, it is a system based on consociational principles (see Lijphart 1996), which means that it includes provisions designed to accommodate cross-community power-sharing, minority protections, community autonomy and equality, and weighted majority decision-making on contentious issues (O'Leary 1999). The power-sharing system is based on a process of "designation", whereby Members of the Northern Ireland Assembly (MLAs) are required to designate as "Unionist", "Nationalist", or "Other". Within the Northern Ireland Executive, the offices of First Minister and Deputy First Minister are shared, with the First Ministerial role going to the nominee from the largest party, and the Deputy First Ministerial role to that of the largest party of the second largest designation.[3] The d'Hondt method is used to allocate the remaining ministerial posts according to the number of seats each party has in the Assembly.[4] This guarantees proportionate representation within the Executive for both unionists and nationalists. Key decisions of the Northern Ireland Assembly require cross-community support, achieved through the use of one of two methods: parallel consent or weighted majority.[5] Critics argue that these kinds of consociational prescriptions formalize, legitimize, and perhaps even entrench ethnic bloc politics (see, e.g., Dixon 1997; Taylor 2009). The Alliance Party is especially critical of how their choice to designate

---

3. As of 2016, the joint office of First Minister and Deputy First Minister has been known as the Executive Office. Under the terms of the 1998 Belfast/Good Friday Agreement, the First and Deputy First Ministers were originally appointed on a joint ticket requiring cross-community consent. These terms of appointment were amended by the 2006 St Andrews Agreement.

4. The Northern Ireland Executive comprises the First Minister, Deputy First Minister and eight departmental ministers. Currently, the DUP have three posts (including First Minister); Sinn Féin have three posts (including Deputy First Minister); the UUP, SDLP and Alliance Party have one ministerial portfolio each.

5. Parallel consent requires a majority of those present and voting, including a majority of the unionist and nationalist designations present and voting. Weighted majority requires that at least 60 per cent of members are present and voting, including at least 40 per cent of each of the unionist and nationalist designations present and voting.

**Table 1.1** The three strands of the Belfast/Good Friday Agreement (1998)

| Stand | Characteristic | Institutions |
|---|---|---|
| Strand 1 | Internal | A directly elected 108-member* Northern Ireland Assembly operates on a cross-community basis with full legislative and executive control over "transferred matters" (and some reserved matters). |
| Strand 2 | North–South | The North/South Ministerial Council (NSMC) comprises representatives from the Irish government and the devolved Northern Ireland administration. It meets in sectoral and plenary format "to develop consultation, co-operation and action within the island of Ireland – including through implementation on an all-island and cross-border basis – on matters of mutual interest within the competence of the Administrations, North and South" (Strand 2, para 1).** |
| Strand 3 | East–West | The British–Irish Council comprises representatives from the UK and Irish governments; representatives of the devolved administrations in Scotland, Northern Ireland, and Wales; and representatives from the Isle of Man and Channel Islands. It was established "to promote the harmonious and mutually beneficial development of the totality of relationships among the peoples of these islands" (Strand 3, para 1). It aims to reach agreement on cooperation on matters of mutual interest*** and does so through discussion, consultation and the exchange of information. In addition, the Agreement creates the British–Irish Intergovernmental Conference (BIIGC) which brings together the British and Irish Governments to promote bilateral cooperation at all levels on all matters of mutual interest within the competence of both governments. |

*Notes*: * The size of the Northern Ireland Assembly was reduced to 90 members in 2016.

** The Belfast Agreement stipulates a range of areas for North–South cooperation and implementation: agriculture, education, transport, environment, waterways, social security/social welfare, relevant EU programmes, inland fisheries, aquaculture and marine matters, health, urban and rural development. The work of the NSMC is supported by a series of all-island implementation bodies – one such body is the Special EU Programmes Body (SEUPB) which oversees cross-border EU funding programmes.

*** The Belfast Agreement is less prescriptive in relation to areas of BIC cooperation, when compared to the NSMC. However, the Agreement does suggest that suitable areas for early discussion may include transport links, agricultural issues, environmental issues, cultural issues, health issues, education issues and approaches to EU issues. The work of the BIC has since expanded to 11 work sectors.

*Source*: Adapted from Murphy (2018a: 5).

as "Other" limits the extent of their influence by affording priority to unionist and nationalist ethnic identities (see Farry & Neeson 1998; see also Chapter 5).

The achievement of relative peace and stability in Northern Ireland after 1998 was linked to "a particular conjunction of underlying circumstances which laid the conditions for agreement" (Coakley 2008: 110). These included a sense of fatigue and stalemate among combatants; an openness to compromise among nationalists and unionists in Northern Ireland; determined engagement by the British and Irish governments; and the role played by external brokers (most especially the US, but also the EU). As violence dissipated and the peace process bedded down, the institutions created by the Belfast/Good Friday Agreement produced "an apparently stable consociational democracy" (*ibid.*: 110).

Public and political interest in Northern Ireland subsequently abated, as the "Irish question" which had – to a lesser or greater extent – helped to shape British politics in the twentieth century was roundly felt, finally, to have been settled. Despite being a historic achievement, however, the 1998 Agreement did not signal the end of the Northern Ireland peace process. The new institutions and political arrangements certainly stabilized relations within Northern Ireland, on the island of Ireland and between the UK and Republic of Ireland, but they did not entirely eradicate the basis for division and disagreement between the unionist and nationalist ethno-political blocs. Indeed, for the first two decades after 1998, Northern Ireland's distinctive ethnic dual party system – in which party politics is polarized around a profound constitutional cleavage and ethnonational parties compete for votes *within* their own blocs rather than across the community divide – stubbornly endured (see Mitchell 1991, 1995, 1999). It had been hoped (and even assumed) that the consociational character of the 1998 Agreement would (gradually) lead to the dissipation of strong communal identities (and parties) (see, e.g., McGarry & O'Leary 2004). Instead however, evidence of ethnic outbidding – where more assertive and strident ethnonational parties outflank their more moderate rivals (see, e.g., Horowitz 1985) – saw the Democratic Unionist Party (DUP) and Sinn Féin electorally overtake the Ulster Unionist Party (UUP) and the Social Democratic and Labour Party (SDLP).[6]

---

6. Some scholars recognize the DUP and Sinn Féin as "ethnic tribune" parties. Using this classification: "[V]oting for [such] parties implies some intransigence in

Until recently, the persistent appeal of ethnic parties, combined with the polarizing effect of the ethnic dual party system, exerted a stifling squeeze on Northern Ireland's "middle ground", preventing its electoral growth and limiting space for the expression and representation of identities other than unionist or nationalist. In the aftermath of the Brexit vote and in the context of increased electoral gains for middle-ground parties (and the Alliance Party of Northern Ireland (APNI) in particular), there are some initial signs that traditional voting patterns and dynamics in Northern Ireland may be mutable in ways that are consequential for when and how the constitutional question might be addressed in Northern Ireland, and with what outcome.

Although the 1998 Agreement sought to de-escalate and demilitarize constitutional conflict, it did not ultimately resolve (nor did it seek to finally resolve) the question of Northern Ireland's long-term constitutional status. Instead, it made the final resolution of this question contingent on the will of the majority, in accordance with the "principle of consent". Northern Ireland remains a part of the UK insofar as, and for as long as, this is the will of the majority of its citizens. If, at any time, it appears likely that a majority in Northern Ireland would wish to leave the Union and join with the South in the creation of an island-wide and independent Republic, then the Secretary of State for Northern Ireland – the British cabinet member with responsibility for Northern Ireland – is mandated to call a "border poll": that is, a referendum on the question of Irish unity.[7] Ongoing conflict about Northern Ireland's constitutional status has found expression in the so-called culture war – marked by disputes over parades, symbols, commemorations and language – and has also bled into other areas of policy-making. As Morrow (2017) has lamented, meaningful reconciliation has proven elusive. The post-conflict period has been punctuated and even defined by sporadic

---

advocating the ethnic groups' interests, but does not necessarily entail the increased overall attitudinal polarization implied by outbidding models" (Mitchell, Evans & O'Leary 2009: 403).

7. The precise way in which the Secretary of State is to gauge whether a pro-unity majority exists, as well as the precise details of a border poll, including the referendum question(s), were not laid out in the Belfast/Good Friday Agreement. The UCL Constitution Unit Working Group on Unification Referendums on the Island of Ireland (2021) has sought to clarify these and other technical details of any "border poll".

moments of crisis and periods of institutional suspension and collapse (Birrell & Heenan 2017; Nagle 2018; Murphy & Evershed 2021). Since 1998, the Northern Ireland Assembly and Executive were suspended or in abeyance for a cumulative total of some eight years. Despite the challenges however, the devolution arrangements endured and a delicate, if incomplete, peace survived.

## "The English have placed a bomb under the Irish peace process"

The effect of the Northern Ireland peace process, the Agreement and, in particular, the North–South institutions which it created, was to soften, to the point of invisibility, the border between Northern Ireland and the rest of the island of Ireland. This was critical for nationalists as it legitimated and gave practical and meaningful expression to their Irish identity. The softening of the border between North and South, however, had been in train before the peace process reached its apex in 1998. Joint UK and Irish membership of the EU since 1973 had long supported conditions that facilitated a soft border between North and South. The drive to complete the single European market – kickstarted in the mid-1980s with a 1992 deadline – was influenced by free market economics and premised on the free movement of trade and people. The single market required the removal of barriers and obstacles to the freedom of movement, and led to the elimination of border checkpoints, customs controls and security installations (although this took a little longer to achieve in Northern Ireland). There was a neat and fortuitous link between the practical operation of the EU single market and the political ambition of the 1998 Agreement. Both projects, in different ways and for different reasons, sought to remove the physical border between North and South. Each initiative organically and mutually reinforced the other.

Although the EU played no explicitly political role in Northern Ireland, the fact of UK and Irish membership was significant in helping to create conditions which gradually aided movement towards a peace process in Northern Ireland and then later facilitated its institutional embodiment, the 1998 Belfast/Good Friday Agreement. Firstly, EU membership helped to alter and improve relations between the UK and

Ireland to the point where a joint British–Irish approach to Northern Ireland became possible (see Hayward & Murphy 2018). The institutional structures of the EU reinforced Ireland's status as an independent and sovereign state, equal in political status to its larger neighbour. This was an important enabling context for the young Irish state and lent credence and credibility to Irish calls to be involved in any resolution of the Northern Ireland conflict. EU membership also facilitated dialogue between the two states. It was usual for British and Irish leaders to meet (often quietly and discreetly) on the margins of European Council summit meetings in Brussels. Given the volatility of the security situation in Northern Ireland after 1973, such bilateral engagement was less likely – and invariably more politically risky – in either domestic setting. However, the value of these meetings was significant in allowing both states to gradually shift and redefine their relationship. The process of discussion, influenced by a slowly growing spirit of British–Irish cooperation, played a role in helping both states to understand each other better and to explore ways and means of addressing the conflict. As Nagle notes: "the EU provided the context for close cooperation between [the] UK and Republic of Ireland to flourish, which laid the platform for their joint approach to the GFA [Good Friday Agreement]" (2018: 412).

UK and Irish membership of the single market created the conditions for a free and open trade border between the two states. This was most manifestly evident in terms of the land border between Northern Ireland and the Republic of Ireland. As security installations were dismantled in the wake of the peace process, the border effectively became entirely invisible with no restrictions to movement or trade. In addition, the open border facilitated the creation of cross-border institutions including the North–South Ministerial Council, its Joint Secretariat and Implementation Bodies, which worked on an all-island basis. This further softened the politically charged meaning and significance of the border in Irish politics. As Hayward (2018: 246) notes: "Perhaps the most successful dimension of Irish cross-border integration through joint EU membership – which has only been fully manifest since the peace process – is its normalization". Gormley-Heenan and Birrell (2015) have similarly examined how multilevel governance at the EU level supported, supplemented and mapped itself on to the new institutions that emerged from the 1998 Agreement.

Less tangible, but nonetheless substantially important, was how the very nature of the EU integration project allowed national sovereignty and identities to be both multidimensional and non-inimical in nature. This impacted directly on issues of identification, which lie at the heart of the constitutional dispute in Northern Ireland: namely the unionist versus nationalist binary. Within the EU context, contested national sovereignties and identities could be viewed as "complementary rather than oppositional" (see Hayward 2018: 239). The EU did not seek to replace or reconstruct national identities in Northern Ireland: instead the EU "reiterate[d] them through the formalization of dual state involvement" (Hayward 2006: 263).

The EU's tangible and practical role vis-à-vis Northern Ireland became more active and supportive once moves towards peace began, and especially so from the 1990s. The fledgling peace process benefited from EU largesse. Dedicated and targeted financial assistance, including in the form of the specially created PEACE programme, sought to support and buttress peace and reconciliation in Northern Ireland. As Lagana (2020) has demonstrated, EU peace funding, and support for cross-border initiatives, in particular, helped to create and sustain new relationships within and between Northern Ireland and the Republic of Ireland. What Lagana has termed the "meta-governmental" frameworks of EU initiatives provided a new context for new all-island connections and networks. This all aided in the creation of a new post-sovereigntist dispensation in the governance of Northern Ireland which, *inter alia*, helped to blur political boundaries and reduce the urgency and salience of the constitutional question as the defining one in Northern Ireland politics.

The devolution of powers to Northern Ireland's power-sharing institutions meant that they assumed responsibility for a number of policies with an EU dimension. This led to greater Northern Ireland engagement with the EU policy sphere and increased interactions between Brussels and Belfast (see Murphy 2014). It is noteworthy that the broad EU context framing the post-conflict period in Northern Ireland was largely uncontested. There was widespread cross-party support for the single market and the freedom of movement of both people and trade that it embodied. Peace funds and other EU financial support were welcomed unreservedly. Northern Ireland's MEPs worked cooperatively across the ethno-sectarian divide, often to the benefit of all of Northern

Ireland. EU policies were dealt with pragmatically by the power-sharing administration and rarely excited attention or controversy. Indeed, of all the policy issues on the agenda of the Northern Ireland administration after 1998, few were less controversial than the EU. This consensual approach was achieved despite political party positions on the EU which spanned the spectrum from the DUP's Euroscepticism, at one extreme (Ganiel 2009; Murphy & Evershed 2020a), to the SDLP's Europhilia (McLoughlin 2009), at the other (see also Hayward & Murphy 2010).

During the 2000s, however, the EU was to become a highly salient and disputed issue for the UK in general, and for the Conservative Party and successive British governments in particular. Growing public, political and electoral pressures to hold an in/out referendum culminated in the 2016 referendum vote. The outcome of the campaign was a narrow victory for the Leave side. This largely unexpected decision was followed by immediate economic fallout (as the value of sterling plummeted) and extended political turmoil (including the resignation of two prime ministers). The largely benign and benevolent, but nonetheless significant, ways in which the EU pervaded and supported first the Northern Ireland peace process, and later its politics, was profoundly challenged. In Northern Ireland (as in Scotland), the electorate voted Remain. On the morning after the vote, columnist Fintan O'Toole (2016) provocatively declared in *The Guardian*: "The English have placed a bomb under the Irish peace process". He proceeded to characterize the result as "an insult to Ireland". O'Toole's depiction of how the referendum result was perceived and understood in Ireland captured the sense of both shock and dismay (particularly among nationalists on the island of Ireland) at the prospect of the UK leaving the EU and how this would bring the border back into Irish politics, challenge the peace process, undermine the Belfast/Good Friday Agreement, and provoke a difficult and divisive discussion about Northern Ireland's constitutional status.

### "Brexit ... represents a critical juncture for the study and practice of politics"

The entire Brexit debacle has been heavily critiqued by the broad social science community. Richardson and Rittberger (2020: 650) have labelled it "an omnishambles of monumental proportions". Social scientists have been especially critical of what are perceived as a series of feckless and reckless decisions by the British political elite, which resulted in the Leave vote, produced years of political turmoil in and for Westminster, and disturbed the UK's constitutional and territorial equilibrium. Nowhere has this turmoil been more evident than in relation to Northern Ireland where the fallout from Brexit has been, and will continue to be, most acutely felt across the economic, political and constitutional spheres.

A key explanation for Brexit's long shadow is based on its character as a "critical juncture". The concept of a critical juncture is well-established in political science and is linked to the study of institutions, and most specifically to theories of historical institutionalism (HI). Rosamond's laconic definition of a "critical juncture" is also instructive. He notes that it is "an intensive period of fluidity and crisis that brings forth a revised institutional equilibrium" (2016: 866). More detailed accounts of "critical junctures" refer to "situations of uncertainty in which decisions of important actors are causally decisive for the selection of one path of institutional development over other possible paths" (Capoccia 2016). Collier and Collier (1991: 29) define a critical juncture as: "a period of significant change, which typically occurs in distinct ways in different countries (or other units of analysis) and which is hypothesized to produce distinct legacies". Mahoney (2002) talks about "choice point[s]" when a particular option, influenced by earlier historical conditions, is chosen from among two or more alternatives. The chosen option then becomes established, and the opportunities for revisiting earlier alternatives is less available, if not impossible.

Importantly, and particularly relevant to this study of Northern Ireland, critical junctures only become "critical" when they generate path-dependent processes and exert long-term effects (Bernhard 2015: 976). The notion of path dependency supports a few key claims (Pierson 2000: 251): "Specific patterns of timing and sequence matter; starting from similar conditions, a wide range of social outcomes may be possible; large consequences may result from relatively 'small' or contingent events; particular courses of action, once introduced, can be virtually impossible to reverse; and consequently, political development is often punctuated by critical moments or junctures that shape the basic contours of social life". Soifer (2012: 1573) observes that a critical juncture that produces a new developmental pathway is influenced by "the loosening of the constraints of structure [which allows] for agency or contingency to shape divergence from the past". Scholars are agreed that Brexit constitutes just such a "critical juncture" for the UK (Jennings & Lodge 2019: 772):

> Brexit … represents a critical juncture for the study and practice of politics. How did a country that a few years earlier appeared to be confident on the world stage and broadly at peace with itself, choose to engage in a divisive referendum and subsequently a snap election campaign, leaving it polarized in terms of public opinion, destabilized in terms of its territorial politics, with a return to two-party politics in England under two far from centrist political leaders, and an electoral map that makes it unlikely that any party will command a large majority in parliament in the near future?

Brexit altered the UK's politico-economic trajectory by breaking its connection with the EU and setting the state on a new developmental pathway. In Northern Ireland specifically, it has also precipitated a "critical *constitutional* moment": a period which may or may not lead to a critical constitutional juncture. As Bulmer and Burch (1998: 605) note: "Historical institutionalism is not only concerned with identifying the type and degree of transformation taking place, but also with examining those 'critical moments' when an opportunity arises for significant change. Such opportunities may not be realized and exploited but, if they are, the outcome is a 'critical juncture' at which there is a clear departure from previously established patterns". In theory, at such "critical moments", opportunities for institutional change and innovation are at their widest (*ibid.*). By destabilizing territorial politics, unravelling existing political-legal frameworks and upending the UK's political equilibrium, Brexit provides a space wherein constitutional change has become more proximate and possible than it was before 2016. However, although the permissive conditions for constitutional change may be present in Northern Ireland, critically, those conditions may or may not produce transformative institutional change. In this context, Brexit has created "a window of opportunity in which divergence *may* occur, and that divergence *may* have long-term consequences" (Soifer 2012: 1575, emphasis in the original). To put it more simply, critical moments do not guarantee critical junctures, but under certain conditions, they can morph into a critical juncture which heralds a new developmental pathway.

The 1998 Belfast/Good Friday Agreement, which was the culmination of a peace process began in the 1980s, represents a critical juncture. That agreement fundamentally changed Northern Ireland's political situation: facilitating a move away from violent conflict and institutional stasis to reach a point of relative political stability and institutional development. This was due to a particular confluence of factors and conditions (Ruane & Todd 2007: 453): "The Good Friday Agreement became possible not because 'slow learners' had eventually grasped the need to cooperate in representative institutions, but because there had been a major shift at once in the communal power balance, in the trajectories of the two states and in the guarantees and support offered internationally". In the case of the 1998 Agreement, these geopolitical shifts provided the conditions – a window of opportunity – where political agents were incentivized (for reasons of rational self-interest) to moderate their preferences and to work towards an agreed solution. The "constructive ambiguity"[8] at the heart of the 1998 Agreement was also important in enabling opposing parties to sign up to its terms (see Bell & Cavanaugh 1999; Dingley 2005; Mitchell 2009). The resulting constitutional "disruption", epitomized by the shift from direct rule to devolved governance, was based on substantive cross-community and bilateral buy-in and this helped to ease the transition from "critical moment" to "critical juncture", and to limit the potential for instability.

Critical junctures typically emerge from crisis or an exogenous shock which alters the perceptions, positions and policies of key actors and can change the path-dependent trajectory (see Roos & Zaun 2016; Collier & Collier 1991). Northern Ireland has encountered numerous periods of instability (including since 1998), many of which are couched in the language of "crisis", but which have not produced a "critical juncture".[9] Hay

---

8. "Constructive ambiguity is a classic manoeuvre when agreeing on a hotly-disputed text. Actors deliberately adopt language that is vague and can, simultaneously, mean different things to different people" (Bell & Cavanaugh 1999: 1356).

9. Those issues, which were often framed as "crisis", included, for example, difficulties in agreeing the decommissioning of paramilitary weapons (1998–2005); the Orange Order marching season (particularly events at Drumcree 1995–2000); the flags crisis (2012–13) (see Chapter 5); and the collapse or suspension of the devolved institutions (sporadically after 1998).

(1999) notes the ubiquity with which the term "crisis" is both used and mis-used. In seeking to address this anomaly, he (re-)conceptualizes "crisis" as "a moment of decisive intervention and not merely a moment of fragmentation, dislocation or destruction" (317). This conception of crisis denotes a range of resulting possibilities or outcomes which represent alternatives to a critical juncture.

This book analyses the potential or likelihood that the Brexit crisis represents a "critical constitutional juncture" for Northern Ireland. It assesses what conditions and driving forces are present at this current "critical moment". This involves analysing the particular political dynamics released by Brexit and determining how they are primed to influence the constitutional futures of Northern Ireland, and of "these islands" more generally, and to what effect. By determining the precise scope of Brexit's impact on key political agents in Northern Ireland, and on the Irish and British governments, and vice versa, we can tentatively offer insights about Northern Ireland's future institutional pathway and the likelihood (or not) of a "critical constitutional juncture".

The following chapter provides an account of how Brexit disrupted stability on the island of Ireland by interrupting a fragile political equilibrium in Northern Ireland. This includes an analysis of how the constitutional status quo was undermined by Brexit's stoking of political and communal tensions – in Northern Ireland, between North and South and between the UK and Ireland. Later chapters focus explicitly on key political agents in Northern Ireland's Brexit story. We explore how Brexit impacted on Irish nationalism, including an assessment of the rise of Sinn Féin, nationalist civil society movements and changing voter sentiment. This is examined in the context of a pattern of growing support for Irish unity (albeit that this growth is neither stable nor unconditional). This is followed by an analysis of Brexit's implications for unionism in Northern Ireland. This focuses on the backfiring of Ulster unionist support for Brexit, and includes an assessment of the uneasy relations between unionists in Northern Ireland and the wider British establishment. Unionism's insecurity, which sits alongside enduring and resilient support for Northern Ireland's constitutional status quo, is unpacked.

The Brexit period has been notable for how it has impacted on the heightened electoral appeal of Northern Ireland's non-aligned middle ground, as represented primarily by the Alliance Party, but also the

Green Party and non-aligned voters (that is, those who do not define themselves primarily as either unionist or nationalist) more generally. The link between Brexit and the rise of the centre ground is explored with a particular emphasis on the consequences for Northern Ireland's constitutional future. The position of the Alliance Party is especially crucial in determining the nature and direction of Northern Ireland's future constitutional path.

As co-guarantors of the 1998 Belfast/Good Friday Agreement, the roles of the British and Irish governments are critical in managing both Brexit and its fallout for Northern Ireland. The contrasting British and Irish approaches to the UK's EU referendum and its aftermath are discussed. In particular, the strategic options available to the two governments in navigating Brexit's "Irish question" are set out and analysed. The final chapter examines, in the round, how and to what extent key political agents are influencing Northern Ireland's "critical constitutional moment" and with what likely consequences for the future of Northern Ireland and "these islands".

## 2

# Northern Ireland and the great Brexit disruption

"Nobody wants to return to the borders of the past, so we will make it a priority to deliver a practical solution as soon as we can."

Theresa May, 17 January 2017

"There will be no border down the Irish Sea ... over my dead body"

Boris Johnson, 13 August 2020

Brexit has created deep economic, political and constitutional uncertainty and instability, and nowhere has this been experienced more acutely, or with more far-reaching effect, than in Northern Ireland. Already unstable and crisis-prone, Northern Ireland's post-Agreement settlement was radically disrupted by the UK's 2016 decision to leave the EU (Murphy 2018a; Hayward & Murphy 2018; Cochrane 2020; Murphy & Evershed 2021). That decision was the culmination of a process that began long before referendum day, and which will continue long after 31 January 2020 (the day the UK formally left the EU). Here, we are concerned with the key episodes which have so-far defined Northern Ireland's Brexit: the important and enduring ways in which, during the UK's exit from the EU, they impacted on Northern Ireland, and vice versa. These pivotal moments are narrated here and further developed throughout this book. This account of Northern Ireland's Brexit experience is a necessary precursor to a more sustained analysis in later chapters of the role of different agents in this process, and how the way it unfolded was determined by the strategic calculations (and miscalculations) and decisions (and mistakes) of different agents, and with what potential long-term political and constitutional consequences.

The description provided here is necessarily partial in both senses of the word – incomplete and subjective – and acknowledges, indeed argues, that Brexit's consequences continue to unfold in both intended and unintended ways. Foregrounding the impetus and motivation for the UK's EU referendum, and analysing its subsequent conduct through a Northern Ireland lens, provides an important context for understanding why the "Irish question" became such a contested and complex issue following the vote. This helps to account for why the Brexit negotiations became bogged down by a British position which had a fatal contradiction at its core: namely, a desire to leave both the EU's single market and customs union (i.e. the desire for a "hard" Brexit) and to simultaneously maintain an open border on the island of Ireland. The incompatibility of these Brexit objectives pervaded the entirety of the subsequent EU–UK negotiations, and chiefly explains why and how Brexit became so politically disruptive, difficult and destabilizing for Northern Ireland.

### "One of the biggest decisions this country will face in our lifetimes"

On 20 February 2016, Prime Minister David Cameron announced that the promised UK referendum on EU membership would take place on 23 June 2016. The announcement followed Cameron's securing what he termed "special status" for Britain during his renegotiation of the terms of UK membership: an achievement which persuaded the prime minister (if not all of his cabinet) to support the UK remaining in the EU (see Smith 2016). The June 2016 date was chosen to accommodate a number of external contingencies, which included an upcoming German federal election. This apparent attention to timing, however, took limited account of internal or domestic factors. And notably, the decision to call a referendum was made without reference to how a constitutionally charged referendum campaign might disturb Northern Ireland's delicate political settlement and its vulnerable and "negative" peace (Murphy 2018a). Unlike in the rest of the UK, and England in particular, the EU was not a hotly contested issue in Northern Ireland. Of all the many policy and political challenges facing Northern Ireland, the question of the UK's membership of the EU was certainly not a priority. No political party in Northern Ireland was actively agitating for a referendum on EU membership. Northern Ireland, however, had no role in influencing Cameron's decision. An Assembly election in Northern Ireland preceded the referendum by just six weeks. This combination of electoral contests constituted a two-part drama marked by political campaigning and emotionally charged appeals to ethnonational identity: all potentially destabilizing for the susceptible peace in Northern Ireland.

At the national level, the contest between the Leave and Remain sides was intense, and particularly concentrated across England. The referendum campaign was ill-tempered and antagonistic, the clarity and accuracy of information provided to voters was weak, and the quality of debate was poor. Feelings, emotions and perceptions jostled with facts and reality. To take one emblematic example, the comprehensive rubbishing of Vote Leave's claim that leaving the EU would save the UK £350 million a week did nothing to diminish its pervasiveness or salience. Key referendum debates revolved around migration, the economy and sovereignty. The Conservative Party, Labour Party, UKIP and the official Leave and Remain referendum campaign groups spent the bulk of the campaign focused resolutely on these issues. The referendum period revealed a telling observation about the UK in terms of the relationships between its constituent parts in general, and between Great Britain and Northern Ireland in particular. The broader political implications of a Leave vote for the UK's devolved regions, and particularly for Northern Ireland, did not enjoy any significant airing during the referendum campaign. The Irish dimension sparked barely a mention during key debates and discussions. There was scant serious attention paid to Northern Ireland's tenuous and delicate political situation and the nature of its contested border with Ireland; little sense that the timing, even the very fact of the referendum, might prove challenging for a region in transition from conflict to peace; nor any appreciation that a Leave vote might revive England's "Irish question" and prove consequential for the cohesion of the UK.

In Northern Ireland itself, the referendum campaign was somewhat muted (see Murphy 2016a, 2018a). Coupled with campaign fatigue (following the recent Assembly election), the politically complex and constitutionally emotive nature of the issues involved turned the electorate off. Additionally, the question of EU membership was never one that excited much attention in Northern Ireland, where Euroscepticism has rarely been vociferous or noisy. Indeed, Northern Ireland was one of the more Europhile parts of the UK, with public opinion consistently recording majority support for UK (and Irish) membership of the EU (see McGowan & O'Connor 2004; Clements 2010). The level and intensity of support for the EU has been influenced by the particular (economic) benefits which EU membership has brought Northern Ireland. Being part of the single European market facilitated the diversification of Northern Ireland trade patterns and an ability to attract inward investment (Barrett *et al.* 2015). The Common Agricultural Policy (CAP) underpinned the viability of the Northern Ireland agri-food sector (House of Lords 2016a: 14). Structural funding support, and in particular the PEACE programmes, offered targeted financial assistance to communities overcoming conflict (Lagana 2020).

Public support for the EU was largely echoed by Northern Ireland's main political parties. By 2016, just one – the DUP – could be legitimately described as Eurosceptic.[1] And even in this case, before 2016, the particular brand of rhetorically trenchant and ethno-religious Euroscepticism to which the party had traditionally subscribed had been moderated as the party had transitioned from protest to power (Murphy & Evershed 2020a, 2020b). Sinn Féin's traditional opposition to the EU – rooted in absolutist understandings of Irish sovereignty and a left-wing critique of European capitalism – has shifted over time to become less Eurosceptic and more "Eurocritical" (Maillot 2009; Evershed & Murphy 2021). The smaller UUP is a self-described "Eurorealist" political party whose approach to the EU is based on "hesitant pro-Europeanism" (Murphy 2009). The SDLP, Alliance Party and Green Party are all, to differing degrees, pro-EU in outlook. In practice, and despite different perspectives, the cross-party power-sharing Northern Ireland Executive and Assembly rarely disagreed on EU issues where some manner of devolved responsibility applied. Conflict and contestation was not a feature of Northern Ireland's approach to the EU policy landscape (see Murphy 2014). The expectation that the referendum would record a Remain result also limited the extent to which political parties were willing to engage energetically with the

---

1. The smaller unionist party, TUV, also has an explicitly Eurosceptic position, and the small far-left PBP has an anti-EU position, informed by a left critique of the EU.

issue, particularly given the need to fight an Assembly election just six weeks ahead of the referendum. Concerns about the consequences of a Leave vote for Northern Ireland did form part of the EU referendum campaign narrative in Northern Ireland, albeit that the campaign was markedly more lacklustre than in the rest of the UK.

On a turnout of 62.69 per cent, 55.8 per cent of the Northern Ireland electorate voted in favour of remaining in the EU (McCann & Hainsworth 2017: 335). The referendum result demonstrated a clear East–West divide (see Murphy 2016b: 849). All constituencies bordering the Irish Republic voted Remain while all Eastern constituencies (bar three of the four Belfast constituencies) supported Leave. In addition, all Westminster constituencies represented by a nationalist MP voted

**Figure 2.1** Electoral map of the EU referendum results in Northern Ireland

*Source*: thedetail.tv (2017) (https://www.TheDetail.tv/articles/data-mapping-shows-northern-ireland-s-divisions-haven-t-gone-away).

Remain. Seven of the ten Northern Ireland constituencies represented by a unionist MP opted for Leave. To a degree, the referendum result in Northern Ireland mirrored that elsewhere in the UK, in that similar demographic and socio-economic trends – what Goodhart (2017) has defined, for example, as the division between "somewheres" and "anywheres" – help to account for the spread of Leave and Remain votes. However, in Northern Ireland, these trends are also both reflective of and mapped onto more specific ethno-political conditions. Research by Garry (2016a: 2) suggests that voter choice in the referendum was driven by "the deep underlying ethnonational divide in Northern Ireland politics". Sixty six per cent of self-described "Unionists" voted to exit the EU while almost 90 per cent of self-described "Nationalists" voted Remain. Northern Ireland's majority vote to stay in the EU, however, was effectively over-ridden by the preferences of English voters who were motivated ultimately by different concerns to those which exercised voters in Northern Ireland and whose motivation for voting Leave generally demonstrated little, if any, cognisance of the "Irish question".

Although the referendum campaign in Northern Ireland was understated, responses to the result were more strident. A mixture of surprise and dismay quickly gave way to contested political interpretations of the outcome. Having campaigned for Leave, DUP leader Arlene Foster saw the result as a sign that: "We are now entering a new era of an even stronger United Kingdom" (BBC News 2016). In contrast, then Sinn Féin president, Gerry Adams, foresaw the weakening of the UK and viewed the Leave vote as providing "a democratic imperative for a 'border poll' to be held" (Sinn Féin 2016a). The two opposing interpretations of the vote in Northern Ireland spoke to the conflation of Brexit with the constitutional question around which Northern Ireland politics hinges. The ensuing period of protracted Brexit negotiations did not challenge or soften this difference of opinion: if anything, proposals to address issues specific to Northern Ireland exposed a widening gulf between unionism and nationalism, and between the UK and Ireland. Cameron heralded the referendum as "one of the biggest decisions this country will face in our lifetimes" (Mason et al. 2016). He (perhaps unwittingly) captured the transformational significance of that decision for Northern Ireland, the island of Ireland, and the UK's own territorial constitution.

## "Flexible and imaginative solutions will be required"

Cross-party unity in Northern Ireland is an elusive thing (Leach *et al.* 2021). Birrell and Heenan (2017: 476) have identified "a running catalogue of difficult or wicked issues that have not been resolved and have undermined the political system". These include highly contested "culture war" issues such as flags and emblems, commemorations and language rights, and marked differences around abortion rights and marriage equality. Before Brexit became a similarly "wicked" issue however, there were tentative signs of cross-party coalescence on specific issues of significance to Northern Ireland. This was detailed in a joint letter from then First Minister, Arlene Foster, and Deputy First Minister, Martin McGuinness, to UK Prime Minister, Theresa May, in August 2016 calling for specific Northern Ireland interests to be protected during the EU–UK negotiation process. The letter noted Northern Ireland's peculiarity in being the only part of the UK to share a land border with an EU member state and noted the importance of ensuring that "the border does not create an incentive for those who would wish to undermine the peace process and/or the political settlement" (The Executive Office 2016a). It also addressed four other issues including: ease of trade with EU member-states and access to labour; the all-island single electricity market; access to EU funds; and protections for the agri-food and fisheries industry. The letter constituted a loose list of key cross-party priorities. It reflected the EU's later call for "flexible and imaginative solutions" in dealing with the Irish border (European Council 2017).

The prime minister responded to the letter in October 2016 and indicated her commitment to "full engagement with the Northern Ireland Executive on the UK's exit from the EU". She suggested that her government would "take full account of the specific interests of the people of Northern Ireland" and she advised that the future of the border was "an important priority for the UK as a whole" (The Executive Office 2016b). These pledges and assurances would be tested (and found wanting) over and over again as the increasingly vexed question of the border plagued the Brexit negotiation process.

The semblance of cross-party consensus on Brexit represented by the First and Deputy First Ministers' letter was not to last. A Northern Ireland Assembly debate on 17 October 2016 discussed an SDLP Proposal on "EU Special Status for Northern Ireland". The motion called for formal recognition of Northern Ireland's unique status, and for the negotiation of a bespoke post-Brexit settlement. All nationalist MLAs supported the motion, and all unionists opposed it, and the proposal was defeated by 47 to 46 votes. The prospect of Northern Ireland being treated as different to or distinct from the rest of the UK was roundly rejected by unionists as an affront to their political identity. In contrast, for nationalists, "special status" was seen as key to protecting the all-island economy, and the openness of the border between Northern Ireland and the Republic which gave expression to their identity. Although all Northern Ireland political parties supported the maintenance of an open border on the island of Ireland, the process and formula for achieving such an outcome was intricately entangled with opposing constitutional positions. The Brexit issue thus crystallized into not just a political disagreement between unionists and nationalists, but one that was also implicitly constitutional in nature (O'Leary 2018).

Relations between the two ethnonational blocs suffered a further setback when in November 2016, the DUP became embroiled in the so-called "cash for ash" scandal. The Renewable Heat Incentive (RHI) scheme implicated senior DUP figures in a failed renewable energy initiative which cost almost £500 million (see McBride 2019a). The scandal was layered over existing tensions between the parties in the Northern Ireland Executive and ultimately led to the collapse of the devolved institutions in January 2017 when then Deputy First Minister, the late Martin McGuinness, resigned in protest at First Minister Arlene Foster's failure to take responsibility for the scandal. Power-sharing ensures that the offices of the First and Deputy First Minister are dependent on each other. This meant that the resignation of the Deputy First Minister forced the First Minister's removal from office. This led to the collapse of the Northern Ireland Executive and was followed by the dissolution of the Northern Ireland Assembly on 26 January 2017. After a snap (and particularly rancorous) Northern Ireland Assembly election in March 2017, no new Executive was formed. The institutions were to remain inactive for almost three years as local political parties and leaders consistently failed to agree a basis for their resurrection.

In early 2017, during this period of intense instability and disagreement in Northern Ireland, Prime Minister Theresa May delivered her Lancaster House Speech. The speech set out the British government's approach to Brexit and committed the UK to leaving both the EU's single market and customs union. This hard-line position provided the genesis of what has been described by Connelly (2019) as "the titanic contradictions at the heart of Brexit: how to leave the customs union and single market and maintain an invisible border on the island of Ireland".

The speech won praise from Brexiters, particularly those within the Conservative Party. The Labour Party was circumspectly critical of the prime minister's approach to Brexit. The harshest criticism, however, came from Scottish First Minister Nicola Sturgeon, who claimed that leaving the single market was "economically catastrophic" and hinted that such a position would hasten calls for a second independence referendum (Staunton 2017). The Irish government noted the potential economic risks and the threat posed to the openness of the Irish border by the hard form of Brexit May had outlined. While it made no secret of its preference for a softer form of Brexit, it also stressed its acceptance of the referendum result, and sought to identify such potential economic opportunities as might emerge. Although the DUP was supportive of (and, as we discuss further below, became increasingly wedded to) the British government's hard-line position, it was greeted with some derision by Sinn Féin President, Gerry Adams: "As she has said before Ms May set the future of the border and any arrangements with the island of Ireland in the context of Britain's determination to control immigration and defend its borders. It is difficult to see how this can be accomplished without significant changes to the current border arrangements" (Sinn Féin 2017a).

As the differences between unionism and nationalism continued to harden, the Brexit juggernaut gained momentum. On 29 March 2017, Prime Minister Theresa May triggered Article 50, commencing a (nominal) two-year period of withdrawal negotiations between the UK and the EU.[2] By activating Article 50, May moved the Brexit process into a challenging negotiation phase with little sign that the British government had given sufficient consideration to the complexity of the withdrawal process, particularly as it applied to Northern Ireland (Phinnemore and Whitten 2021). As was the case for all other devolved

---

2. This initial (and subsequent) deadlines were missed as the UK failed to support different iterations of a withdrawal deal. The UK did not formally leave the EU until 31 January 2020.

governments of the UK, Northern Ireland received no formal notification from the prime minister that she was about to trigger Article 50.

The triggering of Article 50 kicked off a two-stage negotiation process. The first phase involved agreeing the terms of the UK's withdrawal from the EU. The second phase – scheduled to commence following agreement on the terms of a withdrawal deal – would focus on the future relationship between the UK and the EU. One month after May's Article 50 letter, on 29 April 2017, the EU issued its guidelines for the EU–UK withdrawal negotiations. The guidelines highlighted the need for progress on three key issues. Firstly, agreement on a financial settlement covering the UK's EU commitments and liabilities. Secondly, agreement on reciprocal guarantees for EU and UK citizens to safeguard status and rights. And thirdly, the guidelines explicitly referenced the need to protect the Northern Ireland peace process:

> In view of the unique circumstances on the island of Ireland, flexible and imaginative solutions will be required, including with the aim of avoiding a hard border, while respecting the integrity of the Union legal order. In this context, the Union should also recognize existing bilateral agreements and arrangements between the United Kingdom and Ireland which are compatible with EU law.       (European Council 2017: 6)

The UK's view that the Irish border issue could be resolved during the second phase of negotiations was resolutely rejected. Binding legal commitments – established before the start of negotiations on the future EU–UK relationship – were deemed imperative by the European Commission, including to prevent the Irish border being used as a pawn during the subsequent future relationship negotiations (Connelly 2018).

The collapse of Northern Ireland's power-sharing institutions removed any capacity (or need) for the political parties in Northern Ireland to formulate or articulate an agreed position on Brexit as the withdrawal negotiations began. Even if such an agreed position had materialized (and admittedly that was unlikely), the UK government is unlikely to have acted on this (McEwen 2020). Its capacity for doing so was limited by a toxic hard-versus-soft Brexit gulf within the Conservative Party. That toxicity and its impact was to intensify further following May's decision to call a snap general election in May 2017.

The prime minister mistakenly anticipated a strong Conservative Party majority, which she believed would strengthen her Brexit negotiation strategy. The political gamble backfired as May was left short of a majority. The DUP – having secured ten Westminster seats – emerged as king-maker. An extraordinary political arithmetic propelled the DUP into a confidence-and-supply agreement supporting a minority Conservative Party government (Cabinet Office 2017). The terms of the agreement involved approximately £1 billion of additional financial support for Northern Ireland (Tonge 2017).[3] In exchange, the DUP agreed to support the British government on all finance bills and, critically, on Brexit-related decisions.

The DUP's new-found and unprecedented proximity to the British government, and May's reliance on DUP support, were met with both anger and anxiety in Northern Ireland. The Belfast/Good Friday Agreement's stipulation that the British government ought not to assume a partisan position in relation to Northern Ireland was tacitly challenged by the confidence-and-supply agreement. The complexity of the arrangement and its full implications came into sharp focus in December 2017, when Prime Minister May was humiliatingly forced to row back on the original terms of an EU–UK Joint Report outlining agreements reached on the terms of the UK's withdrawal from the EU (Boffey *et al.* 2017). The text of this report detailed the progress made in the first phase of the negotiations, and outlined agreements in principle across the three key areas of protecting the reciprocal rights of EU citizens in the UK and UK citizens in the EU; the financial or "divorce" settlement; and, crucially, the framework for addressing the unique circumstances in Northern Ireland.

On 4 December 2017, RTÉ's Tony Connelly broke the news that on Ireland/Northern Ireland, the text of the Joint Report was to include that: "in the absence of agreed solutions the UK [would] ensure that there continue[d] to be no divergence from those rules of the internal market + customs union which, now or in the future, support[ed] North South cooperation + protection of the GFA" (Connelly 2017a). In effect,

---

3. There has been some debate as to whether the promised funding was fully delivered, given the collapse of the Conservative–DUP deal in late 2019. Although the DUP have insisted that it was paid, Sinn Féin's Conor Murphy, who became finance minister in the newly reinstated Northern Ireland Executive in January 2020, has cast doubt on these claims (Bell 2020).

this would be tantamount to the kind of "special status" for Northern Ireland previously rejected by unionists. While Great Britain would have a hard Brexit, leaving the single market and the customs union, the default would be that Northern Ireland would effectively remain within the EU's customs and regulatory orbit.

The DUP had not been party to the discussions between the UK government and the European Commission about the precise terms of the Joint Report, and was furious. In a statement, DUP leader Arlene Foster noted: "We have been very clear. Northern Ireland must leave the EU on the same terms as the rest of the United Kingdom. We will not accept any form of regulatory divergence which separates Northern Ireland economically or politically from the rest of the United Kingdom. The economic and constitutional integrity of the United Kingdom will not be compromised in any way" (Duffy 2017).

Having failed to view the proposals with an eye to the DUP's likely response to them (let alone discuss them with the DUP), the British government was forced back to the negotiating table to seek to amend the terms of its agreement with the EU. A second version of the Joint Report was produced to address DUP concerns. Specifically, Article 50 of the redrafted report committed the UK to ensuring that no new regulatory barriers would be permitted to develop between Northern Ireland and the rest of the UK without the consent of the Northern Ireland Assembly. This paragraph placated the DUP by providing a guarantee that Northern Ireland businesses would retain unfettered access to the whole of the UK internal market. The episode demonstrated the extent to which the Northern Ireland dimension to Brexit, and unionist constitutional sensitivities in particular, could be unknown and/or readily overlooked by the UK government. Connelly (2017b) notes that: "In Brussels, officials expressed bewilderment that the DUP had not been kept in the loop by Mrs May as the evolving text [of the Joint Report] waxed and waned along the semantic fault-line of regulatory convergence and regulatory alignment".

The subsequent progress of the EU–UK withdrawal negotiations proved fraught and testy. In February 2018, the EU published a draft legal text of a Withdrawal Agreement, which sought to give expression to the December 2017 Joint Report. This included a Protocol on Ireland/ Northern Ireland outlining what became known as the "backstop": a set of measures to ensure the openness of the Irish border by retaining

Northern Ireland's place in the EU's customs union and single market in the event that this could not otherwise be facilitated under the terms of any new trade arrangement between the UK and the EU, or by "alternative" technological arrangements. With December's humiliating *volte face* fresh in her mind, and now fully cognizant of the DUP's feelings on the matter, Theresa May insisted that the backstop – and the potential for a new customs and regulatory border in the Irish Sea which it implied – was something to which no British prime minister could ever agree.

For much of the rest of 2018, the UK and the EU fractiously traded a series of proposals and counter-proposals aimed at preventing a hard border on the island of Ireland. By November 2018, a compromise was reached and the legal text of a Withdrawal Agreement was agreed by EU and UK negotiators. The Agreement included a redrafted Protocol on Ireland/Northern Ireland detailing the agreed version of the backstop. Rather than applying only to Northern Ireland, key elements of the Protocol would apply to the UK as a whole. Specifically, it meant that the entire UK would remain in the EU's customs territory – thus removing the need for customs checks between Great Britain and Northern Ireland. Northern Ireland would still be bound by the rules of the EU's single market, but a series of unilateral commitments to retain alignment on EU standards and regulations was made by the UK in order to minimize checks on goods moving across the Irish Sea (Hayward & Phinnemore 2019). The backstop would apply "unless and until" alternative arrangements to replace it were agreed, or it was otherwise superseded by a new trade agreement between the UK and the EU.

Similar formulae for breaking the negotiating impasse had initially been resisted by the EU, which had reservations about extending the provisions of the backstop to the UK as a whole, and handing over substantial powers to police and protect the integrity of its market and customs union (Boffey & Rankin 2018a, 2018b). Above all, the EU was concerned that a UK-wide backstop would prejudge the outcome of negotiations on its future trading relationship with the UK (Connelly 2019). The all-UK backstop therefore represented a substantial compromise on the part of the EU, and something of a win for the British government. Despite this, May encountered insurmountable difficulties in getting Westminster to support the draft deal.

The most vociferous criticisms came, once again, from the DUP: the very party May's efforts to reformulate the terms of the backstop had sought to mollify. While it removed the need for customs checks between Great Britain and Ireland, May's deal still required a degree of regulatory alignment between Northern Ireland and the EU. This hinted at the possibility of regulatory divergence between Northern Ireland and the rest of the UK, and was viewed by the DUP as an affront to Northern Ireland's place in the Union. Although arch-Brexiters purported to share some of the DUP's constitutional concerns about a regulatory border in the Irish Sea, this constituency was decidedly more alarmed by the provision that the UK remain within the EU's customs territory. Staying in the EU's customs area – potentially indefinitely – meant that the UK would not be able to negotiate its own trade deals with other countries. Initially masked by combined efforts to thwart Theresa May's Brexit deal, this difference in emphasis between Ulster unionist and "mainland" Tory Brexiters was ultimately to prove disastrous for the DUP.

The DUP's opposition to the backstop was not reflective of wider political and public perspectives and positions in Northern Ireland. In fact, the party's rejection of the draft Withdrawal Agreement was at odds with the preferences of the majority of Northern Ireland's other political parties: Sinn Féin, the SDLP, the Alliance Party and the Greens all supported the backstop. It was also contrary to the support which key interest groups in Northern Ireland – including the Ulster Farmers' Union (UFU) and the Northern Ireland Chamber of Commerce – voiced for the draft deal. Moreover, the DUP's rejection of the backstop was not shared by the general public. According to polling conducted by Lord Ashcroft in 2019, for instance, 60 per cent of Northern Ireland's voters favoured leaving the EU with a deal that included the backstop over an alternative "no deal" Brexit. Thirty five per cent said that they had "no problem" with the backstop, while 24 per cent felt that while it was not ideal, it was an "acceptable compromise". This was compared to 40 per cent who viewed it as "unacceptable" (Lord Ashcroft Polls 2019). In the event, the DUP joined a majority of MPs in voting against the deal on each of the three occasions it came before the House of Commons during Theresa May's premiership (see Table 2.1).

Theresa May's failure to galvanize parliamentary support for the Agreement was to prove her downfall. She stepped down as leader of the

**Table 2.1** Timeline of Westminster Brexit votes

| Date | Outcome | Vote breakdown |
| --- | --- | --- |
| 15 January 2019 | MPs voted against the prime minister's withdrawal deal | 432 to 202 |
| 12 March 2019 | MPs voted against the prime minister's withdrawal deal | 391 to 242 |
| 29 March 2019 | MPs voted against the prime minister's withdrawal deal (but on this occasion without the Political Declaration on the framework for the future relationship). | 344 to 286 |

Conservative Party on 7 June 2019 and was replaced by Boris Johnson, who assumed the office of prime minister on 24 July 2019. Johnson came to power vowing that he would ditch the backstop and refuse any deal with the EU that would create any kind of a border in the Irish Sea. Johnson's revised withdrawal deal – thrashed out following a meeting on 10 October 2019 between Johnson and Irish Taoiseach Leo Varadkar – did indeed junk the backstop. But it replaced it with a "frontstop" (Keating 2019). Johnson's deal with the EU (European Commission 2019) affirmed that the UK would leave both the single market and the EU customs union, and guaranteed Northern Ireland's *de jure* place in the UK's customs territory and internal market. However, to ensure no return to a hard border on the island of Ireland, the redrafted Protocol on Ireland/Northern Ireland retained, *de facto*, Northern Ireland's place in the EU's single market and customs union, creating a necessity for some customs and regulatory checks between Northern Ireland and the rest of the UK. In an attempt to leverage some degree of support for the Protocol in Northern Ireland, it also provided that four years after the end of the transition period, Northern Ireland's democratic institutions would be given the opportunity to vote on whether or not they wished for key arrangements under the Protocol to continue.

Johnson faced the same Brexit trilemma as Theresa May. He was unable to simultaneously deliver all three things Brexiters had promised: leaving the single market and customs union, maintaining an open border on the island of Ireland, and ensuring no border between Northern

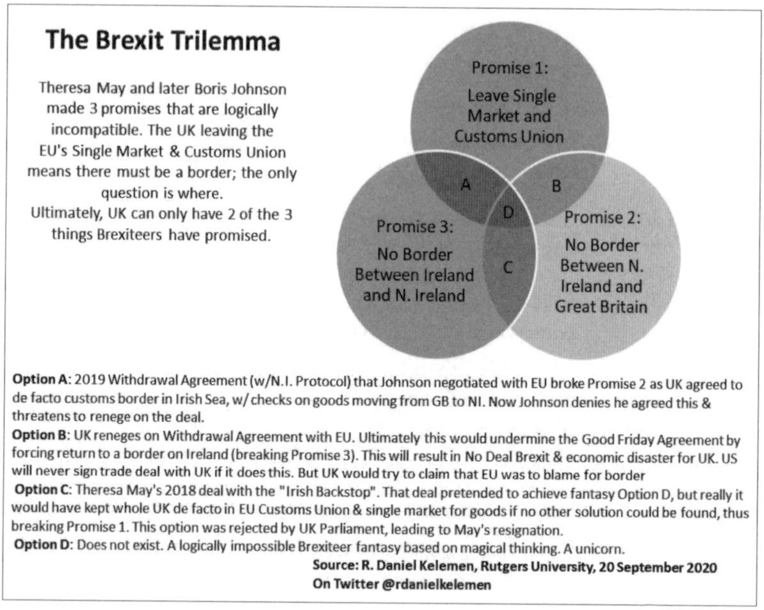
The Brexit Trilemma
Theresa May and later Boris Johnson made 3 promises that are logically incompatible. The UK leaving the EU's Single Market & Customs Union means there must be a border; the only question is where.
Ultimately, UK can only have 2 of the 3 things Brexiteers have promised.
Promise 1: Leave Single Market and Customs Union
Promise 2: No Border Between N. Ireland and Great Britain
Promise 3: No Border Between Ireland and N. Ireland
A
B
C
D
Option A: 2019 Withdrawal Agreement (w/N.I. Protocol) that Johnson negotiated with EU broke Promise 2 as UK agreed to de facto customs border in Irish Sea, w/ checks on goods moving from GB to NI. Now Johnson denies he agreed this & threatens to renege on the deal.
Option B: UK reneges on Withdrawal Agreement with EU. Ultimately this would undermine the Good Friday Agreement by forcing return to a border on Ireland (breaking Promise 3). This will result in No Deal Brexit & economic disaster for UK. US will never sign trade deal with UK if it does this. But UK would try to claim that EU was to blame for border
Option C: Theresa May's 2018 deal with the "Irish Backstop". That deal pretended to achieve fantasy Option D, but really it would have kept whole UK de facto in EU Customs Union & single market for goods if no other solution could be found, thus breaking Promise 1. This option was rejected by UK Parliament, leading to May's resignation.
Option D: Does not exist. A logically impossible Brexiteer fantasy based on magical thinking. A unicorn.
Source: R. Daniel Kelemen, Rutgers University, 20 September 2020
On Twitter @rdanielkelemen

**Figure 2.2** The Brexit trilemma

*Source*: R. Daniel Lelemen, Rutgers University, 20 September 2020 on Twitter @rdanielkelemen.

Ireland and Great Britain (see Figure 2.2). Johnson's willingness to prioritize a hard Brexit and to "Get Brexit Done" (at all costs), led him to agree a deal which sacrificed the promise of no border in the Irish Sea. As the 31 October 2019 deadline for agreeing a withdrawal deal loomed, the complex (and rather convoluted) protocol arrangement broke the political impasse by facilitating agreement on a deal acceptable to both the British prime minister and the EU. Unsurprisingly, however, the revised deal did not meet with DUP approval. In fact, the arrangement was utterly opposed by all swathes of unionism for its supposed impact on the constitutional integrity of the UK (see Wilson 2020).

The revised deal still required parliamentary approval, and any optimistic sense that the withdrawal chapter of the Brexit saga might finally be coming to a close was fleeting. Johnson lost the Westminster vote: 308 in favour and 322 against. Following the vote, the European Council President Donald Tusk recommended that the EU27 accept the UK's request for a third extension of the Article 50 process until 31

January 2020. A general election was seen as the only route to break-ing the impasse. Johnson's attempt to call one, however, was also sub-ject to the agreement of a belligerent and unquiescing parliament. The Labour Party opposed efforts to dissolve parliament by abstaining from a parliamentary vote. The necessary two-thirds parliamentary sup-port (required under the terms of the Fixed Term Parliament Act) did not materialize. Johnson introduced a one-sentence bill to amend the Fixed Term Parliament Act by setting a 12 December election date. The necessary simple majority was secured, setting the scene for the first December general election since 1923.

On 12 December 2019, on a campaign pledge that he would "Get Brexit Done", Johnson led the Conservative Party to its biggest par-liamentary victory since 1987, winning 43.6 per cent of the vote. His 80-seat majority eliminated the need for DUP support and effectively set the scene for his revised withdrawal deal to secure a parliamentary majority. Despite continued protestations from an electorally dimin-ished DUP (the party lost two seats), the European Union (Withdrawal Agreement) Act received royal assent on 23 January 2020. This final move paved the way for the UK to formally leave the EU on 31 January 2020. Prime Minister Boris Johnson's self-proclaimed commitment to the Ulster unionist cause proved to have been short-lived (see Kenny & Sheldon 2021).

## "There is no alternative to the full and correct implementation of the protocol"

Eventual agreement on a withdrawal deal highlighted the clear malle-ability of Britain's approach to Northern Ireland's Brexit situation. The nature of the deal, and the troubled process of implementation which has followed from it, provide a demonstration of how decisions taken by the British government have edged (and continue to edge) Northern Ireland closer to a "critical juncture": how the decisions of key agents have created new structural conditions within which those agents are now forced to make further, consequential decisions. Rather than her-alding a moment of catharsis or closure, the UK's exit from the EU has instead come with renewed political and constitutional conflict. Critical decisions made during Johnson's premiership have decreased stability in Northern Ireland, and provoked spirited reactions from key actors in Northern Ireland, from the Irish government, and from the EU.

By restoring Northern Ireland's voice for the very final act of the process of the UK's withdrawal from the EU, the re-establishment of power-sharing following the *New Decade, New Approach* agreement (DFA 2020) lent greater agency to Northern Ireland and its political representatives after a three-year hiatus during which their collective voices had been muted and marginalized at previous critical Brexit moments. The deal was brokered by Secretary of State for Northern Ireland, Julian Smith, and Minister for Foreign Affairs and then Tánaiste (deputy prime minister), Simon Coveney, and was made possible by the DUP's centre of gravity returning to Stormont following the collapse of its confidence-and-supply arrangement with the Tories. The deal committed the newly restored Northern Ireland Executive, *inter alia*, to passing legislation to promote and protect the Irish language, which the newly chastened DUP had previously refused to support. It is notable that when the Withdrawal Agreement – replete with its Protocol on Ireland/Northern Ireland – became law, it did so against the express wishes of the Northern Ireland Assembly, which had voted unanimously to withhold consent for the UK's withdrawal from the EU on 20 January 2020 (McCormack 2020a). This represented the coming together of Unionists opposed to a Brexit shaped by the Protocol with Nationalists and "Others" opposed to Brexit *per se*.

This was shortly followed by a change of British political stewardship in Northern Ireland, when Secretary of State Julian Smith was replaced by Brandon Lewis in February 2020. Lewis became the fourth Northern Ireland secretary in as many years.[4] The appointment of Lewis, and the sacking of Smith, was met with some dismay in Northern Ireland. SDLP leader Colum Eastwood labelled it a "strategic error" (Walker & O'Carroll 2020) and in a tweet, he condemned the sacking, viewing it as a demonstration of "Johnson's dangerous indifference to us [Northern Ireland]" (Eastwood 2020).

Following Boris Johnson having secured the UK's withdrawal from the EU – achieving what Theresa May could not – by agreeing to a

---

4. His three most-recent predecessors were: James Brokenshire – appointed in July 2016; Karen Bradley – appointed January 2018; and Julian Smith – appointed in July 2019.

regulatory and customs border in the Irish Sea, the focus switched to implementation. Early warning signs of UK government intentions in this regard were evident when Johnson used the occasion of a reception hosted by the Northern Ireland Conservatives in November 2019 to insist that Northern Ireland businesses could throw customs paperwork "in the bin" (BBC News 2019a). In addition to dialling up the political rhetoric, this conveyed false promises in relation to the manner of the Protocol's implementation and its likely impact on trade between Great Britain and Northern Ireland. Johnson's shabby and misleading dismissal of how Brexit would play out in Northern Ireland fuelled an uneasy (and widespread) sense of distrust and apprehension. The resulting confusion further unsettled key relationships: between unionism and nationalism, between Britain and Ireland, and between the UK and the EU, and surreptitiously fuelled both expectations (and fears in the case of unionism) of some element of future constitutional change.

For much of 2020, concerns were expressed by the EU that the UK government appeared less than fully committed to fulfilling its obligations under the terms of the Protocol (Connelly 2020; Rice 2020). This was related to uncertainty about whether the UK really intended to secure a deal on a future trading relationship with the EU, and what shape such a deal could plausibly take. Johnson's resolute refusal to countenance any extension to the post-withdrawal transition period (which he was entitled to request under the terms of the Withdrawal Agreement) – even as his government's resources were being stretched ever more thinly by a global public health emergency and as negotiations on the future relationship were, from March 2020, serially disrupted by Covid restrictions – raised alarm bells. With the UK seeking a deal that prioritized sovereignty above all else and seeking as distant a future relationship as possible from the EU, full implementation of the Protocol and facilitation of all required checks and processes at Northern Ireland's ports would be all the more imperative, in order to protect the integrity of the European single market. The EU's faith in the UK to deliver this was dealt an almost killer blow by the publication of the Internal Market Bill in September 2020, which contained a number of provisions to override key aspects of the Withdrawal Agreement, and the Northern Ireland Protocol, in particular, including in areas such as customs procedures and state aid (Foster, Payne & Brunsden 2020). It marked, by the explicit admission of Secretary of State for Northern

Ireland, Brandon Lewis, an intention to break international law "in a specific and limited way" (BBC News 2020) and the EU began legal proceedings against the UK.

These proceedings fell away, however, when the EU and the UK eventually reached agreement on the phased implementation of the Protocol in December 2020 (Heffer 2020). This agreement was made at a meeting of the EU–UK Joint Committee, established to oversee implementation of the Withdrawal Agreement and co-chaired by then Cabinet Office Minister, Michael Gove and European Commission Vice-President, Maroš Šefčovič. The UK agreed to drop the controversial clauses of the Internal Market Bill, and a grace period was offered to give the UK more time to prepare for customs and certain regulatory checks at Northern Ireland ports, including on medicines, chilled meats and other supermarket products. This new agreement foreshadowed the conclusion of a Trade and Cooperation Agreement between EU and UK negotiators on Christmas Eve (European Commission 2020). This was a thin trade deal, guaranteeing tariff and quota-free trade between the EU and the UK, but also giving the UK the freedom to diverge from EU standards and rules in the future. This form of hard Brexit meant that when the new Irish Sea border came into effect, the need for rigorous checks on goods entering Northern Ireland (and, indeed, the Republic of Ireland) from Great Britain would be maximized. The deal entered into effect on New Year's Day and, despite the temporary mitigations agreed by the Joint Committee earlier in December, the impact was immediate, particularly against the backdrop of a global pandemic.

Having had next to no time to prepare for the precise terms on which the Protocol would be implemented, businesses in Northern Ireland struggled to get up to speed with new trading requirements. There were reports of empty supermarket shelves, of British companies refusing to sell goods to Northern Ireland, and of parcels going undelivered (see, e.g., McBride 2021a, 2021b). Dissent stirred at the unionist grassroots about the new arrangements, and this was both reflected and magnified by unionist politicians. It was also hardened further by the EU's utterly misjudged decision to trigger Article 16 of the Protocol. Article 16 had been inserted as an option of last resort in the event of disagreement between the EU and the UK. A simmering row over supplies of the Oxford/AstraZeneca Covid-19 vaccine to the EU (where the rollout was slower than in the UK) and the UK's possible use of the Protocol to ship vaccines to Britain using Northern Ireland as a backdoor, prompted the EU to trigger the Article 16 mechanism. The highly controversial move was roundly condemned in Northern Ireland, and by the British and Irish governments. DUP leader Arlene Foster called it "an incredible act of hostility" (Quinn 2021); Irish Taoiseach Micheál Martin labelled it a "mistake" (Sheehy 2021); and Prime Minister Johnson expressed "grave concerns" about the EU's actions (McGlynn *et al.* 2021). The EU swiftly reversed course and European Commission President Ursula von der Leyen voiced her deep regret over the ill-advised move. Despite the EU's prompt response and unreserved apology, the political damage was done and unionist scepticism about the EU's sincerity and probity as a neutral Brexit player was (further) undermined. In the wake of the incident, unionist dissatisfaction finally bubbled over into street protests, some of which turned violent. The EU, nevertheless, remains adamant and resolute that "there is no alternative to the full and correct implementation of the protocol" (O'Leary 2021).

The process of agreeing whether and how the new burdens and barriers that the Protocol places on trade in Northern Ireland might be alleviated pitted the UK and the EU against each other, while unionists' demands for the Protocol to be removed clashed with demands from nationalists and others that it be implemented in full. In short, the form that Brexit has taken in Northern Ireland has both created and sustained political conflicts that seem unlikely to be resolved in the short to medium term. In particular, it opened up long-term questions to which there are no easy answers. The contested decisions and developments – some based on ignorance, and others ill-advised, mistaken and even nefarious – which both preceded and followed the EU referendum created conditions under which different agents were forced to make decisions with potentially long-term and path-dependent consequences for Northern Ireland's constitutional future. Brexit's effect in and for Northern Ireland is the product of calculations made and decisions taken by different political agents, which in turn created new conditions to which those same agents were then forced to respond. Brexit is not and likely will not be "done" for Northern Ireland in the short or medium term, and it will have long-term consequences which all of these agents must continue to navigate. The following chapters analyse the strategic positions, forced reactions and calculated reassessments that individual agents (in Northern Ireland, the Republic of

Ireland and Great Britain) pursued in seeking to manage Brexit's impact on their core constituencies. They detail how Brexit changed the conditions underpinning stability and the status quo in Northern Ireland, and so created a highly charged "critical moment" capable of precipitating a "critical constitutional juncture".

# 3

# Irish nationalism

"To the nationalist people in Northern Ireland, I want to assure you … You will never again be left behind by an Irish Government."

Leo Varadkar, 8 December 2017

"I believe we are now in a decade of opportunity and I believe in the next number of years, certainly before the end of this decade, we will have voted for a united Ireland."

Michelle O'Neill, 13 August 2020

"The Government has said that, for the next five years, a border poll is not on our agenda. I've also made it clear that my approach is through consensus and listening and engagement."

Micheál Martin, 22 October 2020

In July 2016, Gerry Adams, Sinn Féin's president of more than 35 years, was interviewed in his Leinster House office by VICE News' Katie Engelhart. Asked, "In a way, Brexit is a gift for you, right? You campaigned against it, but now that it's happening, you're using it to make the case for a United Ireland", Adams responded, "Yeah, well, you always have to never waste a crisis, never waste a difficulty" (VICE News 2016). This question, and Adams' answer, are illuminating. They speak to the somewhat ambiguous position that Irish nationalism, in general, and specifically Sinn Féin – as the largest nationalist party in Northern Ireland and biggest all-island party – found itself in after the Brexit referendum. On the one hand, Brexit posed an intrinsic challenge to the kind of actually-existing North–South cooperation, cross-border connectivity and all-island integration that has given subtle but increasingly concrete expression to nationalist political identity since 1998. On the other hand, the political and constitutional upheaval that the referendum brought in its wake provides perhaps the best chance that nationalists have had in the one hundred years since partition of seeing their aspiration to Irish unification fulfilled.

Brexit has thus created risks and opportunities for Irish nationalism, and different nationalist agents have sought to make sense of and navigate the critical constitutional moment it has represented. Here we define "nationalism" broadly as encompassing those, on both sides of the border, whose primary political identity is Irish, and who share a political aspiration to Irish (re)unification. More particularly, we are concerned here with those political parties and movements whose policy programmes seek, to a lesser or greater extent, to give expression to Irish identity and the aspiration to unification. In Northern Ireland, this is largely (though far from perfectly) reducible to those parties whose elected representatives explicitly designate as "Nationalist". Of these, the largest and most significant electorally are Sinn Féin (see Bean 2007; de Bréadún 2015; Whiting 2018) and the SDLP (see McLoughlin 2010; Farren 2010; Campbell 2015).

Across the border in the Republic of Ireland, where definitions of nationalism rely less heavily on juxtaposition to a unionist other, this is perhaps more of an ambiguous exercise. All of the main parties that contest elections in the Republic of Ireland (as well as the substantial number of independent candidates who also contest these elections [see Weeks 2017]) seek to give some expression to a sense of Irish nationhood, and most, if not all, at least nominally favour a united Ireland (Duffy 2020). This includes Fianna Fáil and Fine Gael, as well as the Social Democrats and the Labour Party, which each aspire to Irish unity in the long term. Sinn Féin is a staunch advocate of Irish unification in the short- to medium-term, and the party contests elections on both sides of the border.

A number of parties similarly organize across jurisdictions, but with more equivocal consequences for their position on the constitutional question. In the Republic, both the Green Party and the hard-left People Before Profit (PBP) stand for election on (rhetorically) pro-unity platforms, but in the North, elected representatives from both parties designate as "Other" (that is, officially neutral on the constitutional question).

A smattering of smaller parties that are organized on an all-island basis are more emphatically nationalist. These include Aontú (whose defining policy is its anti-choice position on abortion) as well as a number of micro-parties on the far right or affiliated to one or other of the "dissident" (that is, anti-Good Friday Agreement) Republican paramilitary groupings (see McGlinchey 2019). Ultimately, when talking about the politics of Irish nationalism in the Republic of Ireland in the wake of Brexit, we are principally interested in the state's three largest political parties:[1] Fianna Fáil (see Whelan 2011; McGraw & O'Malley 2018), Sinn Féin and Fine Gael (see Collins & Meehan 2020). Fianna Fáil was the lead opposition party between 2016–20 and party of government after the 2020 general election. Sinn Féin became the lead opposition party in 2020, following its best ever election result in the Republic of Ireland. Fine Gael was the lead party of government between 2016 and 2020 and is a member of a "grand coalition" government formed with Fianna Fáil and the Green Party after the 2020 general election. The various mobilizations of all of these different nationalist agents on the island of Ireland, their attempts to leverage such opportunities as Brexit's critical moment has presented, and, more particularly, to negotiate its risks, entails enduring consequences for Northern Ireland's future.

## "Irish Unity is our route back to Europe"

Nationalists in Northern Ireland voted overwhelmingly in favour of the UK remaining in the EU (see, e.g., Murphy 2018a: 51–3). All of Northern Ireland's nationalist-majority parliamentary constituencies returned substantial majorities for Remain. Indeed, according to Coakley and Garry (2016), the 56 per cent of the Northern Irish electorate which voted to Remain included fully 89 per cent of nationalist voters. In this regard, nationalists took their cue from Sinn Féin and the SDLP, both of which held pro-Remain positions in the referendum. As Connelly (2018: 12–18) details, the then Fine Gael government also strongly advocated for Remain and made a number of interventions in

---

1. In the 2020 Irish general election, these parties received a combined 67.57 per cent of first preference votes, with Sinn Féin receiving 24.53 per cent, Fianna Fáil 22.18 per cent, and Fine Gael 20.86 per cent (*Irish Times* 2020).

the referendum campaign on both sides of the Irish Sea. The Fianna Fáil opposition also campaigned actively for a Remain vote.

This positioning reflected concerns shared by nationalists of all shades about the potential economic, social and political impact of Brexit on both parts of the island of Ireland. On 3 June 2016, then Deputy First Minister of Northern Ireland, Martin McGuinness, captured the mood when he argued that, "Brexit would be bad for Ireland, bad for business and trade, bad for our farmers and bad for human rights and workers' rights" (*Belfast Telegraph* 2016a). The risk posed by Brexit, as perceived by nationalists, was thus, on one level, very material. But it was also more profoundly existential. The re-imposition of a hard border at what would become a new frontier between the UK and the EU would represent a stark reassertion of British sovereignty in Northern Ireland, which had come to be exercised in more diffuse, subtle and unobtrusive ways during and since the peace process (Gormley-Heenan & Birrell 2015). The blurring of boundaries between North and South, and the invisible land border which the Belfast/Good Friday Agreement has both facilitated and on which its proper functioning is dependent, is a reflection of an Irish nationalist political identity which has increasingly been accommodated and found expression in Northern Ireland in the wake of the peace process. Brexit would necessarily pose an intrinsic threat to this. As Cochrane (2020: 51, original emphasis) suggests, "A pragmatic acceptance that [one] could be Irish within the UK within the envelope of the European Union is *not at all* the same as agreeing to be Irish within the UK, outside the protective influence of EU membership of which the rest of the imagined community in Ireland was a member".

On 24 June 2016, once it became clear that the UK had voted to leave the EU, nationalists on both sides of the border expressed their dismay at the result. Tony Connelly (2018; see also Laffan 2018) has detailed how Ireland's Fine Gael-led government moved quickly to begin lobbying at the EU level to ensure the protection of Irish national interests, including the Common Travel Area, trade links with the UK and the Belfast/Good Friday Agreement. As Murphy (2019a: 540–41) has examined, the Irish government's Brexit priorities informed a "four-fold series of actions". The first and primary focus was on intensive engagement with both the EU and heads of other European states. There was also a focus on consulting with stakeholders across the island, including through a series of All-Island Civic Dialogues. The institutional response included increasing capacity to manage Brexit in and across relevant government departments, while the Brexit Omnibus Act provided a legislative response (and sought to prepare Ireland for the possibility of a no deal Brexit). For his part, Fianna Fáil leader and then leader of the opposition, Micheál Martin, lamented the referendum outcome as "the result of a relentless campaign of attacks on Europe and the promotion of an anti-foreigner agenda". He called for an "inclusive national-approach to the negotiations" (Fianna Fáil 2016a) and subsequently backed the government's negotiating strategy.

In Northern Ireland, the nationalist response to the Brexit vote was to highlight that the will of a majority of Northern Irish voters was to Remain in the EU. The Sinn Féin leadership wasted no time in calling for a border poll, on the basis that the UK government had lost its democratic authority to govern in Northern Ireland. At a press conference outside Stormont Castle, Martin McGuinness told the assembled media,

> Our focus is clearly on the democratically expressed wishes of the people here in the North. And achieving a 56 per cent vote was brought about as a result of Unionists, Nationalists and Republicans voting together to remain in Europe … This is about a decision which has, effectively, in my view, undermined the good work that was done in the Good Friday Agreement … We do believe that there is, against the backdrop of this decision – which has been so detrimental to everybody on this island – a democratic imperative for a border poll.
>
> (*Belfast Telegraph* 2016b)

McGuinness' argument hinged on a maximalist interpretation of the "principle of consent", which holds that the kind of constitutional change that Brexit represents can only take place in Northern Ireland with the support of a majority of its citizens (Harvey 2016; Murphy 2018b). As Cochrane (2020) notes, this recourse to the consent principle has represented something of a departure for Sinn Féin. The principle had been incorporated as a core pillar of the Belfast/Good Friday Agreement largely to assuage unionists' concerns about being levered into a united Ireland against their will, and only reluctantly accepted by Sinn Féin who had historically referred to it as a "Unionist veto" (see, e.g., Sinn

Féin 1994). The consent principle has also been leveraged by unionists to *oppose* any Brexit settlement which marks Northern Ireland as distinct or diverging from the rest of the UK. Its deployment by Sinn Féin in the Brexit process is indicative of how, since 2016, the Leave/Remain divide has been mapped onto – and altered the terms of – the constitutional question which has long defined Northern Ireland politics.

According to Sinn Féin, Northern Ireland's Remain majority provided both the logic for a border poll and a pool of voters from which a majority for Irish unification was liable to emerge. This pool includes what one Sinn Féin MP described as "middle-class" nationalists who had previously been comfortable with the post-1998 dispensation (interview with author, 2018), but also "others" and even unionists concerned about Brexit's ramifications for Northern Ireland's economy. The Irish unity debate no longer hinges on a simple or binary choice between the UK and an Irish Republic: the question of restored EU membership is now also at stake (Humphreys 2018; Harvey & Bassett 2019). As one Sinn Féin MP (interview with author, 2018) noted, for instance:

> I was [recently canvassing] a unionist farmer. And he made it very clear, he said 'look, I'm a DUP voter, I won't vote for you'. But we were just talking before I left, and we started talking about Brexit. And it changed a bit, you know? You could sense that he was worried, anxious. And he said, 'I tell you what, we might not agree on too many things', but he looked over and he says, 'over there', pointing to the South, 'that's never looked as close as it does today'.

In the months and years following the referendum, as the process of the UK's withdrawal from the EU became bogged down in conflict around the potential hardening of the Irish border, some of the trends in polling on the question of unification seemed to support Sinn Féin's view that Brexit had made it more of a live and proximate possibility. In a poll conducted by LucidTalk in 2018, 48 per cent of respondents signalled that they were "100 per cent certain" that they would vote for Northern Ireland to leave the UK in the event of a "no-deal" Brexit (with 55 per cent favouring Irish unification in this scenario if those who would "probably" vote for it were also included). Even in the event that the UK left the EU with a deal guaranteeing an open border on the island of Ireland, some 30 per cent of voters still favoured Irish unification (rising to 48 per cent if "probables" were also included) (LucidTalk 2018: 15–16).

RedC's Local and European Elections Exit Poll in May 2019 found support for Irish unity among voters in the Republic of Ireland at 77 per cent (once undecideds and non-voters were excluded) (RedC 2019: 50), whereas a poll released by Lord Ashcroft in September 2019 found that (once "don't knows" and non-voters were excluded) 51 per cent of Northern Irish voters would vote for Irish unification were a border poll to be held tomorrow (Lord Ashcroft Polls 2019). A major study of some 2,000 Northern Irish voters conducted by academics at the University of Liverpool and published in February 2020 put support for a united Ireland substantially lower, at only 29 per cent (Breen 2020a), but a poll published by the Detail and LucidTalk, also in February 2020, had this figure at 45 per cent. The same poll also found that 75 per cent of voters in the Republic of Ireland and 69 per cent of Northern Irish voters felt that Brexit had made a border poll more likely (Ingoldsby 2020). A further poll carried out by LucidTalk and published in October 2020 had support for Irish unity at 35 per cent, leading by one per cent support for Northern Ireland remaining in the UK (which stood at 34 per cent). In the same poll, 26 per cent said that their support for the Union was determined by their support for the NHS and their desire for an ongoing guarantee to healthcare free at the point of delivery (Breen 2020b).

It is both possible and necessary to question the accuracy, validity and biases of this polling (and, indeed, of opinion polling more generally), and the extent to which it really paints a picture of growing support for Irish unity is unclear (Emerson 2018; Moriarty 2020a; CUWGUR 2021). As Tonge (2020a; see also CUWGUR 2021: 49–55) notes, across polls taken on this question since 2016, the gap between those in favour and those opposed to Irish unification has fluctuated from as little as three to as much as 41 per cent, and overall – despite a narrowing in the polls that ranges from marginal to fairly substantial[2] – the constitutional

---

2. As noted by the CUWGUR (2021), there are sizeable differences between polls on the question of Irish unity conducted face-to-face and those conducted online. Face-to-face polling (which the working group defines as the "gold standard") tends to return smaller percentages in favour of unity than do polls conducted online. Donaghy (2020) has speculated that this may be attributable to a "shy nationalist" factor, whereby "centre ground voters are breaking towards support

status quo still consistently emerges as the preference of a majority in Northern Ireland. However, there is mounting evidence that Brexit has precipitated increased demand for and expectation around constitutional change. Northern Ireland has been taken out of the EU against the express wishes of the majority of its citizens, and it remains the only part of the UK with a clear route back to EU membership. According to LucidTalk polling in February 2020, 48 per cent of Northern Ireland voters would support Irish unity as a route back to Europe (Ingoldsby 2020). Further, Brexit has destabilized the UK constitution more widely (Wincott *et al.* 2020), has re-ignited the question of Scottish independence, and precipitated a rise in what has been termed "indy-curiosity" in Wales. It is highly likely that an "Indyref II" in Scotland would have implications for the constitutional debate in Northern Ireland, particularly if such a referendum was won by the pro-independence side (CUWGUR 2021: 32–3).

To put it plainly, Brexit has made a united Ireland – though far from inevitable, and, according to some polls, only at the margins – a more immediate possibility (Connolly & Doyle 2019a). Research undertaken by Garry *et al.* (2021) intimates that as the form that Brexit has (both potentially and actually) taken since 2016 has increasingly hardened, this has become ever more the case. Thus, as alluded to by Gerry Adams during his VICE News interview, Brexit, in general, and the forms of hard Brexit favoured first by Theresa May and latterly by Boris Johnson, in particular, have presented Sinn Féin members and supporters with what is arguably a once-in-a-generation opportunity to see their constitutional aspirations fulfilled sooner rather than later. It is unsurprising, therefore, that Sinn Féin have publicly called for a border poll within the next five years. Calling for and seeking to win such a poll is, after all, the party's *raison d'être*.

The push for a post-Brexit border poll has not been led solely or exclusively by Sinn Féin. The new momentum which this debate has gathered since the Brexit referendum has both been driven by and given rise to a number of grassroots campaigns, organizations and social media groups which have sprung up since 2016. These include

---

for Irish unity in private polls, but for whatever reason prefer not to disclose this in person". Alternatively, online polling may overstate the number of pro-unity voters.

Think32, Shared Ireland and Ireland's Future. Shared Ireland hosts the "A conversation with …" podcast series, in which guests from across the island of Ireland are invited to discuss the question of Irish unity. Ireland's Future – which is led by Belfast-based lawyer, Niall Murphy – has been responsible for organizing a series of public engagement events throughout the island of Ireland since 2017, including a flagship event at Belfast's Waterfront Hall in January 2019. The Waterfront Hall event was attended by some 2,000 people and featured speeches from prominent commentators and academics, and speakers from each of Ireland's main nationalist parties. Ireland's Future has also coordinated a series of open letters to the Taoiseach – the latest of which was sent on 1 November 2019 and which received more than 1,000 signatures from "civic" nationalists in sectors including academia, the arts, media and business – urging the creation of a citizens' assembly on the question of unification (Ireland's Future 2019a, 2019b). Since December 2020, it has published a series of discussion documents outlining its views on the principles governing and procedures for referendums on Irish unity.

## "The border poll should be the last, and not first, piece of the jigsaw"

Sinn Féin is not the only Irish political party in the (at least rhetorically) pro-unity camp, albeit that theirs has been the most consistent and unequivocal call for an urgent post-Brexit border poll. The SDLP has provided some indication that the party also views Brexit as having fundamentally changed the nature and immediacy of the constitutional question. Senior members of the party – for whom membership of the EU has long been both of profound emotional and personal significance and political-strategic importance (McLoughlin 2009) – have indicated that Brexit has reprioritized and recentred the constitutional question in their politics. For example, one SDLP MLA suggested that,

> Those of us on the more moderate of the nationalist scale were quite content – and I think particularly this generation of elected representatives in the SDLP were quite content, that our project for at least the next couple of decades was making Northern Ireland work … But that has changed quite radically

and quite quickly ... As somebody who doesn't feel very Nationalist, who's not stirred by Nationalistic things – that this is being done to me by these anonymous people in England makes me *feel* very Nationalist. (Interview with author, 2018)

Early in the Brexit process, the party's current leader, Colum Eastwood, also intimated that it was his view that a referendum on Northern Ireland's constitutional status should be held once Brexit negotiations were complete, and this formed part of the SDLP's manifesto for the 2017 UK general election (Moriarty 2017).

However, the SDLP has generally and more consistently asserted that the time is not right for a border poll; that such a poll would be unnecessarily divisive and would further destabilize Northern Ireland in a period already marked by considerable instability;[3] and that it should not be held until it is both conclusively and consensually winnable, and framed by a viable plan for unification (Manley 2020a). SDLP members have been keen to stress that Northern Ireland's pro-Remain majority does not translate automatically either into a majority for unity *or* into a concrete plan for it (Hanna 2019a, 2019b). Since 2016, senior SDLP figures – including former Deputy First Minister of Northern Ireland, Seamus Mallon – have publicly expressed concerns that if a border poll was won by the pro-unity side by a simple majority, then this would mean a sizeable minority in the newly unified state that would feel alienated from and opposed to it (Mallon with Pollak 2019). This would have potentially serious implications for the perceived legitimacy of such a poll, and for the smoothness of any transition to Irish unity that followed. As such, and contra the terms of the Belfast/Good Friday Agreement – which explicitly sets the threshold for victory in a referendum on Northern Ireland's constitutional status at 50 per cent + 1 – some within the SDLP have suggested that a weighted majority or cross-community consent should be required to induce a transfer of

---

3. Mary Lou McDonald, who took over the presidency of Sinn Féin from Gerry Adams in February 2018, expressed similar sentiments in July 2018 when she argued that "It is not ... our preferred option that we deal with the issue of Irish unity in a climate that is unsteady or unstable or chaotic, in other words in the context of a crash Brexit or a very hard Brexit" (*Irish Times* 2018). However, she later reaffirmed that her party's preference was for a border poll at the nearest available opportunity.

sovereignty in and over Northern Ireland. Key figures within the party – including former MLA and current MP, Claire Hanna – have been keen to stress above all that deepening North–South integration and building better relationships within and between North and South should be a precursor to any border poll.

The SDLP's position on the question of a post-Brexit border poll has largely been mirrored in the approach taken by Fine Gael and Fianna Fáil[4] since 2016. Senior figures in both parties have, at times, sought to burnish their pro-unity credentials. Fianna Fáil Senator Mark Daly has played a prominent role in the burgeoning unity debate, including as rapporteur for a report entitled *Brexit and the Future of Ireland: Uniting Ireland and its People in Peace and Prosperity*, adopted by the Houses of the Oireachtas Joint Committee on the Implementation of the Good Friday Agreement in August 2017. Also in 2017, then Tánaiste and Minister for Foreign Affairs, Fine Gael's Simon Coveney, asserted that he would like to see a united Ireland within his "political lifetime" (Manley 2017). Sections of the British press have been keen – often to the point of farce – to paint Fine Gael party leader, former Taoiseach and current Tánaiste, Leo Varadkar,[5] as a rabid Irish nationalist, and one who has sought to leverage Brexit in furtherance of his unity agenda (see Thompson 2020). Indeed, in his opening address to Fine Gael's *ard fheis* (party conference) in June 2021, Varadkar stressed that he "believe[s] in the unification of our island", that it can and should happen in his lifetime, and that Fine Gael "should be proud to say that unification is something we aspire to" (Fine Gael 2021). Also in 2021, Fianna Fáil TD, Jim O'Callaghan and Fine Gael TD, Neale Richmond (both tipped as potential future leaders of their parties) presented their respective visions for a united Ireland at a seminar at Sidney Sussex College, Cambridge (O'Callaghan 2021; Richmond 2021). In part as a response to the electoral growth of Sinn Féin since 2016, and particularly in 2020, both Fine Gael and Fianna Fáil have taken a keener and more sustained interest in the constitutional question, at least rhetorically.

---

4. In January 2019, the SDLP and Fianna Fáil announced a new, formal partnership agreement, including a joint approach on "Uniting Ireland's People" (McCann 2019).

5. Under the terms of the Programme for Government jointly agreed by Fianna Fáil, Fine Gael and the Green Party in 2020, Leo Varadkar will resume the role of Taoiseach in December 2022.

However, in general, both parties have been more than a little hesitant to use Brexit as an opportunity to further the project of Irish unification. According to one Fine Gael Senator, for example,

> I've no interest in a United Ireland in the short term. It's an emotional thing: people like the idea of a United Ireland, but there is no practical way to do it without more or less causing trouble. If you rush it, there will be paramilitary violence, particularly on the Loyalist side. And then, if you have a referendum, 60 to 70 per cent of people here say they would like it, but I think if you started saying, 'well, sure, you'd like it, but are you prepared to pay an extra couple of grand tax a year', people might like it less. And the more you see in Northern Ireland – when you're confronted with the likes of Sammy Wilson and Jim Allister, the less appealing it is. You're thinking, 'well, they're going to be in our Parliament. We're gonna have to change our flag, change our anthem, we're gonna have to make Ulster-Scots an official language: all of these things'.     (Interview with authors, 2018)

Crucially, during the tenure of the governments of the 32nd Dáil (led between 2016 and 2017 by Enda Kenny, and between 2017 and 2020 by Leo Varadkar), there were "no policy documents, no public consultations, no Dáil debates … and no media sources actively agitating for a united Ireland" (Murphy 2019b). As noted above, in 2017 the Oireachtas Joint Committee on the Implementation of the Good Friday Agreement published its report on uniting Ireland after Brexit. The report, which ran to more than 400 pages, included a series of recommendations in preparation for a border poll, including the convening of a "New Ireland Forum 2"[6] and a full legal and constitutional audit. Precisely none of these recommendations were implemented.

---

6. The original New Ireland Forum was held between 1983 and 1984 and sought to facilitate North–South dialogue on solutions to the conflict in Northern Ireland and a new, peaceful and democratic political settlement. Its final report listed three possible alternatives: a unitary Irish state, a federal or confederal Irish state and joint British/Irish sovereignty over Northern Ireland (New Ireland Forum 1984). While none of its recommendations were ultimately adopted, it provided a key impetus for the 1985 Anglo-Irish Agreement.

As a result, and as Humphreys (2018; see also de Mars *et al.* 2018) has highlighted, key legal-political lacunae have been allowed to persist in Ireland's constitution, which will need to be addressed if any transition to a united Ireland is to be facilitated in the future.[7] Indeed, any process of unification is going to involve far more than simply removing the border. From issues such as the symbols of the state – its flag(s), anthem(s) and rituals – to more substantive questions about citizenship, the economy and reform of the health sector, unity would represent a process of profound and contested state restructuring on the island of Ireland. Ireland's governing parties have so far been reluctant to fully grapple with what such a process would entail.

On the face of it, the "Shared Island" unit established in the Department of the Taoiseach – which is underpinned by a "Shared Island Fund" of some €500 million – by the Fianna Fáil, Fine Gael and Green Party government in 2020 represents something of a departure from a previously more hesitant approach to pursuing and preparing for Irish unity. However, the language around the aims and financing of this unit carefully and deliberately eschewed references to "unity" (McGrath 2020), and its mission is couched in a broader approach to stabilizing, repairing and normalizing North–South and British–Irish relations after Brexit (Tannam 2020). The current Taoiseach, Fianna Fáil's Micheál Martin, has ruled out pursuing a border poll within the lifetime of the 33rd Dáil[8] (Preston 2020), and his government's approach to the debate about Irish unity *per se* remains markedly circumspect. The focus instead is largely on deepening all-island economic integration and connectivity through investment in a number

---

7. For instance, as it stands, full voting rights in the Republic of Ireland are only granted to Irish citizens. The Belfast/Good Friday Agreement stipulates that those born in what is now Northern Ireland will remain entitled to claim British or Irish citizenship, or both, in perpetuity and without prejudicing access to the full range of rights and entitlements made available to citizens by whichever government is sovereign there. In order to guarantee this, as Humphreys (2018) outlines, it would therefore be necessary to extend full voting rights to British citizens in the event that sovereignty over Northern Ireland were to transfer from London to Dublin.

8. Although this decision is not ultimately (at least primarily) his to make: the Belfast/Good Friday Agreement and the Northern Ireland Act 1998 stipulate that if the Secretary of State for Northern Ireland is persuaded that there is liable to be a pro-unity majority in Northern Ireland, then it is on this basis that a border poll is to be held. CUWGUR (2021) has explored what this might mean in practice.

of infrastructure and capital projects. These include development of the A5 corridor (which connects Dublin and Derry), the Ulster Canal and Narrow Water Bridge, a series of cross-border greenways, and a scoping exercise on developing cross-border high-speed rail links (Merrion Street 2020).

Despite Brexiters' claims that subsequent Irish governments – as the vanguard of some "new phase of pan-nationalism" (Wilson Foster 2018) – have sought to use or leverage Brexit as a way to usher in Irish unity by the back door, the principal product of the Irish government's role (and, indeed, of the role played by Irish nationalists more widely) in the Brexit process has been the Protocol on Ireland/Northern Ireland. It is noteworthy that this Protocol (in its multiple iterations) has been concerned, insofar as this has been possible, with maintaining the political, legal and constitutional status quo (and its foundational "principle of consent") on the island of Ireland (Hayward & Phinnemore 2019; McGarry & O'Leary 2019; Phinnemore & Whitten 2021). The Protocol is an attempt at compromise, intended to guarantee a minimum level of political-legal stability for Ireland in an unknown and uncertain post-Brexit future, rather than an expression of desire for further disruption. Its primary purpose is emphatically not to bring about constitutional change. Indeed, notwithstanding unionist concerns about the forms of East–West regulatory divergence that it enshrines, the Protocol on Ireland/Northern Ireland explicitly acknowledges Northern Ireland's current constitutional status as part of the United Kingdom.

## "There's no such thing as a good Brexit"

Insofar as there has been a concerted "pan-nationalist" effort to affect the course of the Brexit process since 2016, its principal outworking has been the Protocol, rather than any sustained acceleration towards a border poll. This demonstrates that the perceived risks that Brexit has posed – both material and metaphysical – for nationalism have ultimately been viewed as trumping any of its opportunities, and that it has been met more with cautious technocracy than with tub-thumping renditions of "A Nation Once Again". There has been almost universal agreement that there is no good Brexit outcome for Ireland. Indeed, notwithstanding Adams' claims about never wasting a crisis, and his party's ongoing calls for a post-Brexit border poll within five years, we argue that even Sinn Féin has actually sought to navigate Brexit, and the critical juncture it potentially represents, with more caution than enthusiasm and a deep awareness of the dangers it poses (Evershed & Murphy 2021). As argued by one Sinn Féin Senator in 2018,

> While, yes, a hard Brexit and that recklessness, that chaos would probably strengthen our argument for a United Ireland, we actually haven't taken that path. Because we understand that in the here and now, we have to represent our people. We have to try and protect their health services, education, our economy that funds all of that. So, we have actually taken an approach that I hope is responsible, and is in the best interests of our people … Of course we want a United Ireland, but we don't want one built on the ruins – the economic ruins. We want one in which people are happy and comfortable and have their eyes wide open about what it means, rather than done in a way that's based on fear or chaos. That's not the pathway to a United Ireland that I would want.
>
> (Interview with author, 2018)

In late 2016, Sinn Féin's policy approach to Brexit crystallized around what it called "Special Designated Status for the North within the EU" (Sinn Féin 2016b, 2017b). This policy prioritized continued access to the single market for Northern Ireland; maintenance of EU funding; continuation of the Common Travel Area (CTA); upholding of employment and workers' rights; representation for Northern Ireland in the European Parliament and on other EU bodies; human rights guarantees; maintenance of EU environmental protections and energy laws; and full protection of the Belfast/Good Friday Agreement (Murphy 2018a: 129). Crucially, as an approach to managing the fallout of Brexit for Ireland, North and South, this policy platform is largely indistinguishable from that adopted by the SDLP, Fine Gael or Fianna Fáil (or, for that matter, Alliance, the Green Party or any of the Republic's other main political parties). Notwithstanding some disagreement and squabbling at the margins, and a pinch of what might be termed a "narcissism of minor difference" (Blok 1998), the degree of cross-border policy convergence within Irish nationalism on the question as to how Brexit should be managed has been remarkable. And this shared approach has consistently put continuity and stability above the pursuit of constitutional change. Opposition parties have largely set aside party-politicking around Brexit in order to protect national political and economic interests. The Fianna Fáil leadership persistently put off ending its confidence-and-supply agreement with the then Fine Gael-led government until it became clear that an open border and the Belfast/Good Friday Agreement had been protected by a Brexit withdrawal agreement.

Throughout the Brexit negotiations, Sinn Féin did not seek to oppose – and largely rallied to – the Irish government's negotiating position and strategy (Costello 2021). As it was put by one Sinn Féin TD,

> I think on Brexit, the approach from politicians in Ireland generally – and having that cohesion – has been good, because Europe could then see that there was consistency across the political parties. We haven't taken a confrontational approach with the Irish government. We hold them to account as best we can, where we see that they have been naïve or slow, or where they haven't been as robust as they should be. We do hold them to account, but we're conscious that what we need to do is keep that consistent position in place.
>
> (Interview with authors, 2018)

This involved a number of compromises for the party, including embracing Ireland's EU membership more unequivocally than had traditionally been the case (Costello 2021; Holmes 2021). Spearheaded by the party's then MEP for Northern Ireland, Martina Anderson, Sinn Féin maintained its own (para)diplomatic effort throughout the Brexit negotiations which centred on "working" the European Parliament and Commission to ensure maintenance of an open border and protection of the Belfast/Good Friday Agreement in any Brexit withdrawal agreement. However, this complemented, rather than contradicted, the Irish government's own approach, and was largely subsumed into the wider Irish effort. Further, in Northern Ireland, the party often collaborated with its electoral competitors – the SDLP, Alliance and the Green Party – to lobby the UK government and push for acceptance, adoption and implementation of the Ireland/Northern Ireland Protocol. This found its ultimate expression in a series of "pro-Remain" electoral pacts between these parties during the 2019 UK general election (Whitten 2020a).

Sinn Féin's donning of the "green jersey" during Brexit negotiations came with a considerable political price tag, and blunted the extent to which it was able or even sought to leverage the UK's withdrawal from the EU for electoral gain or for the pursuit of its unity agenda. There was no "Brexit bounce" for the party in the Irish presidential election in 2018 (Duggan 2019), or in local or European elections in the Republic of Ireland in 2019 (Johnston 2020; Quinlivan 2020). The party's vote-share in Northern Ireland in the 2019 UK general election was also down by 6.7 per cent as compared to 2017 (albeit that, for the first time, Northern Ireland returned more Nationalists than Unionists to Westminster [Whitten 2020a]). Indeed, the broad consensus across nationalist parties around how Brexit should be managed has meant that there has been limited political capital to be gained for any of these parties in seeking to trumpet their Brexit policy, as Fine Gael found to its cost during the 2020 general election (Murphy 2021a). It is notable that Brexit was, according to an RTÉ/*Irish Times* exit poll, the most important factor in deciding how to vote in that election for only one per cent of Irish voters (Ó Cionnaith 2020). Instead, the key issues – and those which underpinned an electoral surge for Sinn Féin, which became the most popular party in the state by number of first preference votes – were more "bread and butter". Housing and healthcare were foremost among voters' concerns after years of rising rents and house prices and lengthening hospital waiting lists. The constitutional question featured only marginally in the election campaign.

However, the election result (and the longer-term political trends of which it is indicative) has implications for the constitutional debate on and about the island of Ireland (Murphy 2020). While these were not central to its electoral triumph in February 2020, Sinn Féin's manifesto for the general election did include a number of policy commitments in furtherance of the unity agenda. These included the establishment of a Joint Oireachtas Committee on Irish Unity, an all-island citizens' assembly to discuss and plan for a border poll, a white paper on unification and, ultimately, unity referendums on both sides of the border within five years (Sinn Féin 2020a: 11–12). It is difficult to imagine any government involving Sinn Féin as a senior (or even junior) partner – now a live prospect and, as it stands, a likely outcome of the next Irish general election, which must be held by February 2025 – not implementing at least some version of this platform. Arguably, it has already played an important role in shaping government policy: it is hard not to see the "Shared Island" unit as both a response to Sinn Féin's electoral surge, and as an attempt to (re)capture some of the ground in the constitutional debate that had been ceded to the party (McGrath 2020). As noted above, for at least the duration of the current Dáil, the Irish government's focus will be more on cross-border infrastructure than on the removal of the border *per se*.

At any rate, in the immediate political-economic future, it is arguable that other matters are liable to be more pressing. The work of the Shared Island unit – and, indeed, the tenure of this government more generally – will be framed and shaped by the long-term economic implications of both Brexit and the Covid-19 pandemic. As research by the Economic and Social Research Institute (ESRI) suggests, the challenges presented by these dual economic shocks are different in different sectors, such that the scale of the threat to the economy as a whole in the medium term is both broad and deep (Daly & Lawless 2020). In the longer term, over the next ten years, Brexit has the capacity to dent or stymie any potential post-pandemic recovery (McQuinn *et al.* 2020: 4–9).

As the Constitution Unit's Working Group on Unification Referendums on the Island of Ireland (2021: 52) has noted, the 2019 Northern Ireland Life and Times survey found that "a strong economy in the Republic of Ireland (compared to Northern Ireland) would be the factor that most persuaded people to vote in favour of Irish unification". It might be inferred, therefore, that a weakening of the Irish economy might act to dissuade people of the desirability of a border poll. And given the key role that economic uncertainty can play in shaping decision-making and its underpinning of "status quo bias" in constitutional referendums (Nadeau *et al.* 1999), this will likely have implications for any appetite for constitutional change in the Republic too. A number of models and studies suggest that unification would be economically beneficial (KLC Consulting 2016; Sinn Féin 2020b; Gosling 2020). However, some of the key claims on which this modelling is based are contested (see, e.g., Fitzgerald & Morgenroth 2019; Emerson

2020). Any perceived cost to the Irish taxpayer of unification is likely to face further scrutiny if the constitutional debate continues to gain traction. Indeed, a poll conducted by Kantor for the *Irish Independent* in 2021 found that while 67 per cent of voters in the Republic of Ireland favour Irish unification in principle, a majority – 54 per cent – said that they would be unwilling to pay more tax to facilitate it. Thirty-nine per cent felt that Irish unity would leave them worse off (Sheahan 2021). The upshot of all this is that the political-economic mood music for the next five years, and likely beyond, is liable to be fairly anxious, and not necessarily conducive to the kind of radical constitutional upheaval that Irish unity would represent.

## "Up the Republic, Up the RA and *Tiocfaidh ár lá*"

As the political party most closely identified with the project of Irish unity, how Sinn Féin is perceived by voters on both sides of the border will likely have an important bearing on whether, to what extent and in what ways this project continues to accelerate in coming months and years. In the North, where the party has a track record in government, its performance, perceived competence and social and economic policy platform have some bearing on how the party is viewed by voters (Garry 2016b). However, voter attitudes towards Sinn Féin – and, indeed, party politics more generally – remain shaped more fundamentally by the legacy of the Troubles (Little 2006), competition between competing ethnonational blocs (Tilley, Garry & Matthews 2019) and the political-legal and cultural "war by other means", which lies beneath Northern Ireland's peace (Curtis 2014).

Memorialization and even veneration of the Provisional IRA's campaign remains an important part of Sinn Féin's political culture (and cultural politics) and of Northern Ireland's "culture war" (Viggiani 2014). Senior party members – many of whom are themselves former IRA volunteers – often play a conspicuous role in public commemorations of the IRA. In February 2020, newly re-elected Sinn Féin TD, David Cullinane, courted controversy when he was filmed celebrating his party's electoral success with a victory speech which recalled the Republican Hunger Strikes of 1981 and included the line, "Up the

Republic, Up the RA and *Tiocfaidh ár lá*".[9] Then, in June 2020, thousands of spectators lined the Andersonstown Road in West Belfast for the funeral of prominent Belfast Republican, Bobby Storey. In direct contravention of her own Executive's Covid-19 regulations, Storey's guard of honour included party Vice President and Deputy First Minister of Northern Ireland, Michelle O'Neill. Commemoration and invocation of the armed struggle plays an important function in the maintenance of Sinn Féin's connection with its electoral base (Bean 2007; Brown & Viggiani 2010). But beyond this constituency, Sinn Féin's undermining of its own Covid restrictions at the Bobby Storey funeral was roundly condemned and severely dented perceptions of and approval ratings for the party (see, e.g., Breen 2020c). This was exacerbated in early 2021 by a Public Prosecution Service (PPS) decision not to prosecute any of the funeral's organizers for breaches of Covid regulations (Breen 2021a).

Unionists, in particular, balk at what they claim is Sinn Féin's glorification of terrorism. They are also liable to perceive duplicity and underhandedness in how Sinn Féin has approached governance in Northern Ireland, sought to navigate Brexit, and claimed to want to accommodate British identity in a "new" Ireland. As one senior Fianna Fáil TD viewed it:

> Sinn Féin have used Brexit as a bit of a rallying call to their base: 'let's go for unity!' And that's negative in my view. The Good Friday Agreement provides the framework for Irish unity, but in due course. And evolution is far better than this forced approach which Sinn Féin have adopted: 'let's use Brexit as the wedge to drive this'. And that then drives unionism back into the trenches on the question of the Union ... They're biting off their nose to spite their own face really, in quite a negative way.
> (Interview with authors, 2018)

Even by one senior Republican's own admission, episodes such as Cullinane's "Up the RA!" speech are "counterproductive to the Republican project: it goes against the spirit of engagement" (Sinn Féin Special

---

9. "*Tiocfaidh ár lá*" is Irish for "Our day will come". It is an Irish Republican slogan attributed to Provisional IRA prisoners in Long Kesh/HM Prison Maze, in general, and often to IRA prisoner and hunger striker, Bobby Sands, in particular.

Advisor, interview with author, 2020). Critically, such episodes also play badly with many nationalists and those who are more agnostic or persuadable on the constitutional question, and who Sinn Féin will need to win round to the pro-unity side in any future border poll. The Alliance Party – a newly assertive force in Northern Ireland politics – are wont to attempt to cast Sinn Féin and the DUP as two sides of the same ethno-sectarian coin.

Sinn Féin is the single most important driving force behind the contemporary constitutional debate in Northern Ireland, and stands to benefit from the new political and electoral arithmetic that Brexit has precipitated there. According to polling in February and May 2021, Sinn Féin looks set to become the biggest party in the Northern Ireland Assembly following the next election (Breen 2021b, 2021c). But the legacies of its (para)military past, perceptions of coat-trailing – particularly in the context of the global coronavirus pandemic – and being viewed as a party of Northern Ireland's duopolistic establishment remain as potential obstacles to it achieving its most prized political objective. This is coupled with issues in Sinn Féin's party management in Northern Ireland, which in 2021 included a rancorous process of internal restructuring in Derry, the standing down of sitting MLAs, and what *Belfast Telegraph* political editor, Suzanne Breen (2020c), identified as an issue with succession and "a significant contrast in the talent at the top of the party in both jurisdictions. Sinn Féin's front bench in the Dáil dwarfs that on [the Northern] side of the border".

In the Republic of Ireland, since the 2020 general election, Sinn Féin has continued to poll well, and at the time of writing it remains a prevailing assumption in the corridors of Leinster House that the party will play a leading role in government following the next general election (albeit that this election is not scheduled to take place until 2025). However, Fine Gael's fortunes have also rebounded, in part as a result of its perceived success in the handling of the early phase of the Covid-19 pandemic. Having garnered 21 per cent of first preference votes at the election, Fine Gael has recovered some ground in polling since March 2020. The net result has been a squeeze on Fianna Fáil's polling. This has been accompanied by increased scrutiny of Sinn Féin and probing of its (para)military heritage in the Southern Irish media (see, e.g., *Irish Times* 2020). Added to this has been a belligerent social media campaign from Fine Gael seeking to highlight Sinn Féin's links with the

IRA, irregularities in its finances, and cross-border inconsistencies in its policy programme (McGee 2020).

Fianna Fáil too have been keen to draw attention to the violence of Sinn Féin's past. During a Dáil debate on the Shared Island unit in September 2020, for instance, Fianna Fáil leader and Taoiseach, Micheál Martin, responded to a critical question about the initiative from Sinn Féin TD, Rose Conway-Walsh, with an insistence that he did "not need any lectures from … anybody on the Sinn Féin side of the house". He continued, "You endorsed violence as the way to unify Ireland and what you did was you did more damage than anybody else in relation to a united Ireland. And you continue to endorse that narrative, not understanding that every time you endorse the narrative of violence you make it more difficult than ever to get a united Ireland or to get consent" (Martin, quoted in McGrath 2020).

As indicated by Sinn Féin's sustained and growing polling figures since March 2020, it is not clear that these sorts of rhetorical attacks on the party have (yet) had much purchase or impact with voters in the Republic of Ireland, in general, and the pool of younger voters from which Sinn Féin increasingly draws support, in particular. These voters came of age or were born after the signing of the Belfast/Good Friday Agreement, and do not necessarily see the violence of the Troubles as so enduringly resonant in the political present. Arguably, they also perceive themselves as having a less immediate stake in the kind of ethno-sectarian identity politics that surrounds the constitutional question north of the border. Further, and as indicated above, exit polling during Ireland's 2020 general election suggests that issues other than Irish unity – notably, housing and healthcare – may be of more pressing importance to this cohort (though 75 per cent of voters aged 18–24, 60 per cent aged 25–34, and 80 per cent of Sinn Féin first-preference voters would like to see a border poll within the next five years [Barry 2020]).

Perhaps the most profound challenge confronting those advocating Irish unity in the short term are precisely the different priorities of those living on either side of a border which has – despite persistent predictions about its imminent erasure – endured for a century. In one hundred years of partition, the political cultures of the two jurisdictions on the island of Ireland have diverged: the twentieth- and early twenty-first-century experiences of the two states have been strikingly different. Despite the enduring political division of the island, people across these jurisdictions are, and long have been, connected by a multitude of familial, sporting, artistic, educational and organizational links. But the experience of being "Irish" across them has nonetheless been profoundly different (Todd 2015a). Outside of the border counties, where everyday lives are more meaningfully defined by cross-border relationships (McCall 2021), this has necessarily had consequences for how citizens on either side of the border perceive each other.

After 1998, despite the forms of North–South cooperation enshrined in the Belfast/Good Friday Agreement, Southern political and societal disengagement from the North arguably increased rather than diminished (Todd 2015b; Tannam 2018). More than 20 years since the conclusion of peace talks, the extent to which people in Bandon and Ballymoney, Killarney and Coleraine (or, for that matter, Kilkenny and Letterkenny) *really* know and understand each other remains something of an open question. As it was put by Fine Gael TD, Neale Richmond, during an appearance on *The Bunker* podcast on 3 December 2020: "how many people in Tyrone have friends in Cork, and *vice versa*? Where is that real level of engagement of people going up from Dublin and spending some time in the North, doing business there, and on a personal basis?" As the only nationalist party aspiring to (and seemingly on the cusp of) government on both sides of the border, the challenge that divergent experiences, aspirations and governmental demands on either side of it poses for Sinn Féin is acute (McBride 2020a, 2020b; Breen 2020c). The party itself stresses the importance of developing cross-border relationships and interconnectivity after Brexit and as part of building towards a "new" Ireland (Finucane 2019).

That Irish unity is imminent is thus far from a foregone conclusion, despite (and, indeed, because of) the political and constitutional upheaval that Brexit represents. A range of political, economic and cultural forces militate both for and against it, and there is profound intra-nationalist disagreement as to its contemporary desirability, attainability and sequencing. For nationalists of all hues, the range of challenges that Brexit poses for the island of Ireland has ultimately outweighed any opportunities. This has produced an approach which places political stability above any further change and disruption. The priority across nationalist parties and voters on both sides of the border has been the securing of a Brexit which prioritizes protection of the Belfast/Good Friday Agreement, North–South cooperation and Ireland's economic interests, rather than one which seeks to fast-track unity by any means necessary. In seeking to secure this objective, nationalism has largely "rallied to the flag", falling in behind a strategy led by the Irish government. This strategy has focused primarily on lobbying in Brussels and other European capitals to ensure that Ireland's national interests – above all, an open border and the Belfast/Good Friday Agreement – are protected during and after Brexit. The risks posed by Brexit have also precipitated new forms of collaboration between nationalist parties (and indeed, between nationalists and "others"; see, e.g., Young 2020).

In this context, Sinn Féin's calls for a border poll within five years have arguably been as much rhetorical flourish as firm policy goal. However, this is not to say that such calls have not been without either cause or consequence. Brexit is profoundly unpopular in Northern Ireland, and the (at times, apparently wilful) political, economic and cultural damage that it has wrought on Northern Ireland is considerable. This has undoubtedly given the conversation about Northern Ireland's constitutional future a new urgency. This is reflected in the inception of a number of pressure groups whose deliberate aim is to lobby and prepare for a border poll. A post-Brexit border poll may not be a policy goal currently shared by the island of Ireland's other major nationalist political parties, but calls for it by Sinn Féin reflect that the constitutional question is a live issue which requires a serious and considered policy response (Humphreys 2018). Present policy, as enshrined in the Programme for Government adopted by Fine Gael, Fianna Fáil and the Green Party in 2020, is to pursue a "shared" rather than a "united" Ireland.

It therefore seems likely that the prevailing priority for nationalism-at-large in the short term will be the attempted (re)building of relationships, the deepening of North–South economic integration and the building of new cross-border infrastructure, rather than the pursuit of an immediate post-Brexit border poll. This work will take place in a context shaped by a range of both "known" and "unknown" unknowns, particularly in relation to how Brexit, in general, and the Ireland/Northern Ireland Protocol, in particular, will reshape political economic dynamics on the island of Ireland in the near future, and how this will interact with the economic fallout of the Covid-19 pandemic. That is to say, it will likely be some time before it is known whether the balance of forces unleashed by both Brexit and Covid-19 tilts more towards or away from a united Ireland. Ultimately (and perhaps somewhat ironically) how these forces have been, are and will be interpreted and navigated by Ulster unionists will likely have as much (if not more) bearing on whether and when they may lead to Irish unification as will the choices, strategies and policy programmes of nationalists. It is to Ulster unionists' role in and experience of Brexit, and the constitutional debate that it has catalysed, that we therefore now turn.

# 4

# Ulster unionism

"I don't expect my own house to burn down but I still insure it because it could happen".

Peter Robinson, 27 July 2018

"Preparing for a possible united Ireland is not an insurance policy against something unpleasant happening, it is an invitation to republican arsonists to come in and burn our house down".

Sammy Wilson, 28 July 2018

In October 2018, then DUP party leader, Arlene Foster, used an interview with the BBC to stress that her party had only one red line in the Brexit process, that "there cannot ever be a border down the Irish Sea, a differential between Northern Ireland and the rest of the UK". This red line was, she asserted, "blood red" (see Morris 2018). Having campaigned for Brexit in 2016, by 2018 the DUP had been forced into a position of having to insist that Northern Ireland would leave the EU on the same terms as the rest of the UK. On the face of it, it did so from a position of strength unparalleled in its history, furnished by the confidence-and-supply arrangement, agreed with Theresa May's Conservative Party to give May the majority she needed in order to keep a hold on the reins of government. Nevertheless, the DUP ultimately failed to secure its preferred Brexit outcome, and cast Northern Ireland's constitutional future in an uncertain light.

The focus here is on the political tensions that Brexit's critical moment has produced for Ulster unionism, how unionists have sought to negotiate these, and with what potential consequences for Northern Ireland's constitutional future. For our purposes, "unionism" comprises those in Northern Ireland whose primary political identity is British and, more particularly, for whom the maintenance of Northern Ireland's present status as part of the United Kingdom is a (or, indeed, *the*) primary motivation in their political decision-making. Members of those political parties that seek to protect and promote Northern Ireland's position in the Union designate in the Northern Ireland Assembly as "Unionist". The largest of these, and the largest party in the Assembly (at the time of writing, by one seat) is the DUP (see Tonge *et al.* 2014). The decisions, actions and strategic (mis)calculations of this party have been of immediate consequence for the course of the Brexit process, and are therefore of primary interest to us. The DUP, however, exists in a complex relationship with other Unionist parties and a wide array of other unionist and loyalist[1] political actors.

Traditionally, the DUP's closest rival – and formerly the dominant unionist political force in Northern Ireland, until it was electorally overtaken by the DUP in 2003 – has been the UUP (see Hennessey *et al.* 2019). As of the 2017 Assembly election, the UUP holds 10 seats in the Northern Ireland Assembly, as well as the Health portfolio in the Northern Ireland Executive. To the cultural-political right of the DUP is Traditional Unionist Voice (TUV), whose leader, Jim Allister, left the DUP in protest at its decision in 2006 to enter power-sharing government with Sinn Féin. Allister is currently an MLA and the TUV also has a handful of councillors across Northern Ireland. The Progressive Unionist Party (PUP) is a small party economically to the left of the main Unionist parties. The party is linked to the loyalist paramilitary group, the Ulster Volunteer Force (UVF), in a way which mirrors (albeit inexactly) Sinn Féin's relationship with the IRA. As in the case of Sinn Féin, this paramilitary connection was central to the important role that the PUP was able to play in the peace process. Unlike Sinn Féin, however, the PUP has never enjoyed a post-conflict electoral renaissance, and its electoral base has never expanded beyond sections of working-class loyalism (Edwards 2010; McAuley 2010, 2015). The PUP

---

1. Loyalism – as distinct from wider unionism – is notoriously difficult to define in precise terms. Generally, loyalism is held to be more militant than "mainstream" unionism, and associated with paramilitarism. Arguably, the key thing that distinguishes loyalism is its class-characteristic, with loyalism generally a more working-class phenomenon (see Bell 1990; Shirlow & McGovern 1997; Gallaher 2007; McAuley 2010, 2015; Burgess & Mulvenna 2015).

holds no Assembly or parliamentary seats, and just three of Northern Ireland's more than 400 council seats. Finally, there is also a long tradition of "Independent" Unionism in Northern Ireland (Reid 2008) and a small number of Independent Unionists continue to contest, and win, elections. Claire Sugden served as Minister for Justice in the short-lived Northern Ireland Executive of 2016–17 and still sits as an Independent Unionist MLA for East Londonderry. Sylvia Hermon – who served as the MP for North Down from 2001 until 2019 – sat in the House of Commons as an Independent Unionist from 2010.

Other important independent (that is, not directly or officially affiliated to any particular political party) unionist agents in the overlapping debates about Brexit and the constitutional future in Northern Ireland include, *inter alia*, Sarah Creighton, a writer, lawyer and political commentator; Alex Kane, a commentator and columnist for the *Belfast Telegraph*, *Irish News* and the *Irish Times*; Ben Lowry, deputy editor of the *Belfast News Letter*; and Jamie Bryson, a loyalist blogger and political activist. Theirs are prominent unionist voices on both the left and the right, which range from green, feminist and/or liberal through to ultra-conservative and ethno-chauvinist. Arguments, perspectives and forms of political positioning from across this broad spectrum, from these commentators and others, and from both within and without formal party-political structures, have all been pivotal in shaping the politics of Brexit in Northern Ireland. Often, this has involved critiquing the particular role that the DUP has played in Brexit's fraught political theatre, assessing its fallout, and appraising what it might mean for Northern Ireland's place in the Union in the long term. This is all to say, in sum, that Brexit has been a source of and important vector for intra-unionist political conflict.

### "We can be even stronger if we take back control"

In 2016, unionists tended to support leaving the EU, albeit less emphatically than nationalists favoured remaining. According to Coakley and Garry (2016), 66 per cent of unionist voters backed Leave. Unionist parties were split on the question of the UK's future EU membership, with the UUP leadership backing Remain, while the DUP and TUV backed Leave. At the outset of the referendum campaign, the DUP's support for

Leave appeared very slightly less than full and unequivocal. In February 2016, Arlene Foster announced that it was her party's recommendation "on balance" that the UK should leave the EU, with the full expectation that "DUP members and voters [would] hold a range of differing personal views as to what is in the best interests of the United Kingdom" (*News Letter* 2016). The decision taken by senior party members to back Leave had, however, been unanimous. According to one such member, "I was at the policy-making conference that we had – I say conference, it was a meeting upstairs [at Stormont] – where they said, 'right gentlemen, we need to agree our policy on Brexit' – this was before the referendum. And ten minutes later we had agreed our policy. We just went 'round the room and it was, 'Burn it! Shoot it! Strangle it!'" (DUP MLA, interview with author, 2018). Public opposition to Brexit was voiced by a vanishingly small number of DUP members (see McBride 2019b). By the end of the referendum campaign, the party appeared to have fully claimed the pro-Leave mantle, including by placing a Vote Leave wrap-around advert in the Metro newspaper (which only circulates on the British "mainland") on the eve of the referendum.[2] In the event, 75 per cent of DUP voters, 91 per cent of TUV voters and 58 per cent of UUP voters voted for Brexit (Garry 2016a).

After years of political wrangling over the Irish border and constitutional upheaval across the UK – the result of which has been both the erection of new barriers between Great Britain and Northern Ireland, questions about the long-term viability of the Union and an increased volume and intensity to the debate about Irish unification – it is worth pausing to ask *why* unionists tended, by a margin of 2:1, to back Brexit. Garry (2016a) found that many of the factors that help to explain the Brexit vote elsewhere in the UK, including educational attainment (80 per cent of voters with a postgraduate degree voted Remain, whereas less than 50 per cent of those qualified to GCSE level did so) and "occupational skill" (80 per cent of "professionals" voted to Remain, whereas 52 per cent of manual workers voted to Leave) were also salient in Northern Ireland. However, although it reflects these trends in wider

---

2. This advert is estimated to have cost more that £280,000. Geoghegan (2020) has examined the trails of "dark money" that helped to finance it, and how Northern Ireland's differentiated rules around party financing were used to try and obscure these.

British politics, Ulster unionist Euroscepticism has long been shaped by particular and distinctive ethno-religious concerns (Murphy 2009; Ganiel 2009; Coakley 2020; Murphy & Evershed 2020a), and the unionist Leave vote in 2016 had its own ethnonational framing.

On one level, and as Coakley (2020) suggests, framed by the "Orange" and "Green" politics of Northern Ireland, the sheer fact of nationalist support for Remain in 2016 was, in itself, a driver of unionist support for Leave. As one former DUP staffer suggested, "probably the fact that Irish nationalism in latter years has been so pro-EU, there's probably some hint in the middle of all of that that if they're for it, we're against it" (interview with author, 2018). More substantively, the Brexit referendum provided an opportunity for unionists to engage in a debate about sovereignty in a way that meaningfully connected them with a wider British political community of which they generally form a far more marginal and peripheral part. As it was put by one SDLP MLA in their analysis of Northern Ireland's Brexit referendum,

> One Ulster Unionist [politician] said this to me: 'this is like our border poll'. Lots of leaflets with Union Jacks on them and stuff, and concepts and arguments around sovereignty and stuff. I think [many unionists] thought it would be a bit of a sandpit: that it was never going to go through, and they could do whatever they wanted. They could beat their chests and have flags on leaflets 'til the cows came home, stand up beside 'British' values and that there would be no consequences.
>
> (Interview with author, 2018)

Warnings about the impact of a Leave vote on Northern Ireland's economy and its border with the Irish Republic went largely unheeded by unionist Brexiters. Indeed, there is some suggestion that a prospective hardening of the border was part of the attraction of Brexit for some unionists, in general, and for sections of the DUP, in particular (see, e.g., McDaid 2018). A Leave vote was seen as an opportunity precisely to restate, reaffirm and reinscribe British sovereignty in and over Northern Ireland, which had come to be exercised in fuzzier, decentred and more ambiguous ways as a consequence of both the peace settlement and UK membership of the EU. Despite some concerns from within unionism itself that this could be politically and constitutionally destabilizing (see, e.g., Lowry 2016), Brexit was broadly welcomed by unionists. As one unionist Leave voter put it: "See the next day, after the vote? I didn't think it would go in our favour. I was driving home, and just happened to look up at the sky, and a big grin came over my face. And I just felt, for the first time … a sense of freedom which I'd never had before … I [felt] like the country [was] *ours* again" (Unionist Leave voter, interview with author, 2017).

Following the referendum, in Northern Ireland, the Brexit project came to be closely identified with unionism. Even the (in the event, somewhat unenthusiastically) pro-Remain UUP quickly shifted to a more pro-Brexit position, in line with broader unionist sentiment. Key figures in the DUP, including the party's Brexit spokesperson, Sammy Wilson, became leading proponents of a hard Brexit: one that would see the UK leave both the single market and the customs union, despite this necessarily having adverse implications for Northern Ireland (Phinnemore & Hayward 2017). That Northern Ireland voted as a whole to Remain in the EU was dismissed as incidental at best, as the decision to Leave was made by the wider British *demos* from which, it was asserted, Northern Irish voters could neither be divorced nor disaggregated (Cochrane 2020). This view was ultimately unreciprocated in Great Britain.

Brexit's functioning as a vehicle for reaffirming Northern Ireland's place in the Union seemed to be reinforced by the signing of the confidence-and-supply arrangement between the DUP and the Conservative Party following the 2017 general election. The deal gave the DUP an opportunity – unparalleled in its history – to exercise power at the constitutional centre, and scope to shape the UK government's priorities for the Brexit process in a way not afforded to other parties in Northern Ireland (particularly given the collapse of the Northern Ireland Executive) nor to Scotland and Wales (McEwen 2020). Undermining the spirit, if not the letter, of the Belfast/Good Friday Agreement's requirement for the sovereign government in Northern Ireland to exercise power there with rigorous impartiality, May's reliance on the DUP saw her come to echo the party's interpretative framing of Northern Ireland's place in the "precious Union". Concerns about the implications of the confidence-and-supply arrangement and its implications for the Belfast/Good Friday Agreement, British–Irish relations and the prospect of restoring power sharing in Northern Ireland were voiced by both outgoing and incoming Taoisigh (Enda Kenny and Leo Varadkar, respectively) (RTÉ News 2017), the Sinn Féin leadership, and former prime minister, John Major (Syal & Walker 2017), among others.

Criticism was also levelled by the leaders of both the Scottish and Welsh governments, who complained that the deal's £1 billion of additional funding for Northern Ireland further upset an already flawed framework for distributing resources across the devolved governments (Birrell & Heenan 2020). Critically, and somewhat demonstrative of "mainland" attitudes towards Northern Ireland more generally (and in an ominous foreshadowing of Boris Johnson's later betrayal of the party as soon as it became expedient to do so), the deal was greeted with dismay and even disgust across the British media. Cartoonists and columnists across the British papers were at pains – to the point of farce and even racialized stereotyping (O'Reilly 2017) – to represent the DUP's hallmark social conservatism as out-of-step with the British mainstream (Tonge 2017). Ruth Davidson, then leader of the Scottish Conservatives, signalled her opposition to her party's pact with the DUP on grounds of the latter's structural homophobia (Evershed 2020).

The DUP reached the peak (but also, ultimately, the limit) of its new-found power in December 2017, when it vetoed arrangements designed to guarantee the openness of the Irish border by keeping Northern Ireland in the regulatory orbit of the EU after Brexit, as outlined in the EU–UK Joint Report. Theresa May's doomed quest to find a "backstop" formula that would allow for the maintenance of a soft border on the island of Ireland and also placate the DUP demand that Northern Ireland would leave the EU on *precisely* the same terms as the rest of the UK ultimately proved her undoing. The DUP's strident opposition to the backstop put it at odds not only with May, but also the EU, the Irish government, Northern Ireland's business and farming communities and, crucially, a majority of citizens in Northern Ireland (see, e.g., Lord Ashcroft Polls 2019). The party's approach on Brexit played particularly badly with nationalist voters. Many nationalists came (with a degree of justification) to view the DUP's role in the Brexit process as provocatively anti-Irish and representing a deliberate attempt to unpick key aspects of the Belfast/Good Friday Agreement to which the DUP had never been fully reconciled, including the institutionalization of North–South cooperation (Tonge *et al.* 2014: 77). It also alienated a section of the liberal unionist electorate, pushing these voters further towards the "Other" camp.

In several key respects, the DUP's position on the backstop was contradictory, if not paradoxical. In resolutely refusing to accept even the most modest of enhanced regulatory checks[3] between Great Britain and Northern Ireland, the DUP thereby appeared willing to countenance a no-deal Brexit. Polls recorded that crashing out of Europe without a deal would drastically and rapidly increase support for a border poll and, critically, for Irish unity (Garry *et al.* 2021). Its opposition to the backstop thereby posed an existential risk to the DUP's most cherished political goal: maintenance of Northern Ireland's membership of the United Kingdom. The party's blood-red line that there could be no post-Brexit regulatory divergence across the Irish Sea was also at odds with the policy differences (some of them stark) that existed between Northern Ireland and the rest of the UK *precisely because* of the DUP's preferences (Barry 2018). The DUP's hypocritical insistence on full alignment with Great Britain on trade regulations but not on marriage equality or access to abortion services,[4] for instance, was alienating not only of nationalists and "others", but also of sections of the DUP's own unionist constituency, not to mention the "mainland" British electorate (McDonald 2017).

The party characterized support for the backstop as a necessarily and insidiously (pan-)nationalist policy position and tantamount to an attempt to achieve Irish unity by the back door (Murphy & Evershed 2020b). Unionist politicians were particularly bellicose in signalling that they viewed it as an Irish governmental power-play. One senior DUP figure claimed the backstop was "Dublin [seeking] to fulfil its objective of securing a united Ireland … they believe the more you can

---

3. As Emerson (2017) examined in a video report for TheDetail.tv, the principle of regulatory divergence between Great Britain and Northern Ireland is well established both historically and contemporarily. The island of Ireland was, for example, already treated as a single ecological unit, including for the purposes of key animal and plant health regulations.

4. With Stormont in abeyance, legal reform of both marriage and abortion regulations in Northern Ireland were forced through at Westminster through amendments to budgetary and technical legislation sponsored by Labour MPs, Conor McGinn and Stella Creasy (Walker & O'Carroll 2019). Same-sex marriage is now legal in Northern Ireland, as is abortion. However, in the case of the latter, the Northern Ireland Executive has so far failed to commission the requisite services.

separate Northern Ireland from the UK, the better the chance of achieving a united Ireland" (DUP MP, interview with authors, 2018). This was despite the Irish government's being at pains not to conflate the issue of Brexit with that of the constitutional question, and that it emphatically and explicitly did not regard Brexit as a fast-track to unification. In fact, the backstop was supported by a wide cross-section of Northern Irish society, almost all of its political parties, organized business interests and professional organizations, trade unions and even many unionists,[5] including then Independent Unionist MP, Sylvia Hermon.

## "We are witnessing the birth of a new country called UK-NI or Ukni"

Despite being roundly opposed by a majority in Northern Ireland, DUP belligerence on the issue of the backstop was supported by Brexit hardliners on the Conservative backbenches, most notably by members of the European Research Group (ERG) (Murray & Armstrong 2021). For Conservative MPs, the DUP's opposition to the backstop became totemic: touted as a key reason for their refusal to back May's Withdrawal Agreement. Had the DUP been prepared to support (or at least, acquiesce to) the backstop, then this would likely have been sufficient to win around enough Tory MPs to carry May's Brexit deal (Kenny & Sheldon 2020, 2021). The depth of support enjoyed by the DUP in its staunch opposition to a Brexit deal that would differentiate Northern Ireland from the rest of the UK, however marginally, was reflective of a self-avowedly more "muscularly" unionist politics that had prevailed within the Conservative Party and shaped its policy on Northern Ireland since its accession to government in 2010 (Kenny & Sheldon 2021). It gave an impression of fellow-travelling between the Tories – particularly the ERG – and the DUP, which both sides may have sincerely bought into for a time.

---

5. A poll conducted by John Coakley and John Garry in 2017 found that at an early stage in the Brexit process, 59 per cent of Unionists were willing to accept new border controls between Northern Ireland and Great Britain in order to maintain an open border on the island of Ireland (Coakley & Garry 2017). By late 2019 this had reduced significantly, though according to polling conducted by Lord Ashcroft (2019), at this stage 5 per cent of Unionists had no problem with the backstop, and a further 15 per cent viewed it as an acceptable compromise.

In November 2018, Boris Johnson was received at the DUP party conference in Belfast with rapturous applause. He delivered a keynote address in which he insisted that, unlike Theresa May, he would never countenance any regulatory border between Great Britain and Northern Ireland (Quinn 2019). In the summer of 2019, having forced Theresa May's resignation as prime minister by failing to back her Brexit deal at three times of asking (contra the terms of its confidence-and-supply deal with the Conservatives), the DUP welcomed Johnson's election to succeed her, heralding him as a "committed Unionist" (*Irish Times* 2019). Even at this stage, however, the writing was arguably on the wall. A series of early warning signals should have given the DUP cause to doubt the "unionist" credentials of the new prime minister and the extent of the commitment to Northern Ireland's "integral" place in the Union (at least as it is defined and understood by the DUP) within his wider political milieu.

Despite pledging that he would never countenance any degree of regulatory separation between Northern Ireland and the rest of the United Kingdom, Boris Johnson had in fact voted for May's Withdrawal Agreement at the third "meaningful" parliamentary vote on the deal, as had a number of other Tory Brexiters, including Dominic Raab and Jacob Rees-Mogg. This was reflective of an uncomfortable truth that would come to haunt the DUP: namely, that for the pro-Brexit right of the Conservative Party, Northern Ireland's place in the Union is simply not understood on the same terms as it is by Ulster unionists, nor is it regarded as being as immutable. Indeed, according to a YouGov poll conducted in June 2019 – after Theresa May had been unceremoniously forced from office – 59 per cent of Conservative Party members recorded that they would be prepared to sacrifice Northern Ireland's place in the Union if this was needed to secure Brexit. Sixty-three per cent of those Tories surveyed also said that they would be willing to see Scotland leave the Union in order to secure Brexit, whereas 26 per cent and 20 per cent said that they would be happy to see Scotland and Northern Ireland, respectively, leave the Union regardless of the Brexit issue (Madden 2019).[6] Weighed against a "clean" Brexit for Great Britain

---

6. It is notable that no comparable question was asked about Wales' membership of the Union, which is often taken for granted in ways which, arguably, are becoming less sustainable.

(and particularly, for England), a "muscularly" unionist approach on Northern Ireland – and the Union *per se* – was ultimately revealed to be a second-order concern for Johnson and the other Conservative Brexiters, with disastrous consequences for the DUP. After a few rounds of shadowboxing, the new prime minister eventually acquiesced readily to a redrafted Protocol on Northern Ireland which retained, *de facto*, the latter's membership of the EU single market and customs union, and contravened the DUP's blood-red line by creating a new customs and regulatory barrier in the Irish Sea.

When Prime Minister Boris Johnson called a snap election in November 2019 to break the Brexit impasse and "Get Brexit Done", Northern Ireland voters punished the DUP for its divisive role in the Brexit process, with many splitting for the pro-Remain APNI. In North Down, a traditional unionist stronghold and a DUP target seat, they did so in large enough numbers to see Alliance's Deputy Leader, Stephen Farry, elected. In total, the DUP lost 5.4 per cent of its vote share, and two of its 10 parliamentary seats (including that of its Deputy Leader, Nigel Dodds in North Belfast). It went from holding three of Belfast's four seats to just one. And more generally unionism failed, for the third successive election in Northern Ireland, to win a majority either of votes cast or seats available. For the first time in its hundred-year history, Northern Ireland returned more Nationalists than Unionists to Westminster. Boris Johnson's sizeable Conservative majority meant that the DUP's protestations about the Withdrawal Agreement and its redrafted Ireland/Northern Ireland Protocol could now be decisively ignored. Johnson's "oven-ready" deal passed its final reading in the House of Commons on 9 January 2020 by 330 votes to 231. No Conservative MP voted "no".

Almost from the outset, warnings were consistently given by observers, commentators and academics on both sides of the Irish Sea that the relationship between the DUP and the Conservative Party (and particularly its pro-Brexit wing) was a marriage of convenience for the latter, entertained only for as long as it remained expedient (see, e.g., F. O'Toole 2017). In such warnings were echoes of Edward Carson's[7]

---

7. Edward Carson was the charismatic leader of Ulster unionism during the "Home Rule Crisis" of the early twentieth century. A Dublin-born lawyer, he was resolute in opposing Home Rule not only for Ulster, but for the whole of the island of

post-partition lamentation that Ulster had been "only a puppet … in the political game that was to get the Conservative Party into power" (HL Debs 14 Dec 1921 Vol. 48 c. 44). Albion's perfidy when it comes to Northern Ireland has long been a dominant trope in unionist political culture (Bell 1990; Shirlow & McGovern 1997; Coulter 2015; Evershed 2018a; McKay 2000, 2021a), and many unionists and loyalists were themselves wary of staking too much on the DUP's relationship with the Conservatives. Indeed, during an interview with one DUP MP, he acknowledged that this relationship was only temporary: "it will last for a time … we haven't given the Conservatives *carte blanche* on Brexit" (interview with authors, 2018). Distrust of Tory motives was a key factor motivating the DUP's hard-ball approach to the Brexit process (Murphy & Evershed 2020b).

Why the DUP seemed to take Johnson's claims that he shared its particular brand of staunch and uncompromising unionism at face value and were willing to trust him to deliver their preferred form of Brexit – despite multiple warnings to the contrary from numerous quarters over several months and even years – remains something of a vexing question. The party had the power and position to push for a softer form of Brexit. But despite openly flirting with this option (BBC News 2019b), it ultimately remained (and, indeed, remains) wedded to the kind of hard Brexit which is most economically risky for Northern Irish businesses, detrimental to North–South cooperation and, critically, impossible to reconcile with an open border on the island of Ireland without some kind of unique settlement for Northern Ireland. As was suggested by one Irish official close to the Brexit process, in private, there was even acknowledgement from some in the DUP that a hard Brexit (and even Brexit *per se*) would be detrimental: "private conversations … are about genuine concerns about life after Brexit, and building a relationship and working North–South and working across the islands, and that if that doesn't work then that would be against the interests of unionism" (Irish official, interview with authors, 2018). That the party nonetheless

---

Ireland, and had (incorrectly) believed that the Conservative Party and its leader, Andrew Bonar Law, had been equally committed to this aim. He viewed partition and the institution of devolved government in what became Northern Ireland as a personal and political failure and forsook the opportunity to become Northern Ireland's first prime minister. Sometimes called the "Uncrowned King of Ulster", Carson's statue stands outside Stormont's Parliament Buildings (BBC 2021).

persisted in maintaining its hard-Brexit position might be explained by the overlapping of a number of factors: (1) a perception that a hard Brexit would play a key role in redefining and reasserting British sovereignty, in general, and in and over Northern Ireland, in particular, on terms more agreeable to the party (Murphy & Evershed 2020b); (2) that key figures within the party – particularly Brexit spokesperson, Sammy Wilson – were "paleosceptics" (Shipman 2016), ideologically wedded to the hardest possible Brexit on its own terms and for its own sake; and (3) that these figures were concentrated in Westminster, rather than in Belfast, where they had a particularly close working relationship with the Conservatives, in general, and the ERG, in particular (Kenny & Sheldon 2020).

When the wax in the DUP's wings melted as it flew too close to the ERG's sun, it was to a chorus of "I told you so's" (see, e.g., Kane 2021). Unionist opponents of the DUP were particularly angry at the party for its role in delivering the very Brexit outcome it had claimed to oppose above all else. The UUP's former leader, Reg Empey, for instance, penned a number of scathing op-eds, deriding DUP MPs for having been "asleep at the wheel" (*News Letter* 2020), while PUP leader, Billy Hutchinson, complained that "there are those by mistake or incompetence that have enabled this sea border … What were they thinking? Or perhaps they weren't thinking at all" (PUP 2020). The sense of betrayal within the DUP itself was palpable. During a debate on the Northern Ireland Protocol in the House of Commons on 13 January 2021, DUP MP Ian Paisley implored of Michael Gove, then co-chair of the EU–UK Joint Committee, "what did we do to Members on the Government Benches to be screwed over by this protocol? Ask your hearts, every single one: what did we do?" (HC Debs 13 January 2021 Vol. 687 c. 310). On the political blog, *Slugger O'Toole*, commentator Sarah Creighton (2021a) described watching this denouement of the DUP's relationship with Tory Brexiters as

> like watching somebody go back to the ex who treated them like crap over and over again. When are the DUP going to realize: the Conservatives aren't your friends. Ditch them. Dump them. Appoint a friend to stop you if you go back there again … [a sea border] was put on the table when Theresa May decided to pull the UK out of the customs union and the single market.

The DUP backed that. They also backed every unrealistic solution offered to manage a hard border between Northern Ireland and the Republic. When May proposed a deal that took a sea border off the table, the Remain parties backed it and the DUP didn't. The party hedged its bets to the ERG and here we are.

The all-UK backstop as negotiated by Theresa May was an (albeit imperfectly) unionist solution to the question of the post-Brexit Irish border. It had represented a not insubstantial concession to unionist demands on the part of the EU, which had initially been reluctant to agree to this kind of post-Brexit temporary customs arrangement with the UK. And it had been accompanied by a series of unilateral commitments from the British government that would have ensured, *inter alia*, no regulatory divergence in practice between Great Britain and Northern Ireland (HM Government 2019; Hayward & Phinnemore 2019). Although many in the DUP, as well as many of the party's fellow travellers, maintain that the backstop was nonetheless unacceptable to Ulster unionists, the DUP's decision to junk it and hitch its wagon instead to the English nationalism of a Johnson premiership was a grave strategic miscalculation – perhaps the biggest and most decisive made by any party over the course of the Brexit process (cf. Rutter & Menon 2020).

By January 2021, the party was left humiliated, weakened and isolated as a consequence of its involvement in the Brexit imbroglio. After the restoration of devolved power-sharing at Stormont under the terms of the *New Decade, New Approach* deal (into which the DUP was bounced at least in part because of the loss of its position of influence in Westminster) (Haughey 2020), DUP ministers became responsible for delivering key components of the new Irish Sea border. Arlene Foster began, tentatively, to attempt to sell the Protocol on Ireland/Northern Ireland and Northern Ireland's unique status within the EU and UK markets as a "gateway of opportunity" (BBC News 2021a). Particularly amid news reports of empty supermarket shelves, undelivered Amazon parcels and a slump in business activity in Northern Ireland that marked the initial phase of implementing the Protocol, however, the ship of unionist opinion on the matter – which the DUP had played a heavy hand in building – had arguably already sailed.

### "More perilous to the Union than anything I have witnessed in my lifetime"

The *Belfast Telegraph* published a poll on 1 February 2021 that had been conducted for the newspaper by LucidTalk (Breen 2021b). The numbers made for alarming reading for the DUP, which polled at a 20-year low of 19 per cent, more than 9 per cent down on its result in the 2017 Assembly election. Sinn Féin's 24 per cent, though a 3.9 per cent drop on the party's 2017 result, would likely be enough to see it returned as the largest party in Stormont and thereby secure the role of First Minister. At 18 per cent – an almost 9 per cent growth in support since 2017 – the Alliance Party would be in contention to become the second biggest party in the Assembly, leaving the DUP trailing a possible third. DUP woes were compounded by a more than 7 per cent increase in support for TUV, which polled at 10 per cent. The poll provided an illustration of the vulnerability that the DUP's Brexit entanglement had created for the party on both its left and right flanks. A further poll in May 2021 made for even worse reading for the DUP, as it slumped to just 16 per cent (Breen 2021c).

With liberal unionists increasingly turning to Alliance, to the right, voters were increasingly drawn to the TUV, whose leader, Jim Allister, spent 2020 and early 2021 harrying the DUP in the Stormont chamber, in print and on the airwaves over its role in delivering a new border in the Irish Sea. On 27 January 2021, Allister published a plan to "disrupt the Protocol" which included (1) that Unionists should suspend involvement in North–South institutions; (2) that unionist MLAs should work together to veto new laws pertaining to or required by the Protocol; and (3) that then DUP Agriculture, Environment and Rural Affairs Minister, Edwin Poots, should order the withdrawal of officials from Irish Sea border posts (TUV 2021). The plan was backed and promoted by a number of unionist hardliners, including loyalist blogger and commentator, Jamie Bryson. Like Allister, Bryson used the platform afforded to him by social media, television and radio to foment protest against the Protocol, which he dubbed the "Betrayal Act" (Bryson 2021). This had begun with a series of protest meetings across Northern Ireland in late 2019 (see Lowry 2019), although these had largely petered out in early 2020, in part as a consequence of the

Covid-19 pandemic. Events in early 2021, however, gave a new lease of life to Bryson's nascent protest movement.

The EU's ill-advised and misjudged triggering of Article 16 of the Protocol in January 2021 enraged and alarmed unionists. Already reeling from the LucidTalk Winter 2021 polling results, having faced months of angry criticism from a core section of its own constituency and with Jim Allister nipping at its heels, the DUP decisively abandoned the rhetoric of "working with" the Protocol and reverted to a more deliberately (and familiar) oppositional position. On 2 February, the party revealed a five-point plan to "free" Northern Ireland from the Protocol (see Table 4.1). On 21 February, it also became a co-sponsor – alongside the UUP, TUV, former Brexit Party MEP, Ben Habib, former UUP leader and Northern Ireland First Minister, Lord David Trimble, and arch-Brexiteer, Baroness Kate Hoey – of a legal challenge against the Northern Ireland Protocol: seeking a judicial review on the grounds that it contravened both the Act of Union 1800 and the Northern Ireland Act 1998.[8]

Concurrently, the Loyalist Communities Council (LCC) – an umbrella group representing the three loyalist paramilitary organizations, the UVF, the Ulster Defence Association (UDA) and the Red Hand Commando (RHC) – declared that it was "withdrawing support" for the Belfast/Good Friday Agreement unless and until the Protocol on Ireland/Northern Ireland was overturned (Morris 2021). In the weeks after the Protocol began operating, menacing graffiti appeared on walls across Northern Ireland, signalling loyalists' opposition to an Irish Sea border in the staunchest of terms, and warning that "All border post staff are targets". There were also reports of both Larne and Belfast ports being surveilled by loyalist paramilitary groups. In February 2021, staff at Larne Harbour were removed amid fears over their safety (O'Carroll 2021). In an appearance on BBC Radio Ulster's Nolan Show, also in February, David Campbell, chair of the LCC, had threatened that "if it comes to the bit where we have to fight physically to maintain our

---

8. On 30 June 2021, the High Court in Belfast ruled that the Protocol was lawful. While the Court found that it did conflict with the Act of Union in respect of free trade between Britain and Northern Ireland, it also found that the relevant sections of the Act of Union had been impliedly repealed by the Withdrawal Agreement Act 2018. All of the applicants' other arguments were rejected. The decision will be appealed by the applicants at the Supreme Court.

**Table 4.1** The DUP's five point plan to "free" Northern Ireland from the Protocol

---

- United message from unionists – free us from the Protocol
- Oppose all Protocol-related measures in the Northern Ireland Assembly
- Build support in Parliament to free us from the Protocol
- Launch Parliamentary e-petition, "Trigger Article 16 – We want unfettered GB–NI Trade"
- Stop all Protocol-related North–South activity

---

Source: DUP (2021).

freedoms within the UK, so be it". Eventually, loyalist disaffection with the Protocol and Johnson's "sell out" combined with other grievances – including a perception of "two-tiered policing" in the wake of the decision not to prosecute any members of Sinn Féin for their involvement in Bobby Storey's funeral – and boiled over into protest and rioting over several nights (McKay 2021b).

Representing new and material barriers for trade in goods between Great Britain and Northern Ireland, the Protocol has had a profoundly dislocating impact on unionists. This was exacerbated by what has been referred to as "gaslighting" at Westminster: that is, the UK government's patently false claims that nothing changed, and that there is no new regulatory border in the Irish Sea. This "border" is, however, the natural outcome of the form of hard Brexit that the DUP itself played a key role in delivering. As Murray (2021) puts it, "the terms of the Protocol are the symptom, not the cause, of the barriers which have developed between Northern Ireland and Great Britain". Unionism's sense of alienation and separation from the rest of the UK notwithstanding, the Protocol categorically does not herald – as some unionists are wont to claim – the creation of an "economic United Ireland". As SDLP MLA, Matt O'Toole, has noted, in areas including financial services, banking and immigration, new forms of North–South divergence mean that in key respects "cross-border economic activity will become harder not easier" (McGonagle 2021). Further, the Protocol does not contravene the "principle of consent" underpinning British sovereignty in and over Northern Ireland. A referendum on the specific question of Northern Ireland's constitutional status (that is, a border poll) is still required in order for there to be any transfer of sovereignty (McGarry & O'Leary 2019).

While it undoubtedly reflects tangible concerns, unionism's current strategy of seeking to "free" Northern Ireland from the Protocol is thus predicated on a number of contestable premises. It also seems highly unlikely to succeed. Attempts to overturn the Protocol via the courts are on shaky ground legally, and mass unionist and loyalist protest has not achieved its desired end since the Ulster Workers' Council (UWC) strike brought down the Sunningdale Agreement in 1974 (Evershed 2018b). Westminster politics has long been all but immune to disruption caused by unionists and loyalists on Northern Ireland's streets. And at any rate, while they have undoubtedly provided for troubling scenes, protests against the Protocol have not (yet) reached anything like sustained or critical mass. These are taking place against a backdrop of uncertainty about the Protocol, but in which there is as much support as there is opposition to it. According to polling undertaken by LucidTalk for Queen's University Belfast, 46 per cent of Northern Ireland voters agree that the Protocol "provides appropriate means for managing the effects of Brexit on Northern Ireland", as compared to 42 per cent who disagree. Fifty per cent agreed that it brought economic opportunities to Northern Ireland. Further, as it stands and with the continued application of Articles 5–10 of the Protocol due to be subject to a vote in the Northern Ireland Assembly in 2024, 47 per cent favour continued application of the Protocol, with 42 per cent favouring disapplication (Hayward *et al.* 2021). The operation of the "consent mechanism" seems set to become a key issue in 2022's Assembly election, and it is unlikely that a clear anti-Protocol majority is liable to emerge (or, for that matter, that unionism will regain its majority).

Tweaks to the working of the Protocol, greater flexibility and affordances in its application, and reductions in the bureaucratic burden it has placed on Northern Ireland businesses are, on the face of it, a far more viable proposition. Past experience shows that where unionists, and particularly the DUP, are willing to work pragmatically and collaboratively to address concerns about the functioning of the Protocol, then this can be instrumental in securing EU buy-in for relevant mitigations. For example, in November 2020, then First and Deputy First Ministers, Arlene Foster and Michelle O'Neill issued a joint letter warning about the lack of preparedness for implementing the Protocol in full and a resultant threat to food supplies as of 1 January 2021. This letter played a pivotal role in the EU and UK agreeing a 3-month grace period for the movement of certain kinds of food products from Great Britain to Northern Ireland (McCormack 2020b).[9] Effective management of the Protocol will, as Shirlow (2021) has argued, undoubtedly require reciprocal flexibility on all sides, including from the EU and Irish governments, but this requires cool heads and leadership from within unionism.

Brexit has generally heralded a retreat from this kind of pragmatism, and a return to a more disruptive and paranoid form of politics on the part of the DUP (Murphy & Evershed 2020b). In many respects, this marks the reversal of the political journey on which the party had been embarked since (at least) the late 1990s (Tonge *et al.* 2014). Having gone from a position of unprecedented power and influence to one of renewed marginalization, the party now finds itself in a corner into which it is largely responsible for having backed itself (Tonge 2019). As a consequence, unionism faces something of a "Catch-22". The "Irish Sea border" represents new forms of material and psycho-geographic separation between Northern Ireland and the "mainland" which may, in time, have the effect of lending Irish unity new economic impetus. Facilitated in part by new forms of maritime connectivity between Ireland and the European continent, there is already some evidence that key supply chains are beginning to reorient away from their prior East–West routes in favour of new North–South ones (Campbell 2021a, 2021b; Carswell 2021). Conversely, if (and it is a big if) the DUP is able to succeed in "scrapping" the Protocol then the default option is for a hard border on the island of Ireland. As noted above, this would be liable to be an even greater accelerant of the debate about and desire for Irish unification (Garry *et al.* 2021).

## "Will the centenary year be a reflection, a commemoration or a celebration?"

Northern Ireland was a state created in unionism's own image. And despite decades of violent upheaval and profound transformation, it has endured for one hundred years. As recently as 2016, its existence

---

9. In March 2021, the UK government opted unilaterally to extend these grace periods, triggering legal action by the European Commission (Campbell 2021b).

seemed secure, at least in the medium term. Many "cultural" Catholics and nationalists seemed largely content to live in a post-Belfast/Good Friday Agreement Northern Ireland in which the exclusionary "Orange State" (Farrell 1980) had been all but dismantled; in which opportunities and resources had become more (though very far from completely) equally distributed; and in which the validity and visibility of Irish identity was increasingly protected. Indeed, to date, the retention of Northern Ireland's place in the Union consistently emerges as the preference of a majority of its citizens.

Brexit has, however, called Northern Ireland's long-term durability into question, such that its centenary presents unionists not with an opportunity for celebration, but with deep and unsettling existential questions. Unionists are now likely a permanent electoral minority in Northern Ireland, and support for Irish unification is polling at all-time highs. That this is the case is in large part of unionism's (or, more particularly, the DUP's) own making. Likewise, how unionists seek to respond to new political realities and leverage their agency will have an important bearing on how Northern Ireland's post-Brexit political and constitutional future unfolds.

The unceremonious end of the DUP's central role in Westminster's Brexit drama and its betrayal by Boris Johnson appeared, at the outset, to have had something of a chastening effect. The December 2019 UK general election was followed swiftly by the restoration of power-sharing at Stormont, apparently improved relations between Belfast and Dublin (Irish Foreign Minister Simon Coveney having played a key role in delivering the *New Decade, New Approach* deal) and an apparent willingness to make the best of what new opportunities the Protocol might afford to Northern Ireland. As journalist and commentator, Newton Emerson (2021a, 2021b), has noted, it is precisely this approach – contrite, flexible and pragmatic – which unionism must adopt if it wishes to stave off growing support for constitutional change.

As research by the pro-Union campaign, Uniting UK, revealed, the kind of uncompromising revanchism and reaction embodied by political unionism in general, and the DUP, in particular, during the Brexit process actively repels young people from across the political spectrum, including young and socially progressive unionists. Younger, Protestant, pro-Union voters have the most liberal attitudes of all voters in Northern Ireland, but they are also the least likely to vote (McDonald

2017). Which way these voters – alienated by the social conservatism of "mainstream" unionism – are liable to vote in a future border poll is an increasingly interesting and open question, particularly given the forms of social liberalization which have recently marked Southern Irish politics and culture (McWilliams 2018; McKay 2021a). A number of commentators from unionist backgrounds have publicly questioned whether a Northern Ireland beholden to a regressive unionist cultural politics "makes sense" (see, e.g., C. Mitchell 2018). As lamented by Philip Smith (2021), former UUP MLA and founding member of Uniting UK, "Unionism is seen as backward looking, afraid of change, a thing of the past and embarrassing".

Uniting UK is one of a small number of emerging unionist groups and think tanks seeking to reset and rehabilitate unionism's image post-Brexit. We Make NI – which describes itself as "a platform to celebrate NI and to debate our shared future in an inclusive, imaginative and positive way" – and the "Pro-Union" pages of "Civic Space" – an initiative facilitated by the Institute of Irish Studies at the University of Liverpool – provide further examples. These fora all provide a way for predominately younger and more diverse unionist voices to find expression and promote a vision of Northern Ireland in the Union founded on a more "civic" than "ethnic" conception of unionism. Key figures within these groups, including Sarah Creighton (2020), have also been willing to engage in discussions about a "Shared Island", as promoted by the government led by Taoiseach Micheál Martin, albeit that their focus remains on making the case for a better Northern Ireland within the UK (Creighton 2021b). This is framed by growing recognition in some quarters that unionist agents need to have some sort of plan for and response to the critical constitutional moment that Brexit has engendered. One particularly prominent voice in this regard has been that of former DUP leader and First Minister, Peter Robinson, who has argued that unionism needs to prepare for a border poll, whether it wants to or not.

For the most part, unionists have refused to engage in dialogue around a new or shared Ireland, arguing that to do so simply gives credence to the idea that constitutional change is inevitable. Former leader of the UUP, Steve Aiken, for instance, dismissed the Shared Island initiative as an "unnecessary layer of bureaucracy" and as a "political expediency" designed to "counter the scourge of Sinn Féin" (Manley

2020b). Unionist and loyalist politics are shaped by a profound sense of fear, and a proclivity to identify processes of change as necessarily both threatening and as evidence of Republican plotting (Evershed 2018a). It is telling that at one protest about the Northern Ireland Protocol, held on Belfast's Shankill Road in June 2021, protestors chose to set fire to a Sinn Féin banner which read "A United Ireland is for Everyone", which had previously hung from the Divis Flats across the peace line on the Falls Road. Through the loyalist political prism, the Northern Ireland Protocol is read not (primarily) as a Tory-imposed solution to a problem created at Westminster, but as a Sinn Féin led, pan-nationalist turning of the political and constitutional ratchet. Protests are liable to intensify and become all-the-more volatile if the constitutional conversation continues to intensify and accelerate. There are, quite simply, a number of unionists and loyalists who will never be willing to engage with discussion about, let alone accept, a united Ireland, with potentially destabilizing and even violent consequences (Reinisch 2019).

In addition to street-level agitation, the post-Brexit period has seen the emergence of a number of platforms from which a new generation of working-class loyalists is seeking to make its voice heard, both on and offline. Let's Talk Loyalism, for instance, is a grass-roots social media initiative led by a group of young loyalists who, as Hudson and Spencer (2021) have put it, "have no interest in street violence – even if they understand the reasons for it. They want a coalition of activists able to use social media to promote wider education and to inject a sense of optimism and confidence and to help envision a better future". Particularly interesting is Her Loyal Voice, which seeks to foreground the perspectives of loyalist women, whose voices are often doubly marginalized in political discourse in and about Northern Ireland. Her Loyal Voice deliberately profiles pro-choice and pro-LGBT rights views from within loyalism, in an attempt to push back against perceptions that loyalism is necessarily socially conservative.

These platforms seek to raise awareness of and address the issues confronting loyalism, which include a perceived lack of representation; deprivation and the lack of any perceptible "peace dividend"; educational under-achievement and lack of opportunity; and other forms of profound alienation in working-class communities, all of which have periodically contributed to, catalysed or found expression in recent patterns of protest (cf. Nolan *et al.* 2014), including in the spring of 2021.

Let's Talk Loyalism and Her Loyal Voice also seek to promote a more positive and accommodating image of loyalism. However, whether and to what extent these initiatives also represent a willingness on the part of those involved in them to listen to and engage meaningfully with contrasting perspectives on Northern Ireland's political and constitutional futures is an important question. It is noteworthy that some of those involved in these projects are among the staunchest and most immovable public critics of the Protocol. Loyalists' complaints that proponents of the Protocol are failing to listen to unionist and loyalist concerns about its impact are rarely, if ever, matched with practical or workable suggestions as to what should replace it.

Far from moving to embrace either a more pragmatic approach towards managing the Protocol, unionism, and particularly the DUP, has instead seemingly doubled-down on a regressive and grievance-stoking politics of protest.[10] What contrition the DUP demonstrated following the passage of the Withdrawal Agreement Act was hastily abandoned. The party's Brexit hard-liners have ultimately refused to concede that the final form that Brexit has taken in Northern Ireland owes more than a little to their overplaying the hand they were dealt in 2017. Key figures within the DUP have also been conspicuous in their attempts to associate themselves with socially regressive figures and movements on both sides of the Atlantic. In 2020, DUP MPs Ian Paisley, Paul Givan and Sammy Wilson publicly supported the re-election of Donald Trump. In January 2021, then Agriculture Minister, Edwin Poots, took to Twitter to thank Arron Banks, founder of Leave.eu, for his role in delivering Brexit. Against the backdrop of Electoral Commission investigations into Leave.eu's referendum spending and data management, it had increasingly become a platform for other hard-right and deeply conservative campaign issues (Geoghegan 2020).

Over the course of the global coronavirus pandemic, key figures in the DUP have been vehement and outspoken in their lockdown scepticism, and have consistently undermined and derided key public health measures. Sammy Wilson was photographed a number of times refusing to wear a face-covering, and in 2021 leant public support to

---

10. The UUP's Doug Beattie, who took over as leader of the party in May 2021, has sought to position his party as more "liberal" on issues such as abortion, but he too remains resolute in his opposition to the Protocol.

Covid-sceptic conspiracists as they protested in London. Ian Paisley Jr has long courted controversy,[11] and in June 2021 he was filmed on stage at a Van Morrison concert protesting lockdown restrictions and calling Health Minister – and fellow unionist – Robin Swann "very dangerous". More generally, and following global trends, Covid-scepticism has added itself to the socially conservative positioning which shapes DUP policy. Having overseen the transgression of her blood-red line on Brexit, it is noteworthy that what finally forced the resignation of Arlene Foster was her decision to abstain rather than vote against a ban on so-called gay conversion therapy.

There seems little prospect of the DUP seeking to occupy a more pragmatic or liberal political space after Brexit. That Arlene Foster was ultimately considered too progressive and conciliatory to continue leading the party is telling. The successful heave against her potentially heralds the party's retreat into an ever more retrogressive and ethno-chauvinist cultural politics. As Sarah Creighton (2021c) has observed, this is liable, in the end, to be self-defeating:

> From a progressive unionist perspective, the idea that Arlene Foster hasn't been sufficiently staunch is laughable. And yet, there are voices out there calling for the new DUP leader to not co-operate with north-south bodies and bring down Stormont. They are getting louder. I worry that Foster's replacement could take the DUP down a dangerous path. Pragmatism is needed when it comes to the protocol … It would be disastrous for unionism if the DUP were to bring down the Assembly and take the obstructionist path.

Indeed, the extent to which the DUP can ultimately survive the fallout from Brexit is currently something of an open question. In 2021, the party underwent two divisive changes of leadership in as many months. The internal coup led by DUP Agriculture Minister, Edwin Poots, against Arlene Foster unravelled when Poots himself was deposed on 17 June, only 20 days after having been elected party leader. He was

---

11. For example, in 2018, Paisley was suspended from the House of Commons after it was revealed that he had not declared a number of visits to Sri Lanka paid for by the Sri Lankan government.

replaced on 22 June by Jeffrey Donaldson, who has doubled down on the party's (likely undeliverable) pledge to "free" Northern Ireland from the Protocol. The immediate cause of Poots' rapid dethronement was his acquiescence to a deal on legislating for Irish language protections in Northern Ireland, in order to secure the nomination of his candidate for First Minister, Paul Givan MLA (see McKay 2021c). However, his defenestration is also emblematic of a deeper crisis and divisions within the DUP. Abandoned by its pretended friends on the "mainland", facing steep electoral decline and all-but powerless to reverse the consequences of its previous mistakes, the DUP has been profoundly weakened by the decisions it has taken during Brexit's critical moment, perhaps terminally so.

Its role in the Brexit process conclusively demonstrated the DUP's disastrous misjudgement of its own agency. The outcome has been precisely that which the party most stridently opposed, and in the end it has presaged a form of existential crisis in and for the party from which – and, as a consequence, unionism more widely – may not recover. To retreat further into the kind of "never, never, never" politics associated with the DUP of old at this critical Brexit moment will exacerbate rather than alleviate the problem that the party now finds itself confronting and do little to prevent the critical constitutional juncture which unionists most fear. It is also likely to hasten the drift of more liberal unionist voters towards parties of the centre- or middle-ground, and further unendear "others" to the prospect of maintaining Northern Ireland's place in the Union. And as we explore in the next chapter, it is precisely on the preference of Northern Ireland's "others" that the answer to the constitutional question ultimately hinges.

# 5

# The "middle ground"

"Let's be blunt, leaving the EU would be a massive step backwards for the UK, including, if not especially, Northern Ireland. A backward step we simply can't afford to take".

David Ford, 5 March 2016

"Like many others, Alliance doesn't want to see any new borders anywhere in these islands".

Stephen Farry, 7 March 2020

"I'm not a nationalist, I'm not an Irish republican, but I am Irish and I am British and the future of this island is my future and so I want to be part of any discourse about what shape that's going to take and I'm always open to those conversations".

Naomi Long, 30 December 2020

In May 2019, the Alliance Party of Northern Ireland made history following the election of their first ever MEP to the European Parliament. The party's leader Naomi Long took the second of Northern Ireland's three seats in an electoral contest which had historically been dominated by Northern Ireland's two political traditions: unionism and nationalism. It was a stunning victory for the middle ground and greeted as such by the Alliance Party's new MEP (quoted in Clark 2019): "An amazing result for the Alliance Party and a watershed moment for [Northern Ireland] politics. So grateful to everyone who voted to make the Alliance surge a tsunami! This can be the beginning of a new politics and a new future for all of us". The impressive result signified not just a recent pattern of growing support for cross-community parties (see

Tonge 2020b; Haughey & Pow 2020), it also confirmed opposition to Brexit among a majority of Northern Ireland voters (two of the three successful candidates – Long and also Sinn Féin's Martina Anderson – were anti-Brexit).

Historically, Northern Ireland has been shaped by a battle between unionism and nationalism which has squeezed the so-called middle ground. In this unique political and electoral setting, the middle ground represents a space which is neither unionist nor nationalist. It relates to those parties and voters who designate as "Other", as set out in the Belfast/Good Friday Agreement; and rather than being an indication of where a party lies on the left–right political spectrum, in Northern Ireland the label "middle ground" or "centre party" implies – first and foremost – neutrality on the constitutional question. A number of political parties are associated with this tradition, and they include the Green Party and the centrist Alliance Party: although each party occupies its own particular position on the left–right political spectrum, both are non-aligned on the constitutional question.[1] Alliance explicitly adheres to the belief that a third tradition, post-nationalist or post-unionist, can be established in Northern Ireland (see Evans & Tonge 2003).

The political centre ground in Northern Ireland is a curious place. It has long been the "poor relation" in terms of its electoral and political muscle. Historically, parties espousing a liberal or non-sectarian politics and avowedly neutral on the constitutional question have failed to mobilize a critical mass of voters. The Alliance Party has historically been the largest of Northern Ireland's middle-ground parties, but even its electoral success typically hovered around the 10 per cent mark, with representation normally confined to local councils and the Northern Ireland Assembly. Brexit, however, presented the Alliance Party with an opportunity to fashion a policy position appealing to both unionists and nationalists, consolidating its cross-community attraction, and potentially heralding the start of a more permanent reshaping and even normalization of Northern Ireland's (ethnic dual) party system to the benefit of the centre ground. Brexit has, therefore, at least partially

---

1. The small PBP self-designates as "Socialist" which means that the party is officially designated as "Other" in the Northern Ireland Assembly. PBP however, does not represent the middle-ground tradition as understood in Northern Ireland in that, unlike the APNI, it is an island-wide party which takes a position on the constitutional question and supports a 32-county socialist republic.

helped to arrest a stagnant electoral trend and demonstrated an appetite for moderation among a sizeable (and growing) constituency of voters from across the political divide who have switched their allegiance to the middle ground in general, and to the Alliance Party in particular. This development has been to the particular (although not exclusive) detriment of unionism. Alliance has accommodated pro-Remain unionists frustrated with how political unionism, and particularly the DUP, has navigated Brexit, but critically the party has not required those voters to abandon or reject their unionist constitutional preference. APNI also garners support from Catholic/nationalist voters who continue to aspire to a united Ireland. However, the largest single proportion of Alliance Party voters – 51 per cent – claim to be "neither unionist or nationalist" (Tonge 2020b: 465). This means that Alliance appeals to a trilogy of (ultimately incompatible) positions on the constitutional question: unionist, nationalist and non-aligned, which complicates the party's agency on the constitutional question. The growing size and increasing political muscle of Northern Ireland's middle ground challenges traditionally neutral stances on constitutional change as espoused by the Alliance Party and the Green Party. How the Alliance Party (as the larger of the two) positions itself on the developing constitutional debate is consequential for the outcome of that debate, and ultimately for the future of Northern Ireland. For Alliance, Brexit represents a very real critical moment with potentially transformative consequences for both the party and for Northern Ireland.

## "It makes sense for Northern Ireland and the UK to remain in the EU, politically, economically and socially"

In 2010, the Alliance Party scored an important electoral win. For the first time in its 40-year history, the party won a seat in Westminster. In the staunchly unionist constituency of East Belfast, APNI deputy party leader, Naomi Long, defeated the incumbent DUP MP, party leader and First Minister Peter Robinson. Robinson was a DUP stalwart who had held the East Belfast Westminster seat since 1979. In 2010 however, his electoral prospects were severely compromised by a political and financial scandal involving his wife and family. This resulted in a 20 per cent fall in the party's vote share in East Belfast and handed victory to the much smaller, more "middle class", and avowedly non-sectarian Alliance Party. Although Long's victory may be partially attributable to the DUP leader's personal troubles, it was nevertheless impressive for having successfully attracted support away from the UUP[2] and for having appealed to a predominantly working-class base not normally attracted to a party such as the APNI.

The Alliance Party's first foray into national politics coincided with another historic development when the Conservative Party and the Liberal Democrats agreed to form a coalition government (the first peacetime coalition since the 1930s). Although the Liberal Democrats is the APNI's sister party in Westminster, "[c]ognisant of her new [working-class] support base, Long declined to take the whip" (Tonge & Evans 2010: 744). This, however, did not prevent Long from sharing the Lib Dems' strong and strident support for the EU. Although the issue of Europe had long dogged British politics, it became an increasingly toxic and divisive subject during the coalition's period in office. Less than a year after the election, calls for a UK referendum on EU membership gathered pace. The APNI's opposition to a referendum was unequivocal. In response to David Cameron's Bloomberg Speech in 2013, in which the prime minister endorsed an in–out referendum, the APNI Chief Whip, Stewart Dickson (Alliance Party 2013), rejected the idea: "It makes sense for Northern Ireland and the UK to remain in the EU, politically, economically and socially". In 2016, the then party leader David Ford admonished the prime minister whom he said "was entirely wrong to get us to this position, attempting unsuccessfully to appease the UKIP tendency in the Tory party". Long (2021a) later noted: "I genuinely believed that an in–out referendum choice without a properly informed electorate and the opportunity to know what out would mean was a false choice".

As the debate on a possible referendum continued in Westminster, the APNI was facing considerable and intense political challenges in Northern Ireland that were unconnected to the looming Brexit debate, but linked instead to the flying of flags. Flags are an important symbol

---

2. In 2010, the UUP fought the Westminster election under the Ulster Conservatives and Unionists – New Force (UCUNF) banner following an alliance with the Conservative Party. Having failed to return a single MP to Westminster, the pact was short-lived.

and expression of cultural identity in Northern Ireland and decisions around when, where and which flags are flown have been a source of enduring division. In December 2012, the Alliance Party councillors on Belfast City Council proposed a motion that the Union flag no longer be flown every day at Belfast City Hall, but instead on 18 "designated days" (in line with practice across the rest of the UK). The motion was in fact a compromise position proposed by Naomi Long in response to an earlier proposal from Nationalist councillors who had wanted the complete removal of the British flag. The slimmed down Alliance Party motion was supported by Sinn Féin and the SDLP, but opposed outright by Unionists. In the weeks before the vote, DUP and UUP activists distributed thousands of leaflets across East Belfast criticizing the motion, and encouraging residents to protest, claiming the proposal was "an attack on the cultural identity of the unionist community, and part of a wider 'culture war' by nationalists/republicans on 'Britishness' in Northern Ireland" (Halliday & Ferguson 2016: 527). A wave of street protests across Belfast and beyond followed and continued into 2013. Many were largely peaceful although they did serve to increase and proliferate tensions. A minority of protests, however, did turn violent and led to clashes with the the the Police Service of Northern Ireland (PSNI).

The Alliance Party bore the brunt of unionist/loyalist anger. APNI offices were picketed; the party's offices in East Belfast and Carrickfergus were attacked and vandalized; and a number of Alliance Party members' homes were targeted by protestors. Despite the danger and the intimidation, the Alliance Party refused to back down and stuck determinedly to its position. The flags protest was indicative of the lingering tensions in Northern Ireland where the communities remain polarized on "culture-war" issues linked to flags, symbols and parading. The impact and effect of the flags protest was consequential for the Alliance Party. This was because unionist/loyalist mobilization on the issue sought to damage and discredit party members (O'Dochartaigh 2021: 9): "The flags campaign sought to make it impossibly difficult for Alliance to combine with nationalists by intimidating activists and eroding the party's support among Protestant voters". Alliance Party MLA Chris Lyttle argued that the flags protest was an attempt by ethnonational parties "to re-sectarianize politics in Northern Ireland in order to quell cross-community politics" (as quoted in Murtagh 2015: 558). The effect of the flags protest on the party however, was not electorally damaging.

In the May 2014 local elections, the party's vote largely held up and in the 2014 European Parliament election, the APNI won 7.2 per cent of the vote recording its highest ever share of the vote in a European election.

Nevertheless, the flags protest highlights the immense difficulties facing a centre-ground party in Northern Ireland when it comes to navigating highly divisive cultural and constitutional issues. Horowitz (1985) makes the point that parties which attempt to reach across the divide in (post-)conflict environments have tended to be "fragile" and their progress transient. Historically, this has been a feature of the experience of cross-community parties in Northern Ireland: their electoral success has been stagnant and their political clout limited. Research by Murtagh (2015) links this to the significant barriers faced by cross-ethnic parties, like the Alliance Party, in terms of both the formal pillars of institutional politics and the informal structures that shape daily politics.

Constraints linked to the consociational power-sharing system, including the inequality and disempowerment felt by Alliance Party MLAs compelled to self-designate as "Other" for the purposes of cross-community voting, are keenly felt to be disadvantageous to the party. Key decisions made by the Northern Ireland Assembly require cross-community support and are therefore based on attaining specific levels of support from those identifying as "Nationalist" and "Unionist". Alliance views this arrangement as a form of discrimination (even sectarianism) because it places greater value on the votes of ethnonational parties than non-ethnonational parties identifying as "Other", as Alliance does. It has been explicitly argued by Farry and Neeson (1998: 1237) that: "Both Unionists and Nationalists are granted greater political rights than 'Others'. This institutionalization of sectarianism works against center parties: there are disincentives for voters to support them as they will at times have less influence in the Assembly. This could create barriers to the growth of the important center-ground in Northern Irish politics". Against the backdrop of the Brexit crisis however, these institutional barriers have not been detrimental to the growth of the centre-ground in Northern Ireland, although the Alliance Party's recent electoral surge has brought into sharper focus the question of how "Others" are represented in the Assembly and the Executive.

A LucidTalk poll carried out in January 2021 (which showed Sinn Féin as the most popular political party) saw Alliance commanding third place and closing the electoral gap on the DUP with just one percentage point between the two parties (LucidTalk 2021a). The May 2021 LucidTalk poll placed the DUP and Alliance neck-and-neck (LucidTalk 2021b). The institutional significance of such an electoral shift (if it materializes) is considerable. By way of example, should Alliance emerge as the second largest party following the 2022 Assembly elections, the party's right to claim the post of Deputy First Minister is potentially (if not likely) precluded by the terms of the Northern Ireland Act 1998. Article 16A(5) stipulates that the largest political party of the second largest political designation shall nominate an MLA to be Deputy First Minister. It is possible that Alliance may well emerge as the second largest party, but will not be entitled to nominate for the post of Deputy First Minister because the party will not be the largest in the second largest political designation (likely to be one of the ethnonational political designations). Alliance has also voiced concerns about Northern Ireland's power-sharing "grand coalition" based on the use of the d'Hondt mechanism which allocates ministerial posts according to party size. Instead, the party favours an Executive which is created voluntarily by those parties that can command (weighted) majority support within the Assembly. To date however, the party's small size and limited political clout has not allowed it the opportunity to push forcefully or effectively for these kinds of institutional reforms.

Also significant in terms of limiting the Alliance Party's reach and appeal are the dynamics of the ethnic dual-party system, which has historically squeezed the centre ground; a polarized political culture has tended to limit the space for the kind of moderation that the Alliance Party espouses; and a divisive political discourse has, in the past, fuelled mistrust of Northern Ireland's centre. This combination of multiple forces has generally constrained the Alliance Party's ability to mine cross-community support, to increase its electoral and political appeal and to be an agitator for significant institutional change.

The challenges facing Northern Ireland's main centre-ground party are also compounded by its image as a quasi-unionist party. This is linked to the Alliance Party's position on the constitutional question, which is based on the principle of consent, i.e. that Northern Ireland should remain a part of the UK until a majority wish otherwise. It is also related to the historic tendency for the party's membership and voters to be drawn more from the Protestant than the Catholic tradition.

As D. Mitchell (2018: 338) notes: "Alliance has, inevitably, struggled to convey and convince that its non-aligned identity is genuine and coherent". In this context, the party's experience of the flags protest was especially important (and enabling) because its impact on the Alliance Party's political and electoral fortunes was not injurious or damaging, but moderate. The episode suggested that taking a party position on difficult and sensitive issues linked to the unionist–nationalist divide did not necessarily alienate the party's voter base, rather: "It showed the resilience and strength of a non-nationalist voter base that was prepared to be part of a non-unionist coalition even on issues of constitutional sensitivity" (O'Dochartaigh 2021: 9).

The party's ability to maintain the support of its Protestant/unionist constituency in the face of intense opposition from unionist parties is linked to some gradual, but important developments. Evidence of political dealignment in Northern Ireland has become more marked in recent years (see Hayward & McManus 2019). Polling demonstrates that strong identification with nationalist and unionist identities is decreasing to the benefit of the centre ground. In addition, Northern Ireland society is becoming more secular and more socially liberal. The UUP and DUP's conservative positioning on a number of sensitive issues has led some liberal unionists to shift their support to the Alliance Party, which supports same-sex marriage and takes a conscience position on abortion. Here again, the APNI did not shy away from taking (what might be deemed) a controversial position. In advance of a similarly divisive and also constitutionally sensitive UK referendum on EU membership, Alliance was buoyed by the knowledge that adopting a strong position on a contested and polarizing constitutional issue did not necessarily mean alienating itself from either unionist or nationalist voters or risking electoral losses, and this is causally important in terms of enabling the party to be an agent of change.

## "An extremely disappointing decision [which] leaves Northern Ireland in a significantly weakened position"

The Alliance Party is a stridently pro-EU party. It is a member of the Alliance of Liberals and Democrats for Europe (ALDE) (previously the European Liberal Democrat and Reform Party) and also a member of

Liberal International.[3] The party's support for the EU is grounded in its liberal and internationalist outlook. It regards the EU as having played a pivotal role in securing peace on the European continent after the Second World War and was a strong advocate for European economic integration, including UK membership of the eurozone (under the correct circumstances). The party was similarly supportive of the EU single market and viewed membership of it as having been "essential to Northern Ireland's future economic growth" (Alliance Party 2014: 8). The EU was also valued for its contribution to peace and stability in Northern Ireland. According to Naomi Long (2021a): "we believe that the EU was good for Northern Ireland; that it was vital for peace, for prosperity and for open borders".

Unsurprisingly, the Alliance Party was a strong advocate for Remain during the referendum campaign. The party's 2016 Assembly election manifesto (2016a: 82) devoted very little to discussion of the referendum, but was nevertheless unequivocal in its commitment to continued UK membership of the EU: "We absolutely reject claims that Northern Ireland would be better if the UK left [the EU]. This is especially true here in Northern Ireland because of our links with Great Britain and our close economic relationship and land-border with the Republic of Ireland. As a result, we will support continued membership of the EU and advocate a 'Remain' vote in the upcoming referendum". Like many other parties in Northern Ireland, Alliance was limited in terms of its ability to engage actively with the referendum campaign. Murphy (2016a, 2016b) has noted that the referendum campaign in Northern Ireland was muted. Elections to the Northern Ireland Assembly took place some six weeks before the Brexit vote and the Alliance Party's resources and efforts were disproportionately focused on the electoral rather than the referendum contest.

Post-referendum analysis notes that Alliance Party supporters were overwhelmingly Remainers. This placed APNI voters in a similar category to SDLP and Sinn Féin voters who were also strongly in favour of Remain. However, it meant that the party was at odds with the Leave position being expounded by the DUP and TUV, and the rather limp support for Remain articulated by the UUP. Similar to the earlier flags

---

3. Liberal International is the world federation of liberal and progressive democratic political parties.

protest, the Alliance Party was taking a position on a contested and polarizing issue. Following the referendum Leave result, the Alliance Party did not temper or moderate its position. Indeed, party leader David Ford was clear that the Leave result was a source of regret for his party. In his response to the vote, he noted (2016): "This is an extremely disappointing decision and leaves Northern Ireland in a significantly weakened position". Navigating the post-referendum period posed considerable challenges for Northern Ireland's centre ground. Adopting and adhering to its anti-Brexit position would bring the Alliance Party into conflict with unionism and loyalism and test the limits of its ability to confront and challenge the traditional sectarian binds of Northern Ireland politics.

## "To attempt and paint every one of those [Remain] people as nationalist is plainly wrong"

The Alliance Party was decisive and arguably measured in its response to the Leave vote. Having been acutely attuned to the potential fallout from Brexit for Northern Ireland, the party's reaction to the vote was based on respecting the democratic will of the people but noting that the democratic will in Northern Ireland did not mirror the UK-wide vote. Immediately following the vote, Alliance positioned Northern Ireland as being distinct not just in terms of its preference to Remain, but also its differential governance arrangements and its evident special circumstances which, the party argued, provided a basis for tailoring Northern Ireland's future relationship with the EU (Alliance Party 2016b): "While Alliance regrets the result, as democrats we respect the outcome of the referendum. We are not here to refight the referendum but instead are seeking assurance the negotiations both within the UK, and between the UK and EU, will reflect the fact most people in Northern Ireland [and Scotland] want a very different relationship with the EU than do England and Wales". The party was proactive in seeking to push and to mainstream the view that Northern Ireland should be treated uniquely during the subsequent EU–UK negotiation period. The party's logic for supporting special arrangements was explicitly linked to Northern Ireland's distinctiveness relative to the rest of the UK. As the Alliance Party saw it, key differences between Northern Ireland and the rest of the

UK supported the necessity for bespoke arrangements. These included: the majority Remain vote in Northern Ireland; the automatic right of people in Northern Ireland to be Irish citizens and, therefore, EU citizens; Northern Ireland's right to determine its own constitutional status; the North–South organization of aspects of the economy; and the existence of a physical border between Northern Ireland and the Republic of Ireland/EU (see Alliance Party 2017: 7). Exiting the EU risked disrupting key aspects of Northern Ireland's tenuous political and economic situation, and in this way, there were concerns that Brexit challenged the values and framework of the Belfast/Good Friday Agreement. The rationale for supporting bespoke arrangements for Northern Ireland was, therefore, grounded primarily in practical concerns about the political and economic impact of Brexit on the island of Ireland and the need to protect the 1998 Agreement.

The form of special deal favoured by the Alliance Party was extensive and included: Northern Ireland participation in the single market and customs union; adherence to the four freedoms of movement; access to structural and competitive funds; rights to EU citizenship for all born in Northern Ireland; Northern Ireland covered by EU regulations; and Assembly control over EU Directives (Alliance Party 2017: 7). In the context of a soft Brexit (which the Alliance Party favoured), there would be limited and minimal differences between Northern Ireland and the rest of the UK. However, in the event of a hard Brexit, Northern Ireland would be all the more detached and distinct relative to the rest of the UK were it to be subject to special arrangements. A soft Brexit, therefore, was not just politically and economically necessary to best protect Northern Ireland interests, it was also electorally desirable for the party. Keeping Northern Ireland closely aligned with both the EU and the rest of the UK reduced the chance of offending or repelling existing and prospective Protestant/unionist voters.

The Alliance Party's support for special treatment for Northern Ireland, however, meant that it shared a similar platform to both the SDLP and Sinn Féin, but was at odds with the unionist approach in general, and the DUP's position in particular. This lack of consensus across the political spectrum about how to deal with Brexit irked the Alliance Party and was linked to what it perceived as a marked lack of leadership in Northern Ireland, and in particular a failure of leadership on the part of the DUP First Minister (see McCann & Hainsworth 2017: 337).

APNI councillor Kate Nicholl explicitly called on Arlene Foster to "recognise and represent the views of the majority in Northern Ireland who wanted to remain part of the EU, and who have now been left feeling lost and concerned for the future … The First Minister must go into any negotiations with the aim of accommodating the democratic will of the people of Northern Ireland, not the political will of the DUP" (Alliance Party 2016c). Calls for the Remain majority vote in Northern Ireland to be respected were championed by the Alliance Party and meant that the party was closely aligned to the broader nationalist position. However, a wider conception that opposition to Brexit was a solely nationalist position was roundly rejected by the party. Alliance was vociferous in attempting to correct the depiction of Brexit as a dichotomous, nationalist versus unionist issue. APNI MLA Stewart Dickson noted that: "Last week, 56 per cent of people in Northern Ireland voted to remain in the European Union. For Arlene Foster to attempt and paint every one of those people as nationalist is plainly wrong. Those who voted remain here cut across all demographics of age, gender, class and otherwise" (Alliance Party 2016d). The party's efforts to take the constitutional politics out of Brexit included supporting UK-wide calls for a second referendum.

## "The clearest, most coherent and most democratic route through this impasse lies with a People's Vote"

On 20 October 2018, around 2,000 people gathered in front of Belfast City Hall in a show of opposition to Brexit. The event coincided with a massive rally in London demanding a second referendum on the terms of the Brexit withdrawal deal. The Belfast "Rally for Remain" was organized by the Alliance Party's Sorcha Eastwood and SDLP activist Séamus de Faoite. Speakers included Belfast's Lord Mayor, Sinn Féin's Deirdre Hargey, university professor and Green Party activist John Barry, and the SDLP's Brexit spokesperson, Claire Hanna. According to Eastwood, the rally aimed to deliver a united cross-community message of opposition to Brexit (McGonagle 2018): "Northern Ireland voted to remain – opposition to Brexit here is cross-community; this is a chance for people to have their voice heard and to send a message as a united community: that they want an internationalist, positive future within the European

Union". Portraying opposition to Brexit as being cross-community in character was a key issue for the Alliance Party, but it was one which enjoyed – at least initially – little traction. Instead, the party was routinely depicted (albeit predominantly by unionists) as aligning with the nationalist position on Brexit. This made it difficult for Alliance to assert its credentials as an anti-Brexit party legitimately representing voters from both sides of the community divide.

As the process of agreeing a withdrawal deal ran into difficulty in Westminster, the Alliance Party's opposition to Brexit concentrated around calls for a second referendum and in so doing, tacked closely to the similar position adopted by its sister party, the Liberal Democrats. This move also saw the party support the UK-wide People's Vote campaign group[4] which was lobbying hard for a second referendum on British membership of the EU. Alliance was vocal in questioning the extent to which the slim majority in favour of Leave provided a mandate for the harder form of Brexit which was materializing under Theresa May's premiership (Long 2019): "The clearest, most coherent and most democratic route through this impasse lies with a People's Vote, including both the prime minister's deal and the Remain option". The party called for the UK electorate as a whole, and not just MPs, to be given the opportunity to decide on the acceptability of the negotiated deal. The position got an early airing when Naomi Long referenced the possibility in her contribution to the Assembly debate immediately following the referendum vote. It was also included in the party's 2017 manifesto which had called for "a referendum with an explicit choice: the negotiated deal or membership of the European Union" (Alliance Party 2017: 8). At a People's Vote rally in Belfast's Ulster Hall on 14 September 2019, Naomi Long was one of a number of Northern Ireland and UK politicians to address a crowd of hundreds.

Efforts to show that the Brexit issue was not a partisan issue was an important plank of the Alliance Party's post-Brexit strategy. The party harboured genuine concerns about the potentially grave political and economic consequences of Brexit for Northern Ireland (as a whole). Reducing the issue to one which pitched nationalist against unionist risked damaging Northern Ireland leverage during the withdrawal negotiations. APNI's support for the softest possible Brexit, plus

---

4. The SDLP and the Green Party of Northern Ireland also supported People's Vote.

special arrangements for Northern Ireland, and based on an agreed cross-community approach, was viewed as being consistent with the principle of consent enshrined in the Belfast/Good Friday Agreement. It was a position grounded in pragmatism, rather than partisan politics.

The party's pragmatic approach sought to detach the issue of Brexit from wider constitutional questions. This enabled the party to defend the backstop and later the Ireland/Northern Ireland Protocol by pitching them as the most practical (if not the most appealing) means of maintaining political and economic stability in Northern Ireland. The party was categoric in rejecting the unionist view that the backstop and the Protocol altered Northern Ireland's constitutional position. According to Naomi Long (2021a): "I think it was fairly obvious that a few sea crossings and air connections were a lot easier to police from a border perspective than 280 odd crossings between north and south … [and] we haven't dismissed that border checks and interfaces caused frictions in communities". This practical perspective on Brexit also allowed the party to engage with the Irish government, which shared similar views on the border issue. Alliance Party members participated in the Irish government's All-Island Civic Dialogue, which was boycotted by unionist parties. In 2019, Taoiseach Leo Varadkar addressed the party's annual conference and warmly praised Alliance saying: "I salute you, for your commitment and support for EU membership". The party also publicly allied with other parties in Northern Ireland, including the SDLP and Sinn Féin, to lobby London and Brussels in support of the backstop and later the Protocol.

The Alliance Party's position, and its willingness to work with nationalist political parties and the Dublin government, put it decidedly at odds with the unionist and loyalist positions on Brexit. In this context, unionist suspicion of the *bona fides* of nationalist intentions vis-à-vis Brexit was similarly applied to the Alliance Party and fuelled severe criticism of the party. Unionist attacks on the party questioned its commitment to the Union and the constitutional status quo. During the 2019 general election campaign, for example, Alliance Party candidate Stephen Farry was portrayed "as part of a pan-nationalist front" and his party regarded by some unionist detractors as "useful idiots" for Sinn Féin (Kane 2019). It was also customary for the DUP, in particular, to attempt to discredit the party by explicitly grouping it with the Irish government and other nationalist parties when criticizing the Protocol.

Unionist condemnation of the Alliance Party's position on Brexit, however, was not electorally detrimental. Indeed, it appears that the party's anti-Brexit position is, at least, partially responsible for an increase in electoral support for the centre ground since 2016.

## "In several predominantly Protestant constituencies thousands of erstwhile unionist voters turned to the Alliance Party"

Having been a party which struggled to win double-digit support, the Alliance Party's vote-winning capacity began to gradually increase after the Brexit referendum. In fact, the growth of the centre ground in Northern Ireland has been one of the most intriguing features of the Brexit period and it is evident across all electoral contests.

In 2017, Northern Ireland voters twice went to the polls against the backdrop of a collapsed Northern Ireland Assembly and intensifying Brexit rancour. The Alliance Party won 9.1 per cent of first preference votes in the 2017 Assembly election. This was up 2.1 per cent on its 2016 Assembly election tally. Given that there were 18 fewer seats on offer in 2017 than in 2016,[5] holding on to its eight seats was a strong electoral outcome for the party. The smaller Green Party also retained its two seats. The 2017 Westminster election was less electorally fruitful for the APNI. The party failed to win a seat and its share of the vote dropped slightly. In 2019 however, as the difficulties around Brexit and the Irish border issue deepened and with Northern Ireland still without functioning devolved institutions since January 2017, the Alliance Party "doubled its vote across three elections … [to become] the third largest party in [Northern Ireland]" (Tonge 2020b: 461).

Although the local government elections on 2 May 2019 were largely dominated by local issues, Brexit and its fallout pervaded the electoral contest. Both the DUP and Sinn Féin alluded to the constitutional question and existential threats during the election campaign. The centre ground – including the Alliance Party and the Green Party – were more focused on local government issues, although these were often

---

5. The Northern Ireland Miscellaneous Provisions Act 2014 reduced the number of Assembly seats from 108 to 90. The act also increased the term of the Assembly from four to five years and ended dual mandates for MLAs.

contextualized with reference to Brexit. The APNI's cross-community character, however, did come under attack during the election campaign. A campaign leaflet supporting UUP candidates in East Belfast "alleged links between the Alliance Party and the Provisional IRA" (Whitten 2020b: 68). The leaflet noted that on Belfast City Council, the Alliance Party's voting record demonstrated a close alignment with Sinn Féin. Although the UUP distanced itself from the leaflet, which had not been sanctioned by the party, the episode nevertheless was an example of unionist figures seeking to discredit the Alliance Party and to suppress Protestant/unionist support for the centre ground. It highlighted the challenges facing the Alliance Party in seeking to mobilize and grow its support across both communities. The controversy, however, had little negative impact. The party's share of the vote increased to 11.5 per cent and it won 65 per cent more seats than in 2014.

The European electoral arena proved similarly fruitful. APNI contested all European Parliament elections between the first direct elections in 1979 and 2019.[6] The European arena, however, has not traditionally been fertile electoral ground for the Alliance Party. The party candidate in 1979 was Oliver Napier who won a 6.8 per cent share of the vote. This was the highest European vote obtained by an Alliance Party candidate until 2014 when Anna Lo won a 7.1 per cent vote share. The most significant breakthrough, however, came in 2019 when Naomi Long won the party's first European Parliament seat.[7] Her victory represented the party's "highest share of the vote in any election that it has contested since its foundation in 1970" (Haughey & Pow 2020: 38). Long secured 18.5 per cent of first preference votes, up 11.4 per cent since 2014. Her victory also came at the expense of the UUP who for the first time since 1979 failed to win a seat. And interestingly, Long secured the second seat – behind the DUP, but ahead of Sinn Féin. This was due to Long being "transfer friendly", i.e. she succeeded in attracting a steady rate of transfers from across the political spectrum. In fact, almost twice as many of SDLP candidate Colum Eastwood's transfers went to the

---

6. In 2004, APNI, the Workers' Party, Conservatives, Labour and a number of independent councillors backed an independent candidate. John Gilliland was the outgoing president of the UFU and he scored 6.6 per cent of the popular vote.
7. Former party leader John Cushnahan did win a European Parliament seat in 1989, but he contested the seat in the Republic of Ireland. Cushnahan ran on the Fine Gael party ticket (in the Munster constituency) and served as an MEP until 2004.

centrist Alliance Party as to Sinn Féin (Haughey & Pow 2020; see also Tonge 2020b). Long also secured support from many pro-Remain unionist voters. In 2019, that category of unionist was not represented by either the DUP or UUP. As O'Dochartaigh (2021: 13) notes: "The most striking result of the election was that in several predominantly Protestant constituencies thousands of erstwhile unionist voters turned to the Alliance Party". The party's opposition to Brexit proved appealing to voters across the community divide.

In December 2019, APNI scored another significant electoral victory. For only the second time in its history, the party returned an Alliance Party MP to Westminster having doubled its share of the vote since the previous election in 2017. The strong showing for the party was not solely based on Stephen Farry's new Westminster seat. His party leader, Naomi Long, and party colleague, Sorcha Eastwood, may not have secured seats, but they both came a close second in their respective constituencies. Overall, the most striking feature of this election was "the rise from fifth to third place, in vote share, of the Alliance Party" (Tonge 2020a: 14). This election was billed the "Brexit election" and, to some extent, it lived up to this label. All of the political parties focused heavily on the issue and the election was notable for the pro-Remain pacts which helped to secure electoral victories for parties opposed to Brexit. The Alliance Party did not participate in pro-Remain pacts, and instead ran a candidate in each of Northern Ireland's 18 constituencies. This was a determined attempt to project its cross-community credentials: an effort "to protect its 'brand' as neither unionist nor nationalist" and to distance itself from other ideological traditions (Tonge 2020b: 464).

Over three elections, and despite unionist slurs and slights, the Alliance Party platform, and in particular its approach to Brexit, did not alienate its existing centre-ground electoral base. Instead, the party successfully mobilized previously disenchanted voters; grew its support among working-class voters; attracted voters from both communities; secured the youngest voter base of any Northern Ireland political party; and increased its membership (see Tonge 2020b). Critically, the party's position on the constitutionally sensitive Brexit issue was not punished by its unionist/Protestant supporters. Rather, the party tapped into and capitalized on looser unionist and nationalist levels of identification in Northern Ireland. Of particular note is the fact that increased support for Alliance is not simply a case of the party attracting greater support from liberal-leaning unionists. Research by Tonge & Evans (2020) (examining the 2019 Westminster election) demonstrates that 18 per cent of APNI voters had voted for the DUP in the previous Westminster election in 2017, whereas 12 per cent had voted for Sinn Féin. The party's appeal is increasingly capturing support from right across the political divide.

The Alliance Party's upward electoral swing shows no sign of abating. Polling evidence since 2019 consistently demonstrates that support for the party continues to grow and solidify. Given the party's longstanding critique of elements of the consociational Belfast/Good Friday Agreement (see Farry & Neeson 1998; D. Mitchell 2018; Murtagh 2015), an increased presence within a future Northern Ireland Assembly offers an opportunity to address Northern Ireland's perceived "institutionalization of sectarianism". Institutional reforms of this magnitude – including changes to the designation of identity, cross-community voting and the d'Hondt mechanism – however, would challenge fundamental features of the Belfast/Good Friday Agreement and may be met with objection and hostility by other political forces and identities. The elevation of the Alliance Party therefore, cannot be understood as a ready panacea for reinforcing stability in Northern Ireland. Pushing for institutional reform is not something the party intends to shy away from, but there is an acknowledgement that such changes do involve risk (Long 2021b). The growth of the centre ground therefore comes with its own potentially destabilizing baggage, in ways that overlap with to the constitutional issue. Importantly, the timing and context for such an electoral shift and (possible) political agitation for institutional reform in Northern Ireland is likely to coincide with an Assembly led by a Sinn Féin First Minister, which would bring its own element of disruption in the form of deepening pressures for a border poll (and especially so, should Sinn Féin also be in power in the Republic of Ireland). However, assuming there is a viable opportunity to push for causally decisive developments, the Alliance Party becomes a highly important agent, not just for institutional change in Northern Ireland, but also for triggering wider constitutional change and a critical juncture.

## "We're not anti-unionist or anti-nationalist. We're just not unionist or nationalist in our stance"

In addition to demonstrating distinctive signs of weakening ethnonationalist identity, recent elections also suggest that the priorities of the Northern Ireland electorate are changing. A growing number of voters are less focused on, and less motivated by constitutional issues, "culture wars" and identity: a post-Westminster election poll demonstrated that for Northern Ireland voters the most important election issue in 2019 was healthcare (Whitten 2020a: 325). Given the Alliance Party's neutrality (and lack of fixatedness) on the constitutional question, it is well-placed to respond to these kinds of changing voter demands and expectations. However, the constitutional issue is not going away and much as the Alliance Party attempts to remain neutral on the question of constitutional change, there is increasing pressure on the party and its leadership to adopt a position. However, because it requires addressing a political question that polarizes (at least some of) its cross-community base, the constitutional issue poses pronounced challenges for the non-aligned Alliance Party.

Adherence to the consent principle remains the foundational basis for the Alliance Party's engagement with the constitutional question. The long-term absence of sufficient support for a border poll eliminated the need for the party to be more expressive on the issue. However, the party has nonetheless been subject to persistent suspicion in relation to its position on the constitutional question: it has simultaneously been accused of being both a unionist party and more recently, a front for the nationalist cause. There is an evident frustration (among APNI leaders in particular) that the party has had such difficulty in asserting its neutrality on the constitutional question. Long (see Smith 2019) articulated this frustration when she said: "We're not anti-unionist or anti-nationalist. We're just not unionist or nationalist in our stance. It's relentless that people just won't accept it".

Although there remains a lack of majority support for a border poll, Brexit has provided some impetus for enlivening the discussion around Irish unity. As pressure builds for a referendum, remaining neutral on the issue becomes an increasingly less sustainable position and the Alliance Party has acknowledged the evolving political discourse around Irish unity. Speaking at the party's fiftieth anniversary annual conference in 2020, deputy leader Stephen Farry noted that adherence to the principle of consent sits alongside an openness to "civilised, rational and evidence-based discussions" on the issue (Moriarty 2020b). Party leader Naomi Long has also voiced a willingness to engage with discussions about Irish unity, suggesting that a failure to engage would be letting Alliance Party voters down (Manley 2020d). In March 2021, Long participated in a high-profile televized discussion of the subject alongside other political leaders from Northern Ireland, and including the Taoiseach, Tánaiste and president of Sinn Féin, Mary Lou McDonald.

The constitutional issue, however, is not at the forefront of the APNI's agenda. Instead, the party is much more resolutely focused on operationalizing the Belfast/Good Friday Agreement and on achieving reconciliation in Northern Ireland before it begins to seriously contemplate the prospects of a united Ireland. Long has stated that her focus as leader is on "uniting our community" and "trying to build a shared society" in Northern Ireland before engaging with discussions on Irish unity (see The Literific 2021). Overcoming segregation in Northern Ireland in terms of education, services and housing is something the Alliance Party believes must be squarely confronted and addressed in order to prepare Northern Ireland for a challenging and likely divisive constitutional debate. In short, the party believes that uniting Ireland is not a responsible or realistic prospect for as long as Northern Ireland itself remains divided and segregated. The party is effectively advocating for a united Northern Ireland as a forerunner to a border poll and suggesting that no referendum should take place until Stormont is stable and functional.

There is a risk, however, that the party's sidestepping of the united Ireland discussion is misjudged and out of sync with a broader appetite for contemplating constitutional change against the backdrop of Brexit-bred instability. In 2019, 1,000 representatives of civic society across Ireland and among the diaspora signed an open letter to Taoiseach Leo Varadkar calling for a "new conversation" and a citizens' assembly to consider the constitutional future of the island of Ireland (see McClements 2019). It included high-profile signatories drawn from across Northern Ireland's traditional political divide. Civic society groups – which, similar to the Alliance Party, are (ostensibly) non-aligned – have begun to form and campaign on the issue of constitutional change. There have even been calls from within its own party ranks for more considered contemplation of a united Ireland. Former Alliance Party chairman, Trevor Lunn, who left the party in 2020 and describes himself as "a slightly unionist-leaning politician" and one of "a group of undecided citizens", has called on the Irish government to set out the case for a united Ireland (Devlin 2020). Judging by recent polling data, which demonstrates a sizeable number of "don't knows" on the Irish unity question, Lunn may well be representative of a small (but growing cohort) of voters in general, and APNI supporters in particular, who may welcome moderate, nuanced and reflective discussion of the Irish unity question.

There is a sensitive and difficult challenge here for the Alliance Party. Engaging with the question of Irish unity risks the party being accused by unionist opponents of supporting the nationalist united Ireland agenda, and possibly alienating a part of their Protestant/unionist constituency. However, avoiding or delaying input to the debate may have a negative impact on the tone, character and direction of the wider discussion and limit the space for moderation and balance, which the centre ground can help to elicit and shape.

For now, the Alliance Party has set a high bar in terms of justifying future Irish unity. More than a bare majority is deemed necessary to support constitutional change (see Moore 2020). Convincing the party to support a united Ireland would also require irrefutable evidence that Northern Ireland would not be less well off as a consequence of constitutional change, whereas the question of how a united Ireland would reflect and respect both British and Irish identities is particularly important for a party which represents the two communities in Northern Ireland. Although these are highly salient issues, the party has not produced any commentary, research or proposals expanding on points or seeking to clarify particular ideas and positions. The party's propensity to be an agent of change at this current critical moment is highly circumscribed.

What is clear however, is that the Alliance Party's pro-EU stand continues to be a central component of its identity. In that context, the party wishes Northern Ireland to rejoin the EU at the earliest possible opportunity (see Long 2021a; Moriarty 2020b). This policy position sits uneasily with the Alliance Party's neutrality on the constitutional question. This is because the most realistic prospect for Northern Ireland to rejoin the EU is in the context of Irish unity:[8] indeed this is a logic frequently used by Sinn Féin in pushing for a border poll. According to the party leadership, however, pressure to rejoin the EU is lessened in the event of closer EU–UK alignment. In this context, Alliance is supportive of the full implementation of the Protocol and of keeping Northern Ireland (and the UK) close to EU standards. In effect, the closer the relationship between Northern Ireland and the EU, the easier it is for the Alliance Party to live with Brexit, to resist pressure for a united Ireland and to counter a critical constitutional juncture.

The Alliance Party's approach to Northern Ireland's current critical constitutional moment is situated within a tricky electoral space. Although the party and its voter base may be seen as instrumental and influential in terms of navigating the constitutional question, it is nevertheless subject to challenges, contingencies and timings neither of its choosing nor its making. These have the potential to diminish and even to disable the centre ground at a time when its capacity for balance and moderation is vital. This prospect would be particularly grievous given that in fragile societies, civic parties like the Alliance Party are deemed to "constitute durable actors in post-settlement contexts with distinct and potentially important, parts to play" (Murtagh 2020: 85). Therefore, as has consistently been the case before in Northern Ireland, preventing such a scenario requires external attention and input. The next chapter examines how the British and Irish governments are key agents in shaping Northern Ireland's constitutional future. Their actions and the relationship between them provide the space in which constitutional conversations take place.

---

8. The Irish unity declaration (attached to the EU's negotiating mandate) facilitates Northern Ireland becoming part of the EU in the event of Irish unity (see also Chapter 6).

# 6

# The British and Irish governments

"Northern Ireland is the frontier zone in which all that is conflictual in British–Irish relations has been concentrated."

Frank Wright (1989)

"Put simply, Brexit is high politics for Ireland. Brexit re-opens Ireland's 'English Question' in ways that are difficult to predict."

Brigid Laffan (2018)

Any understanding of Brexit's impact on Northern Ireland necessarily needs to begin with an understanding of the historic relationship between Britain and Ireland. This relationship is grounded in protracted conflict, including during the early twentieth century, when a period of anti-colonial agitation by Irish nationalists and counter-mobilization by unionists in Ulster ended with partition, and the creation and consolidation of two new states on the island of Ireland: the independent Irish Free State and Northern Ireland, which remained a part of the Union.[1] Partition was intended as a solution to the "Irish question" which had been an obdurate feature of British politics since the late nineteenth century. The creation of the Irish Free State (later the Republic of Ireland) precipitated a marked shift in the character of the British–Irish relationship. What had previously been a colonial relationship between Ireland and Britain changed to become (in theory at least) a relationship of sovereign equals. However, the birth of an independent Irish state in the midst of violent conflict would leave an enduring mark. In particular, the legitimacy of the border separating the Free State from the North

---

1. For a comprehensive examination of the events which defined the Irish Revolution, see Crowley *et al.* (2017).

was a key issue at stake in the Irish Civil War (1922–23), and it would remain essentially contested.

Shortly after the foundation of the Irish Free State, the Irish party system crystallized into an unusual form where political parties were based primarily on a constitutional rather than a socio-economic or class cleavage. As Ó Beacháin (2018: 5) notes, even to this day: "Ireland's party system remains a product of the civil war of 1922–1923". Right from the state's foundation therefore, the constitutional question was embedded in the Irish political system, shaping party competition and framing state structures and institutions.

Thus, Irish politics has been implicitly framed by consideration of Northern Ireland. This was evident in the early years after the foundation of the Irish Free State, following the signing of the Anglo-Irish Treaty in 1921, when politics, communities and even families were torn apart by the pro- versus anti-Treaty dichotomy. This political and societal divide persisted long after 1921 and was evident throughout and beyond the period of the Troubles. In this context, Ireland is different to its neighbour. For mainland British politics, the question of Northern Ireland has not been as mobilizing, or as emotive. Northern Ireland's role in British politics has long been defined by a paucity of understanding, a lack of institutional knowledge and a degree of disregard.

## "A half century of mutual antagonism"

The creation of the independent and sovereign (26-county) Irish state marked a watershed in the relationship between Britain and Ireland. However, differences in terms of size, Irish economic dependence on British markets, and condescending attitudes towards Ireland in British political culture created a marked asymmetry in the relationship. Political and constitutional tensions between the two states lingered long after 1921, most pointedly around the question of partition, which "was seen on the Irish side as a festering injustice" (Mansergh 2002: 96). All political parties in the new Irish state blamed London for partition: "Britain had imposed partition and so, the argument went, only Britain had the power to reverse it" (Ó Beacháin 2018: 49).

For its part, post-partition British political culture did not demonstrate any sustained interest in Northern Ireland's bitterly divided society.

British understanding of Ireland and Irish nationalism, in general, and empathetic engagement with Northern Ireland's nationalist community, in particular, was negligible. The British political establishment largely turned a blind eye to the forms of ethno-sectarian discrimination which devolution in Northern Ireland served to embed. During those early years after 1921, the Irish government was also guilty of being unfamiliar with all the dimensions and dynamics of Northern Ireland's brewing ethnonational conflict. This was most especially evident in relation to a lack of engagement with Ulster unionism and Northern Ireland's political institutions (though the Irish state's approach to the issues facing Northern nationalists after partition was, despite rhetorical flourish, also largely hands-off). In addition, for the half century after partition, the relationship between Britain and Ireland was marked by a lack of diplomatic and political contact. This increased what can be characterized as a gulf of misunderstanding between the two states which was further antagonized by a lack of trust.

When the Troubles broke out in August 1969, neither the UK nor Ireland had settled on a clear analysis of the Northern Ireland problem and their respective positions "were conditioned by a half century of mutual antagonism" (Coakley & Todd 2020: 4). The Irish government's acute concerns about civil rights abuses in Northern Ireland, and how these were being disproportionately experienced by the Catholic/ nationalist community, were coupled with concerns about a deteriorating security situation in Northern Ireland, which was also disproportionately impacting on Catholics. London was not initially minded to regard Dublin as a legitimate stakeholder in addressing or resolving the escalating Troubles. But as the security situation deteriorated, the British government moved to explore political proposals which involved Ireland as a means to resolving the conflict in Northern Ireland.

In December 1973, the Irish and British governments, the UUP, SDLP and Alliance Party contributed to the negotiations leading to the Sunningdale Agreement.[2] The agreement demonstrated how "the British government's position on Northern Ireland had substantially converged with Dublin's during the early years of the Troubles" (Ó Beacháin 2018: 123). However, the later abandonment of the Sunningdale Agreement

---

2. The DUP and other Unionists opposed to power-sharing were not involved in these negotiations.

in the face of intense opposition from unionists ended an initial period of British–Irish rapprochement on the vexed question of Northern Ireland.

Between Sunningdale and 2014's Stormont House Agreement, there were 11 further attempts, including, most importantly, the 1998 Belfast/ Good Friday Agreement, to support political settlement in Northern Ireland (see Coakley & Todd 2020). In all cases, issues of sovereignty, identity and consent were central to the various proposals and prescriptions and, for the most part, both governments maintained a broadly united front in how they approached and managed discussions and decisions (see Tannam 2001, 2011).

What was also not in question during this period was UK (and Irish) membership of the European Union. The EU provided not just an element of external constancy, it also provided a space and a forum where Ireland and Britain could consider and reflect on the Northern Ireland problem (see Hayward & Murphy 2012). To a significant extent, therefore, EU membership helped to address the troubled relationship and provided a framework within which a political settlement could be agreed and British–Irish relations could improve. Meehan (2000: 87) notes that "the 'equalization', as it were, of the status of Ireland and the UK as EU members and the familiarity induced by interactions between their 'European' civil servants" played a role in facilitating understanding and then later settlement.

The UK's decision to leave the EU in June 2016, however, upended the political context for British–Irish relations and disturbed the institutional framework within which the 1998 Agreement was situated. This included, critically, a radical disruption of the UK's territorial constitutional infrastructure, which had undergone a substantive process of restructuring in the late twentieth and early twenty-first century. The consequences of new, post-Brexit political and institutional realities were understood differently in Britain and Ireland, where there were opposing perspectives on and understandings of the relationship between shared EU membership, devolution, and peace and stability in Northern Ireland. There were very different views, in particular, on how best to manage the re-emergent "Irish question" (before, during and after the Brexit referendum). This pointed to the consequences of British political upheaval for Ireland, and the durability of historic

British–Irish misunderstandings – a factor which proved to be highly consequential for how Brexit came to take the form it did.

## "Taking back control of our borders"

Ireland, North and South, featured remarkably little in the debate surrounding the UK's 2016 Brexit referendum (Murphy 2018a; Cochrane 2020). As former Downing Street press officer and current SDLP MLA, Matt O'Toole (2017), lamented, the potential consequences of Brexit for Northern Ireland (and the island of Ireland more generally) were poorly understood and largely overlooked by both the Leave and Remain campaigns:

> Vote Leave had virtually nothing to say on Ireland or the Border, but sustained no identifiable damage to their cause as a result … the Remain campaign was based on focusing swing voters' minds on a narrow proposition: that a vote to leave the European Union was too economically risky. That approach had worked in the 2014 Scottish referendum and the 2015 UK general election. That strategy was also a rational response to polling data. English voters were going to win or lose the 2016 referendum … My colleagues on Cameron's political team were certainly sympathetic – many of them were also angry about Leave's approach to the Irish question – but the truth was that not enough target voters cared enough to make it a central campaign issue.

It is worth remembering, of course, that Brexit was never supposed to happen. David Cameron had called the referendum on the UK's EU membership in order to lance his own party's Eurosceptic boil and stop the Tories, finally and definitively, from "banging on about Europe" (Shipman 2016). He did so expecting to win, and to do so reasonably comfortably by replicating the "project fear" playbook that Westminster had deployed to what was felt to have been good effect during the 2014 Scottish independence referendum.[3] No serious preparations were

---

3. Whether and to what extent Better Together's "project fear" was actually successful in winning the Scottish independence referendum for the "No" side is a matter

made for a possible Leave result. Brexit's consequences for Northern Ireland (or, for that matter, for the rest of the UK) were not seriously considered in part because it was not really thought that there would be any such consequences to manage. To an extent then, the Remain campaign's blind-spot on Ireland – as bemoaned by Matt O'Toole – was reflective of a wider casualness of approach to the referendum. For their part, where and when concerns about the possible impact of Brexit on Northern Ireland and the Irish border did emerge, Leave campaigners – including then Secretary of State for Northern Ireland, Theresa Villiers – dismissed these out-of-hand (Murphy 2018a: 39-41). The implications of "taking back control of our borders" where the existence of those borders is the source of protracted and unresolved conflict, and where what "our" means is essentially contested, were studiously ignored by (and, on the whole, did not cross the minds of) Leavers on the "mainland" (Hayward 2020a; Sandford & Gormley-Heenan 2020). The fractious form that the Brexit process eventually took, and the conflicts that have defined it, stem in large part from this original sin of having systematically ignored Northern Ireland and the concerns of its citizens before, during and since the referendum.

When Theresa May assumed the mantle of prime minister, it was left to her to articulate a vision of what, precisely, Brexit meant, and how the issue of the Irish border was to be dealt with. She was particularly sluggish in outlining a coherent position on the latter. Indeed, in defining her preferred form of Brexit – which centred on a perceived need to restrict freedom of movement and "take back control of our laws, our money and our borders" – she adopted an approach that would necessarily make the question of the Irish border all the more difficult to solve. As Phinnemore and Whitten (2021) outline, Northern Ireland and its border with the Republic featured little in May's earlier Brexit speeches, which provided precisely no clarity on *how* the UK proposed to guarantee that there would be "no return to the borders of the past". As a number of contributors to UK in a Changing Europe's (2021a, 2021b) Brexit Witness Archive – including former Chancellor of the Exchequer, Philip Hammond, and David Lidington, who served as

---

of some dispute. Walker (2016), for instance, has highlighted how more positive identity- and values-based appeals, including in interventions by former prime minister, Gordon Brown, were key to securing working-class "No" votes.

Theresa May's *de facto* deputy prime minister – have attested, while she eventually came to take it seriously, the precise nature of the "problem" of Northern Ireland was one that only gradually and painfully dawned on May (see also Cochrane 2020). It is clear that it never fully dawned on other senior members of her party, its outriders and fellow travellers, who were at pains throughout to deny that such a problem really existed, or that it was entirely a figment of Leo Varadkar's imagination (see, e.g., Singham *et al.* 2017; Rees-Mogg 2018; Gudgin & Bassett 2018). Playing on long-running trends in British political culture, the Brexit process was shaped and largely defined by Brexiters' ignorance of the Irish peace process and indignance that the Belfast/Good Friday Agreement might be allowed to stand in their way.

Already severely constrained, the space for May to resolve Brexit's "Irish question" was narrowed even further by a catastrophic result for her Conservative Party in the snap general election of 2017, and its resultant tryst with the DUP. The confidence-and-supply deal was a red flag to the UK government's interlocutors in both Brussels and Dublin, who already had cause to question its understanding of and commitment to its obligations under the Belfast/Good Friday Agreement (de Mars *et al.* 2018; Birrell & Heenan 2020). The closeness of May's relationship with the DUP, and her persistent echoing of its insistence on the "preciousness" of the Union undermined the probity of the UK government's approach to Northern Ireland, where it is required by the Belfast/Good Friday Agreement to exercise its sovereignty with "rigorous impartiality" with respect to "parity of esteem and … just and equal treatment for the identity, ethos, and aspirations of both communities" (DFA 1998: 4; see also Tannam 2018). May's (incorrect) assertion that a border in the Irish Sea was something that no British prime minister could ever accept locked her into what Kelemen christened her "Irish border trilemma": a set of three overlapping promises on Brexit which simply could not all be delivered simultaneously, and at least one of which would have to be broken (see Chapter 2).

Thus, the UK government's approach to the question of Northern Ireland gave rise to a clumsy mix of incompatible Brexit red lines and a negotiating position defined by inconsistent, contradictory, and even false claims. The upshot was that the UK government was, at best, a difficult and unreliable negotiating partner, and at worst, an actively duplicitous one. In the end it alienated everyone. May's weak grip on power within her own party, her contradictory promises, and her need to supplicate the DUP made it difficult for the EU to deal with her, or to trust that she would be able to secure domestic agreement on any deal that was eventually concluded (Connelly 2019). May was allegedly upset and angered by allegations that she did not take her responsibilities under the Belfast/Good Friday Agreement seriously (Kelly 2018). But her perceived untrustworthiness in this area was not helped by the furtive and belligerent approach she took to the negotiations more generally. Nor was it enhanced by the bellicose and boorish position on Ireland/Northern Ireland adopted by other senior members of her party. Intermittent assaults on the Belfast/Good Friday Agreement in the pages of Tory-supporting newspapers were led by, among others, Owen Patterson MP and then MEP, Daniel Hannan. One-time Brexit Secretary, Dominic Raab, admitted that he had never even read it (Kelly 2019). And former Secretary of State for International Development, Priti Patel, argued that the UK government should use the threat of Irish food shortages to force concessions on the backstop (Ní Aodha 2018).

Under Boris Johnson, the UK became an even more deliberately bad-faith actor. Having definitively disproven May's assertion that no British premier could ever agree to a border in the Irish Sea, Johnson then lied about it by telling Northern Ireland businesses that they could put customs declarations forms "in the bin" (Stewart, Rankin & O'Carroll 2019). This was followed by the publication of the Internal Market Bill, which threatened to override and disapply key parts of the Ireland/ Northern Ireland Protocol (Foster, Payne & Brunsden 2020; Hayward 2020b). In the early phase of its implementation, Secretary of State for Northern Ireland, Brandon Lewis, insisted that the new Irish Sea border did not in fact exist (McBride 2021a). And with Johnson's government having then unilaterally moved to extend post-Brexit grace periods on the regulation of goods moving across this border from Great Britain to Northern Ireland, Irish Foreign Minister, Simon Coveney, warned that the EU was left "negotiating with a partner they simply can't trust" (Connelly 2021a).

A lack of trust in the UK government is also a striking feature of post-Brexit politics in Northern Ireland, and it is acutely felt by unionists, nationalists and "others" alike. According to polling commissioned by Queen's University Belfast in April 2021, fully 86 per cent of Northern Irish voters do not trust the UK government to manage Northern Ireland's post-Brexit interests (Phinnemore & Hayward 2021). Insofar as Brexit has presaged a growing appetite for constitutional change in Northern Ireland, this really has less to do with Irish nationalist agitation than it does with the UK government's wilful failure to meaningfully engage with or seek to understand – let alone mitigate – the particular problems that Brexit has engendered there. Indeed, the Tories' perceived duplicity, and their willingness to ride roughshod over the concerns of those who do not conform to their particular, narrow and Anglo-centric world-view, has contributed to the wider turmoil which has characterized the UK's post-Brexit constitutional politics (Henderson & Wyn Jones 2021). The Conservative government's cavalier approach on Northern Ireland before, during and since Brexit is reflective of a wider disregard it has shown for devolved governance arrangements across the UK, and its ignorance of the ways in which the UK's constitution has evolved in the almost 50 years since accession to the EU.

## "The precious, precious bond between England, Scotland, Wales and Northern Ireland"

In 2017, the House of Lords European Committee noted that,

> The European Union has been, in effect, part of the glue holding the United Kingdom together since 1997. The supremacy of EU law, and the interpretation of that law by the Court of Justice of the EU, have in many areas ensured consistency of legal and regulatory standards across the UK, including in devolved policy areas, such as environment, agriculture and fisheries. In practice, the UK internal market has been upheld by the rules of the EU internal market.
>
> (HL EC 2017: 12)

Brexit removed the supporting constitutional infrastructure that had become increasingly central to holding the UK together as a coherent political and economic entity (Bogdanor 2019). Critically, of course, it did so without the consent of the electorates of two of the UK's four constituent parts: Scotland and Northern Ireland. In the case of the latter, Europeanization – the deterritorialization of domestic law and politics, and their deepening entanglement with multilevel European processes and frameworks – was a particularly important aspect of governance arrangements, to which Brexit was particularly damaging (Murphy 2014, 2019a). But by removing key pieces of the homogenizing legal scaffolding shoring up the UK's haphazard and "improvized" constitution (Weale 2018), processes of de-Europeanization have also posed important and destabilizing questions for the UK's territorial constitution and its devolution settlement more widely.

As Wincott (2018) has highlighted, describing the way in which devolution has evolved in the UK in terms of "settlement" is something of a misnomer, inaccurately reflecting the uneven, asymmetric and constantly evolving ways in which the British state has undergone "partial disintegration" (Jeffrey 2009: 92) since 1997. In addition to the binding effect of EU membership, in the early years of devolution, this disintegration was masked or elided by an "unusually benign" (Wincott 2018: 23) political environment and a high degree of convergence among the four constituent parts of the UK. As it was put by one Irish official who had worked in British–Irish relations over a number of years: "It was Labour in government in London with a huge majority, Labour in government in Scotland with a huge majority, Labour in government in Wales with a huge majority, and the SDLP as the second major party, holding the Deputy First Minister's job in Belfast. So, it was this sort of homogeneous Labour-land. And I think that there was a sense that this would never end" (interview with authors, 2018). Undermined by Labour's fall from power in Westminster in 2010, and in the context of the politics of austerity which followed the global banking and financial crises (McKinnion 2015), the post-devolution integrity of the British state was fundamentally challenged by the political ascendance of the Scottish National Party (SNP) and the Scottish independence referendum in 2014 (McHarg *et al.* 2016; Walker 2016). By the time of the Brexit referendum in 2016, the SNP were in government in Scotland, Labour in Cardiff, the DUP and Sinn Féin in coalition in Belfast (in an arrangement which would collapse a few months later), and the Conservatives at Westminster. The result was a fragmented political geography less conducive to buttressing the British state against the centrifugal forces unleashed by Brexit, which has become little short of a constitutional crisis (or what Wincott *et al.* (2018) would prefer to term a "tipping point") for the UK.

This crisis has been exacerbated by the way in which the Conservative government in Westminster managed the process of withdrawing from the EU, which saw devolved governments in Scotland, Wales and Northern Ireland systematically excluded from having any meaningful involvement (McEwen 2020; Hunt & Minto 2017). As McHarg (2018: 962) suggests, despite "having initially promised that the devolved governments would be fully involved in establishing the UK's negotiating position, resistance to the assertion of a devolved veto seemed to harden the UK government's position that Brexit was a matter for it alone". Intergovernmental meetings – that is, meetings between the central and devolved governments – during the Brexit negotiations, including through a Joint Ministerial Committee (Europe Negotiations) (JMC (EN)), were ad hoc and frustrating for Scottish and Welsh participants, who raised serious questions throughout as to the true extent of the UK government's commitment to working with them on withdrawal from the EU. Broad dissatisfaction was expressed at the government's lack of responsiveness to the concerns of the devolved administrations (McEwen *et al.* 2018) and the final form of hard Brexit eventually agreed by the UK and the EU was fundamentally at odds with the preferences of the devolved administrations.

In the case of Northern Ireland, the hiatus in devolved government from 2017 to 2020 and the closeness of May's relationship with the DUP combined to further constrain the extent to which Northern Ireland's voice was able to make itself heard in the Brexit process. While they represented the majority of people in Northern Ireland, pro-Remain, pro-backstop parties were forced to make their interventions in this conversation outside of formal intergovernmental channels. The Northern Ireland Executive was represented in intergovernmental meetings by senior civil servants, who were severely constrained in what they were able to say and what decisions they could make. As de Mars *et al.* (2018) have speculated, this probably largely suited the UK government, giving it one less awkward partner to have to worry about. Had devolution in Northern Ireland been functioning, then the imperative of obtaining the Northern Ireland Assembly's consent for Brexit legislation would have been "undeniable and the Nationalist parties would, in all likelihood, have had the votes to frustrate it" (*ibid.* 124). With the Assembly and Executive both in abeyance, Westminster was able incrementally to return key regulatory powers needed to implement Brexit from Belfast to London, and pass legislation in areas of devolved competence with only limited pushback (see Emerson 2019).

The devolved governments and legislatures in Wales and Scotland could not be so quietly sidelined. Neither the Scottish (led throughout by SNP First Minister, Nicola Sturgeon) nor the Welsh (led from 2016 to 2018 by Labour's Carwyn Jones and from 2018 by his successor as Welsh Labour leader, Mark Drakeford) governments were willing meekly to quiesce to the UK government's approach on Brexit, and there were important instances of collaboration between Edinburgh and Cardiff in seeking to oppose moves to centralize key Brexit processes and outcomes in London (McEwen 2020). There was sustained conflict between Holyrood and Cardiff Bay and Westminster, in particular, over what would happen to key powers in areas of devolved competence (such as environmental regulation, agriculture, food standards, animal welfare, public procurement, justice, transport, and energy) once these were returned from Brussels and transposed into "retained EU law". When the Scottish parliament voted to preserve its power to legislate in these areas by passing the Scottish EU Continuity Bill in 2018, this was ruled to be illegal by the Supreme Court, which determined that authority to decide whether and what powers in areas of "retained EU law" were to be devolved, when and how resided at Westminster.

This episode was just one among many demonstrations of the ways in which Brexit effectively functioned to recentralize power in London, and how it served to disrupt and undermine the functioning of devolution. The "Sewel Convention" (see Institute for Government 2020) – which holds that the Westminster parliament will not normally legislate with regard to devolved matters without the express consent of the devolved legislature(s) – was contravened on a number of other occasions over the course of the Brexit process. It is notable that when – following the Tory landslide in the December 2019 general election – parliament finally passed the Withdrawal Agreement Bill in January 2020, it did so without the consent of *any* of the devolved legislatures. This was followed in late 2020 by the passage of the Internal Market Bill. As well as raising alarm bells in Brussels and Dublin as to the UK government's intentions vis-à-vis implementation of the Northern Ireland Protocol, the Bill reserved competence for state aid and subsidies at Westminster and restricted devolved governments' capacity to meaningfully legislate on standards and regulations, stymieing their capacity to pursue their own priorities on trade, investment and industrial policy. It also gave the UK government express new funding powers in devolved areas, giving it the option to circumvent or bypass the devolved governments and fund projects and organizations in Scotland, Wales and Northern Ireland directly (Dougan *et al.* 2020). The net result was a serious diminution of trust in the UK government and what is potentially (and even likely) an irredeemable deterioration in intergovernmental relationships within the UK; a growth in nationalist resentment and anti-Union sentiment in Scotland, Wales and Northern Ireland; and the raising of profound questions as to whether and for how long the Union state can endure. These questions are ones with profound implications for Ireland and for British–Irish relations.

## "What we have to recognize is that the Union, as it is, is over"

Giving evidence to the House of Commons Welsh Affairs Committee on 4 March 2021, First Minister Mark Drakeford lamented that,

> There is no institutional architecture to make the United Kingdom work. It is all *ad hoc*, random and made up as we go along. I am afraid that that really is not a satisfactory basis to sustain the future of the United Kingdom ... At the moment, we have a Prime Minister who, I would say, clearly displays outright hostility to the fact of devolution. We heard what he told a group of Conservative Members of Parliament, that he thought devolution was Tony Blair's greatest mistake. I am afraid that, while there is a mindset of that sort at the centre of the Government, the break-up of the Union comes closer every day.

What is critical about this contribution from the Welsh First Minister is that he is himself an avowed believer in the Union. That even he has cause to be so scathing about its current state should be a source of alarm for any unionist.

Since Brexit, pro-independence sentiment in Scotland has grown to consistently out-poll the 45 per cent of the vote which the Yes side achieved in the referendum of 2014. There has also been a growth in what has been termed "indy-curiosity" in Wales, alongside a new urgency to debates about Irish unity on both sides of the Irish border (see, e.g., Shipman & Allardyce 2021). The pull towards disintegration has been exacerbated by the Covid-19 pandemic, which the leaders of devolved governments in Scotland and Wales have generally been seen, rightly or wrongly, as having handled better than has the government in Westminster.

For much of 2020, support for Scottish independence was consistently polling at more than 50 per cent, and in 2021, pro-independence parties won a majority of seats in the Scottish parliamentary election. In Wales, the pandemic has coincided with the growing prominence of grassroots independence campaigns like YesCymru, and support for independence has polled at historic highs. Although, unlike in Scotland, pro-independence Nationalists were not returned as the largest party in Welsh parliamentary elections in 2021 (in fact, Plaid Cymru finished third, behind the Welsh Conservatives), commentators have noted how Labour's return to government represented the "maturation" of a distinctly Welsh politics with its own dynamics, separate to those pertaining in England (see, e.g., Hiraeth 2021). Labour also campaigned on a manifesto committed to seeking forms of constitutional change which, although short of full independence for Wales, would nonetheless represent a radical shake-up of the British state (Welsh Labour 2021: 66). For their part, Irish nationalists have stressed, with some validity, the illogic of attempting to manage the pandemic across two jurisdictions on an island that could usefully have been treated as one epidemiological unit, and have continued to proffer Irish unity as a solution to the new bureaucratic and administrative burdens represented by the Ireland/Northern Ireland Protocol. Sinn Féin look set to be in government on both sides of the Irish border, possibly as the largest party both North and South, in the short to medium term, with a programme that will include pushing and preparing for a border poll within the next five years.

The UK government's response to these centrifugal forces which are threatening to tear the Union apart has been the adoption of an even more "muscular" unionism. On becoming prime minister, Boris Johnson appointed himself "Minister for the Union". In October 2020, he established a new "Union Unit" in Downing Street, with a view to promoting the benefits of the union, including in terms of managing the response to the coronavirus pandemic. One of its first recommendations was that the Oxford/AstraZeneca vaccine should be labelled with union flags. Amid a series of conflicts (both personal and political) within Johnson's No. 10 operation, the unit was eventually wound up and replaced with a new cabinet committee with the same remit. The broad aim throughout has been to reassert Westminster's centrality and dominance, culturally, politically and legally. As noted above, the Internal Market Act gives Westminster new powers to fund projects in devolved areas, and the products of any such investment are to be clearly marked with the symbolism of the union. It is increasingly common to see Conservative politicians speaking in front of union flags; more frequent royal visits to Scotland have been proposed; and UK diplomats have been instructed to refer to the UK in singular, unitary terms, rather than as a "union of four nations" (Deerin 2021).

In Northern Ireland, the UK government took a direct stake in coordinating the commemorations of the state's centenary, and more substantively has refused to countenance the holding of a border poll, or even to outline under what conditions it would be prepared to call one (*Irish News* 2021). This approach to protecting and promoting the Union is, however, entirely counterproductive. Like Boris Johnson himself, it is strikingly unpopular outside of England. Indeed, and as Geoghegan (2021) suggests: "In trying to force a unionism into a single form, Johnson and his colleagues are inadvertently flagging up its weaknesses. The union has always worked best when nobody talked about it. Johnson's muscular unionism increasingly serves to highlight – and accentuate – the union's underlying tensions".

Growth in pro-independence sentiment in Scotland and some flourishing of "indy-curiosity" in Wales – both given greater impetus by the UK government's ham-fisted efforts at buttressing the Union – have encouraged a reorientation of relations between Ireland, Scotland and Wales. Efforts to institutionalize and deepen relations between the Irish state and the constituent units of the UK is premised on ensuring that connections and cooperation are "strengthened in a changing international environment" (DFA 2021a, 2021b). High-level Irish political support for bilateral reviews of the Scottish–Irish and Welsh–Irish future relationships demonstrates how the UK's simmering constitutional crisis is arguably as significant for Ireland as it is for the UK, and that it may require potentially rapid further political and diplomatic pivoting in Dublin. However, it is more particularly in the context of its role as co-guarantors of the Belfast/Good Friday Agreement where Ireland's primary British–Irish interests are concentrated and where the import of Brexit for the Irish government's relationship with its British counterpart is most profoundly experienced. The very decision to call a referendum on the UK's EU membership served to throw a spanner into the workings of this relationship. And as a consequence of the UK government's mismanagement of the Brexit process both internally and externally, it has deteriorated rapidly since 2016.

## "The relationship between our two countries has never been stronger or more settled"

Prior to Brexit, the 2011 visit of Queen Elizabeth II marked the high-point of British–Irish relations. The Queen's first ever state visit to Ireland, and the first visit to Ireland by a British monarch in one hundred years, *appeared* to signal what Coakley has characterized as "a sign of collective British–Irish rapprochement" (2018: 320). Less than a year later, in March 2012, following a meeting in Downing Street, Prime Minister David Cameron and Taoiseach Enda Kenny referenced the Queen's visit as "a symbol of a modern, deep and friendly relationship" in a joint statement which hailed the normalization of the British–Irish relationship. The statement included the shared British–Irish view that: "The relationship between our two countries has never been stronger or more settled, as complex or as important, as it is today" (Merrion Street 2012). The joint statement, however, was more than just an expression of mutual respect, it also "established a new hierarchy of issue areas and common interests between the two states in a policy regime that goes wider than the Northern Ireland issue" (Gillespie 2014: 50). It included mechanisms and activities to further solidify economic and political relations between the two states; and made explicit reference to UK and Irish membership of the EU as a forum for cooperation and consultation: "Our two countries have shared common membership of the European Union for almost forty years. As partners in the European Union we are firm supporters of the Single Market and will work together to encourage an outward-facing EU, which promotes growth and jobs ... We will continue to consult each other on key EU issues" (Merrion Street 2012).

However, as the British prime minister was negotiating a deeper and more structured relationship with Ireland, and one premised on shared EU membership, the UK's constitutional moorings were beginning to shift. Just two months after the Queen's visit to Ireland, the European Union Bill completed its passage through Westminster and became law. The legislation was agreed and approved in the context of a growing debate about a possible UK–EU in–out referendum. A key feature of this new legal provision was the creation of "a so-called 'referendum lock' on any future transfers of power (competencies) from the UK to the European Union" (Wellings & Vines 2016: 311).

High-level attempts by Cameron and Kenny to strengthen the British–Irish relationship also coincided with the continued electoral rise of the SNP and growing calls for a Scottish independence referendum. As the British government was negotiating closer and deeper relations between Ireland and the UK, it was simultaneously working on plans to facilitate a referendum on Scottish independence (see Mullen 2014). This prompted Gillespie (2014: 38) to note: "Paradoxically, however, just as the official discourse of transformation [of the British–Irish relationship] reached its height the normalization on which it was based was challenged by the dual constitutional question facing the UK: Scotland's vote on independence and a likely referendum on the UK's membership of the EU". The strength and settledness of the British–Irish relationship, of which both prime ministers fondly spoke in 2012, would be profoundly impacted by the UK's looming "dual constitutional question".

Following the calling of the Scottish independence referendum in 2014, there was high-level political awareness in Ireland that a vote in favour of independence "would of course have both political and policy implications for Ireland, reshaping our relations with Scotland as well as relations with the United Kingdom and European Union" (Irish Minister of State, Paschal Donohue, cited in Walker 2014: 744). The Irish government nevertheless chose not to comment on the referendum itself preferring instead to respond to, rather than to anticipate, the result. In contrast, the Irish approach to the UK's EU referendum was decidedly different and based on a position of outspoken concern and determined opposition.

### "Ireland has a legitimate reason for getting involved"

A function of Ireland's familiarity with Britain meant that Ireland was aware of the complexity of Britain's historically antagonistic relationship with the EU and understood the invidious nature of the Eurosceptic challenge facing successive British governments. In the years before 2016, Ireland was mindful of, and attentive to, a growing anti-EU narrative in Britain which was coalescing around increased political pressure for an in-out referendum. Enda Kenny voiced these concerns as early as 2012 in response to the UK's decision to remain outside the Fiscal Stability Pact agreed between EU leaders in December 2011. The Irish government's strategy in response to the UK decision was to work to ensure that: "the links between Ireland and Britain, which have been historically so important from a trading point of view, be maintained, and that it be clearly understood that Britain is an essential part of the European Union and that the European Union needs Britain insofar as full membership is concerned" (Kenny, cited in McGee & Scally 2012).

Ireland's strong support for the UK's "essential" position within the EU was premised on the severe problems and issues that a UK exit from the EU would produce for Ireland in general, and for Northern Ireland in particular. More bluntly, from the perspective of its nearest neighbour, and from an early point, the prospect of the UK leaving the EU was identified as anathema to Irish interests and to Northern Ireland's stability in particular. This reflected the immense depth of concern about the potentially catastrophic impact of a UK exit from the EU on the island of Ireland. In contrast to the prevailing mood in Britain, there was a near visceral anxiety among the Irish elite about how Ireland, and in particular how Northern Ireland, would fare (economically, but more especially politically) if its nearest neighbour were outside the shared EU framework. Writing in 2014, Gillespie (50) noted: "Irish policymakers have been watching the UK's intensifying debate on membership of the EU and Scottish independence with growing fascination and alarm ... The prospect of a UK withdrawal [from the EU] is alarming for Irish policymakers because it would jeopardize key conditions that have brought Britain and Ireland closer together in a complex interdependence regime over the last generation". Irish concerns about such a referendum were also shaped by Irish familiarity with referendums,[4] and an acute sensitivity to how risky such plebiscitary tools can be. According to a senior Irish official, Enda Kenny offered "friendly advice" to Cameron along the lines of: "We have some experience of this kind of thing. On referenda, people are voting on everything. It's a free kick at a government. If it's voting about you as Prime Minister they'll take that very seriously, but they don't always take referenda very seriously, or think about the consequences" (Connelly 2018: 13). In an address to Chatham House in London, the Irish Foreign Affairs Minister Charlie Flanagan openly reflected on Ireland's experience of EU referendum campaigns and hoped that his thoughts and observations might "prove helpful … as [the UK] referendum begins to appear in the horizon" (Flanagan 2015). In a similar vein, Barrett (2016) detailed the kinds of lessons the UK might glean from the Irish experience of EU referendums. He noted – rather presciently – that: "Statistically, winning European referendums in particular has become increasingly difficult". He also cautioned against complacency and urged that close attention be paid to turnout, campaign expenditure and the role of the media. There is little evidence to suggest that the British establishment paid heed to Irish experience and advice.

Rather than being reactive in its approach to a possible Brexit, the Irish state was proactive in preparing for the possibility of such an outcome. Official concerns about a Brexit vote, and its potential impact on Ireland, were first contained in the state's 2014 *National Risk Assessment* (Government of Ireland 2014) where a UK vote in favour of leaving the EU was deemed a strategic risk. The Department of the Taoiseach also produced an internal paper in late 2014 looking at the possible consequences for Ireland of a British vote to leave the EU (RTÉ 2021). This first study of the implications of a possible Brexit followed from David Cameron's 2013 Bloomberg Speech which promised a referendum on UK membership of the EU in the event of a Conservative Party majority after the 2015 Westminster election. Even before that election however, the Irish government was preparing the groundwork for navigating a future UK referendum on EU membership.

---

4.  Ireland has held 38 referendums on a variety of issues including EU membership and treaties; marriage equality; abortion; reform of the electoral system; abolition of Seanad Éireann (Irish Senate), etc.

In early 2015, the Taoiseach reorganized his department specifically to prepare for the issue and established a new departmental division "to focus specifically on relations between Ireland and Britain, including bilateral issues that arise in the context of the EU–UK debate" (see Oireachtas Debate, 21 April 2016). This included cross-departmental work which aimed to identify strategic and sectoral issues that would inevitably arise for Ireland in the event of a UK vote to leave the EU. The Irish parliament, through the Joint Committee on European Union Affairs, also considered the implications of a Brexit vote for Ireland. Its report *UK/EU Future Relationship: Implications for Ireland* (Houses of the Oireachtas 2015) published in June 2015 was based on eight dedicated meetings, evidence from 15 witnesses and a fact-finding visit to London. The report establishes Ireland's "right" to take a detailed interest in any future UK–EU referendum: "The Committee believes that Ireland has a legitimate reason for getting involved, namely because it matters more to us than to any other country in Europe" (5). This strong and unapologetic statement of intent underlined the severity of the Brexit threat for Irish interests.

Also in 2015, the ESRI conducted an early scoping study of the possible economic implications of Brexit for Ireland. The analysis suggested that the most significant economic impact of Brexit for Ireland "is likely to be concentrated in the [UK–Irish] trade relationship" (Barrett *et al.* 2015: 60). During this early phase of Irish engagement with the Brexit issue, the government focused its efforts on outlining and widely communicating Irish concerns. From 2015 onwards, senior Irish political figures, including the Taoiseach and Minister for Foreign Affairs, addressed a number of diverse and influential British audiences including the Confederation of British Industry (CBI) (23 March 2015), Chatham House (7 September 2015), the British–Irish Chamber of Commerce (25 January 2016) and the British Irish Association (4 September 2015) among others. In addition to numerous blogs, op-eds and speeches, the then Irish ambassador to the UK, Dan Mulhall, also addressed the House of Commons Northern Ireland Affairs Committee (2016) as part of its report on *Northern Ireland and the EU Referendum* where he outlined the government's concerns.

In tandem during this period, Irish officials and politicians were working towards an EU–UK deal which might assuage British concerns about EU membership and convince UK voters to support a

Remain vote. In oral evidence to the House of Lords European Union Committee (2016b) inquiry on *The EU referendum and EU reform*, the Irish ambassador to the UK was broadly sympathetic to UK calls for (some) reform of the EU and was positive about the EU's capacity to accommodate reasonable reform objectives. Although it was cautious in relation to one of the UK's EU reform objectives, namely support for welfare reform, Ireland was broadly supportive of three of its four proposed reforms – competitiveness, sovereignty and subsidiarity, and a formal setting out of the relationship between those within and outside the eurozone (see O'Mahony 2015). Speaking at a press conference with David Cameron in January 2016, Taoiseach Enda Kenny doubled down on Irish support for the UK's EU reform agenda (10 Downing Street 2016): "People are aware that President Tusk will table a paper, probably next week in regards to the four issues that the Prime Minister put on the table. I actually believe that all of these are solvable in a really positive sense because you know our position in Ireland, Europe will be much stronger with Britain as a central and fundamental member". Throughout Cameron's negotiations with the EU, Ireland's support for the UK's position was steadfast to the point where Kroll and Leuffen (2016: 1314) categorize the Irish government as "one of the most vocal supporters of the British reform ideas in the EU".

## "At the very top of the new Government's agenda"

Following the setting of a date for the UK's EU referendum, phase two of the Irish government's strategy commenced. As the referendum date neared, senior Irish civil servants confirmed that the Brexit issue was "at the very top of the new Government's agenda"[5] and that nothing on the government's agenda was more important (Leahy 2016). In the weeks preceding the referendum vote, this was illustrated by the intense mobilization of the apparatus of the state and the escalation of Irish political efforts to emphasize Ireland's unique relationship with the UK and to communicate Ireland's preference for a Remain vote. Between April 2016 and referendum day on 23 June 2016, senior Irish government

---

5. Enda Kenny was returned as Irish Taoiseach following a general election on 26 February 2016.

ministers conducted 14 visits to Britain and Northern Ireland encouraging voters (and the Irish community in Britain) to support the UK
remaining in the EU (see Oireachtas Debates, 22 June 2016).

Irish civil society and sectoral interests also became increasingly
engaged in the Brexit debate during this pre-referendum period. Reports
by the Irish Congress of Trade Unions (ICTU) (2016), the Irish Business
and Employers Confederation (IBEC) (2016), and the agricultural sector (see, e.g., Donnellan & Hanrahan 2016; Bergin 2016) all painted a
negative picture of how a Brexit vote would impact on the Irish economy and society. By the time of the referendum itself, the Irish political
system and key economic sectors were acutely aware of the implications
of a UK vote to exit the EU.

At the level of Ireland's political and civil service elite, the result of the
referendum was a shock, but it was not entirely unexpected: "As referendum day approached, [the] analysis was getting darker. At a gathering
one evening of embassy staff and an Irish government minister, a straw
poll was held. Of the eight people present around the table, seven of them
predicted a Leave victory" (Connelly 2018:14). Immediately following
the announcement of the Leave result, and based on a pre-agreed cho-
reography, the Irish government rolled out a series of responses which
included: the convening of an emergency cabinet meeting; a statement
by the Taoiseach; consultation with opposition parties; the publication
of preliminary contingency planning; and the recalling of parliament.
The Irish government, all of the main political parties and key social
partners regretted but respected the referendum outcome and committed to work to moderate its worst effects for Ireland. As Murphy
notes (2019a: 535; see also Connelly 2018): "The tone of the broad Irish
response to the UK referendum result was informed by an acute awareness and sensitivity to the possible consequences of the Brexit crisis for
Ireland; many of which had been highlighted in Ireland and by Irish
interests long before the referendum campaign".

In its initial response to the Brexit vote, the Irish state was addressing a number of different audiences. Calming nerves in Ireland was
critical, respecting the UK decision was important, but it was also vital
for the Irish government to affirm and avow Ireland's commitment to
continued membership of the EU. In his statement responding to the
Brexit vote, the Taoiseach explicitly noted that EU membership "is profoundly in [Ireland's] national interest" (Merrion Street 2016). This was

a message that was repeatedly communicated by the Irish government in the days and weeks following the Leave vote. This strategy of aligning Ireland with the EU was deliberate: it demonstrated loyalty to the EU and allowed Ireland to position itself to influence and shape the EU's negotiating position from the get-go.

On the back of extensive pre-referendum research, contingency-planning, scenario-building, strategizing and networking, the Irish government was well-positioned to pursue key national objectives in the context of the EU–UK negotiations. Among its initial practical responses was the decision to roll out an extraordinary diplomatic effort aimed at educating EU capitals about how Brexit would impinge negatively on Irish political and economic interests (see O'Brennan 2019). The endeavour was supported by revised civil service structures and roles; expanded diplomatic teams; additional staff appointed to key state agencies; the creation of a dedicated cabinet committee; civil society consultative dialogues; and an extensive programme of communication (see Rees & O'Brennan 2019; Laffan 2018). By March 2017, four key priorities were clarified, and these formed the basis for Ireland's approach to the negotiations on the UK's withdrawal from the EU. They included: (1) protecting the Northern Ireland peace process; (2) minimizing the impact on trade and the economy; (3) securing the Common Travel Area; and (4) strengthening the EU and Ireland's influence in it (Government of Ireland 2017: 3). The priorities were guided by a central unifying theme, namely, preventing the imposition of a hard land border on the island of Ireland. In its simplest form, this meant that the Irish government supported a soft Brexit: one that would see the UK remain in the EU's single market and customs union. This was conceived as being the least politically and economically disruptive Brexit because, broadly speaking, it would mean the maintenance of existing UK–Ireland trade arrangements and so would avoid the need for the erection of regressive border controls between Ireland and the UK.

Ireland's clear, unambiguous and straightforward position and messaging paid dividends. As former senior Irish civil servant Rory Montgomery (2021) notes: "Ireland was remarkably successful in persuading the EU member states and institutions to accept its analysis and adopt its objectives". The EU's negotiating guidelines contained explicit recognition of Ireland's key Brexit priorities, and specifically aimed to avoid a hard border between Northern Ireland and the Republic of

Ireland. This effectively meant that the EU–UK negotiations were bound and framed, from the outset, by an agreed need to maintain an open border on the island of Ireland and this position had been shaped and moulded by Irish preferences.

The Irish government's success in ensuring that its key Brexit objectives were prioritized as part of the EU–UK negotiating process, however, represented both triumph and test. Although this starting point for negotiations accommodated Irish interests, particularly in relation to protecting the open Irish border, its narrowness limited the options available to the UK and effectively forced the British government into a choice between the softest of Brexits, i.e. membership of the EU customs union and single market, or a differentiated Brexit allowing the UK to remain outside the customs union and single market, but requiring that Northern Ireland be treated differently. The problem for the British government, and latterly for unionism, was that the British government was not strategically engaged with (or even well-versed in) the challenges of how best to deal with the Irish border issue as part of the EU–UK negotiating process. Unlike the Irish government, there was an absence of institutional memory of the Irish question and the Belfast/Good Friday Agreement at the highest political and civil service levels. Former UK Permanent Representative to the EU, Ivan Rogers (UK in a Changing Europe 2021c) has talked of a "system failure" and notes that: "[The sequencing of the negotiations] was over well before [the British government] realized it, and Dublin had also totally outplayed them on what became, by later in 2017, the backstop question … So they [Dublin] had a really very good team, they knew what they were doing. They had a really good diplomatic operation on it. They were much superior to Whitehall, which should give London pause for thought".

Eventually, in a move which infuriated unionists in Northern Ireland, the British government settled on the Ireland/Northern Ireland Protocol as a means to manage the Irish border issue. In addition to feeling betrayed by the British government however, unionists also railed against the Irish government for what they perceived as its original insistence on an overly rigid EU–UK negotiating mandate. Former DUP First Minister Arlene Foster accused Irish Foreign Minister Simon Coveney of being "tone deaf to unionist concerns" and of not fully appreciating or acknowledging wholesale unionist opposition to the Protocol in Northern Ireland (Press Association 2021). For its part, the Irish government demonstrated some appreciation of the difficulties facing unionism and was quietly working to facilitate greater flexibility in the implementation of the Protocol: "With Boris Johnson's Protocol now in place, the Irish Government is, ironically, taking a more proactive role in quietly lobbying capitals on its difficulties, and facilitating contacts between those capitals and stakeholders in Northern Ireland" (Connelly 2021b).

A key challenge for the Irish government, however, is balancing its support for greater flexibility towards Northern Ireland with its ongoing commitments as an EU member state. The extent to which the Irish government can push an alternative agenda which is aligned more closely with unionist/British preferences risks upsetting its EU partners who are concerned first and foremost to protect the integrity of the single market. Offending or aggravating the EU is neither wise nor judicious given that the Republic of Ireland's future is determinedly situated within the European Union camp.

The priority attached by the Irish government to Brexit is built around a trio of highly sensitive challenges. Firstly, and most importantly, there is a primary and overriding objective to safeguard the open border on the island of Ireland, thereby protecting the Belfast/Good Friday Agreement and securing stability in Northern Ireland. Secondly, and similarly important, there is an express need to prioritize and protect Ireland's position as an EU member state. And thirdly, the Irish government is concerned to be mindful of Ireland's constitutional aspiration for Irish unity, a possibility revived by the very fact of Brexit. Detailed planning, and dexterous political and diplomatic manoeuvring have been instrumental in allowing the Irish government to best manage all three challenges simultaneously. It is, however, the issue of a border poll and possible future Irish unity which is especially politically tricky for the Irish government and has proved the least amenable to careful control and management.

### "I hope it moves us towards majority support for unification"

Less than a month after the Leave vote, Taoiseach Enda Kenny outlined his preference that the EU–UK negotiations include some acknowledgement of the possibility of future Irish unity materializing in the aftermath of Brexit: "discussions and negotiations that take place over the next period should take into account the possibility – however far out it might be – that the clause in the Good Friday Agreement might be triggered, in that if there is clear evidence of a majority of people wishing to leave the United Kingdom and join the Republic, that that should be catered for in the [Brexit] discussions that take place" (RTÉ News 2016). His comments were echoed (somewhat more forcefully) a few short weeks later by then leader of the opposition, Micheál Martin (Fianna Fáil 2016b), who characterized the Leave result as an "English-driven anti-EU" vote which he viewed as constituting a defining moment in Northern Ireland politics. Although Martin accepted that evidence of majority support for constitutional change in Northern Ireland did not currently exist, he added: "I hope it moves us towards majority support for unification, and if it does we should trigger a reunification referendum".

Irish political leaders had long been aware that a Leave result might lend new impetus to the project of Irish unity, and could hasten the calling of a border poll. There was, therefore, an eagerness on the part of the Irish government to ensure that Brexit would not act as an impediment to any such future scenario. In this context, the Irish government sought to remove any ambiguity in relation to whether Northern Ireland would be part of the EU or not in the event of popular support for a future united Ireland. Following extensive Irish government lobbying, the April 2017 European Council summit meeting of EU leaders agreed a *Declaration on Irish Unity* which stated: "The European Council acknowledges that the Good Friday Agreement expressly provides for an agreed mechanism whereby a united Ireland may be brought about through peaceful and democratic means; and, in this regard, the European Council acknowledges that, in accordance with international law, the entire territory of such a united Ireland would thus be part of the European Union" (see Staunton & Leahy 2017). The British had sought to delay agreement on the declaration until after the 2017 general election for fear that it might damage the prime minister's election campaign (which was underway at that point) (see Connelly 2018). Despite those objections however, the Irish proposal was supported unanimously by all of the other 26 EU member states. The achievement of the declaration, which Connolly and Doyle (2019b: 166) characterize as "a long-term safety net", highlights the foresight of the Irish government. It is a clear demonstration of the extent to which the Irish authorities were antic-ipating longer-term (constitutional) issues linked to the UK exit from the EU.

Although the UK exit from the EU was (and is) recognized as a seismic event for the Irish economy, state and society, this does not automatically signal a political appetite (never mind an inevitability) for large-scale domestic institutional or constitutional change. Ireland's Brexit story is testament to a general resistance on the part of political actors to large-scale and rapid change (see, e.g., Steinmo 2008). Irish government moves to shore up and safeguard the aspiration for Irish unity were symbolically important, but critically, they were not indica-tive of support for the short- (or even medium-term) pursuit of such an agenda. Immediately following the Brexit referendum, the Irish govern-ment rejected Sinn Féin calls for a border poll, as did other nationalist parties in Ireland including Fianna Fáil and the SDLP (McBride 2016).

What emerged instead in the aftermath of Brexit was not a deter-mined political effort to achieve Irish unity, but a more moderate attempt to foster constructive and inclusive dialogue between North and South. This effort is being led by the new Shared Island initiative created by Taoiseach Micheál Martin and anchored in his department. The unit has a budget of €500 million to support infrastructural projects which deepen North–South cooperation. In evidence to the Houses of the Oireachtas Joint Committee on the Implementation of the Good Friday Agreement (2020), the head of unit outlined:

> the Government's approach to a shared island involves working in partnership with the Executive, through the North-South Ministerial Council, and with the British Government to address the strategic challenges faced on the island, further developing the all-island economy, an enhanced connectivity and deepening co-operation in areas such as health and edu-cation and investing in the north-west and border regions. It also involves fostering constructive and inclusive dialogue, as well as developing a comprehensive programme of research to support the building of consensus around a shared future.

Launching the initiative in October 2020, Martin noted that: "The [Belfast/Good Friday] Agreement is the indispensable framework for our political relationships. It is the foundation stone upon which we build" (Merrion Street 2020). The explicit aim of the initiative is "to strengthen social, economic and political links on the island", and its work is grounded in the language of reconciliation and the spirit of the Belfast/Good Friday Agreement. Tannam (2020) notes that its key significance is "not just about practical policy, but identity – a self-critical reappraisal of who we are on the island and what futures we seek post-Brexit". The range of foreseeable futures is not confined to a binary choice of partition versus Irish unity. Rather the initiative embraces dialogues, conversations and choices which may lead in the direction of Irish unity, but that is not its express purpose or its vision.

The Shared Island initiative has included some engagement with civic unionism in Northern Ireland. The problem for the Irish government, however, is that *political* unionism is not persuaded that the exercise is constitutionally or politically neutral. Unionists have accused the initiative of replicating the work of existing institutions created by the Belfast/Good Friday Agreement. In contrast, the Shared Island initiative has been welcomed by Prime Minister Johnson who has encouraged unionists to engage with it "in a confident way" (Manley 2020c). Unionist distrust of both the British and Irish governments, however, is undermining the inclusiveness (and therefore the legitimacy) of all-island efforts at discussing and managing the re-emerging constitutional question.

If realized, the achievement and enactment of Irish unity would represent not just a critical juncture for Ireland, but one which may possibly lead to a period (or even multiple periods) of instability (see Murray & O'Donoghue 2019). The Shared Island initiative can be read as an effort to stave off this potential for constitutional upheaval and instability by taking a slower and more incremental approach to questions related to the future of the island and relationships between North and South, and between Britain and Ireland. The British government has arguably been less sensitive in its appreciation of, and reaction to, the potentially transformative impact of Brexit on Northern Ireland's constitutional future and on both communities there. As detailed earlier, Theresa May's reference to "our precious union" and Boris Johnson's assertion of a "muscular unionism" rings hollow for many UK (and in particular Northern Ireland) unionists, while for Scottish and Irish nationalists, "muscular unionism" presents a vision of Britain which is more alienating than inclusive.

## "The Irish border will ... remain an unsettled issue long after the UK's exit"

Institutional and constitutional uncertainty coupled with the apparent weakness of the British state in confronting processes of constitutional upheaval and the resurgence of the "Irish question" has exacerbated long-running British–Irish tensions. Having undergone a process of rapprochement as co-members of the EU, the experience and trajectory of Brexit suggests that the British and Irish governments now perceive each other differently and harbour different perspectives about how best to manage and mediate the resulting vulnerability and instability in Northern Ireland. Post-Brexit constitutional politics in Northern Ireland is complicated by the destabilization of the UK's wider territorial constitution and by the disjuncture in the British–Irish relationship; a situation which stands in stark contrast to an earlier "critical juncture" when both governments were at one in their negotiation of, and support for, Northern Ireland's current constitutional playbook, namely the Belfast/Good Friday Agreement. The recent rupture in the British–Irish relationship which is both linked to Brexit, and exacerbated by it, makes the process of dealing with any future constitutional fallout decidedly more difficult.

The post-Brexit implosion of UK constitutional politics represents a moment of uncertainty and vulnerability for both the UK and Ireland. The crisis creates the conditions associated with a "critical moment" by extending the space wherein transformative constitutional change is an option. The roots of this critical moment are linked to the political agency, interactions and decisions of successive British governments, which were decisively influenced by internal party-political Eurosceptic wrangling and attentiveness to English considerations, to the detriment of larger political and constitutional considerations of relevance to Ireland, North and South. This contributed to the gradual corrosion of British–Irish relations. Indeed, for the entirety of Brexit, from the pre- to the post-referendum period and across the full panoply of complex withdrawal and future relationship negotiations and formulations, the British–Irish relationship has been challenged and tested. This is most evident in terms of respective responses to Brexit which have seen Ireland reaffirm the principles of the Belfast/Good Friday Agreement, while the UK has challenged those very same principles (see Murphy 2021b).

The policy and political choices made by recent British prime ministers have, therefore, produced consequences for the UK polity and for relations with its nearest neighbour. As Laffan (2018: 574) notes: "The Irish border will continue to play a pivotal role in the Brexit negotiations and will remain an unsettled issue long after the UK's exit". Different decisions and courses of actions grounded in a more nuanced awareness of (the intensity of) tensions in Northern Ireland, the Republic of Ireland, and across the devolved regions, were "historically available" (Capoccia & Kelemen 2007: 355). The choice of a softer form of Brexit or acceptance of the "backstop", although opposed by unionists, were heartily supported not just by the Irish government, but also by the devolved governments and other key constituencies in Northern Ireland and across the UK. The adoption of these alternative strategies would have maintained more fluid trade arrangements between the UK and the EU, represented a less disruptive form of Brexit generally, and quelled the intensity of current constitutional agitation in Northern Ireland, Scotland and Wales. In rejecting such formulations, however, the British political establishment misunderstood (or at worst ignored) the totality of the constitutional risks associated with Brexit and displayed a wholesale insensitivity to the re-emerging "Irish question". By prioritizing (Conservative) party issues and also specifically English priorities and interests, and simultaneously sidelining legitimate Irish concerns, the British government's political agency during this period has in fact propelled the constitutional conversation and will therefore be causally decisive in determining how orderly (or not) the UK and Ireland's future constitutional trajectory will be.

# 7

# Conclusion: what prospects for the constitutional future(s) of Northern Ireland, and of "these islands"?

## The state of play

The particularly belligerent and vexing form that the Brexit process has taken since 2016 emanates from the British government's original sin of having failed adequately to account for Northern Ireland's specific and unique political and constitutional status. British disengagement from the "Irish question" had started long before the Brexit vote and was a defining feature of British politics during the 2000s, as the Northern Ireland settlement eased into a period of relative peace. This was the case even as the Belfast/Good Friday Agreement and the wider processes of devolution, of which the Agreement formed part, worked to reshape the British territorial constitution. The British government's failure to embrace devolution, and all its policy and political consequences, created a false perception of constitutional stability. It was against this backdrop that the decision to hold an in–out referendum on the UK's EU membership was taken. No thought was given to the potentially profound consequences of such a vote for the UK's territorial constitution and particularly for Northern Ireland. In the event, the referendum produced differential territorial outcomes, with constitutional implications. The opening up of a fractious constitutional conversation in and about the UK has, since 2016, haunted the British political system and had knock-on implications for Ireland and the EU more widely. Brexit has prompted profound political disquiet in Scotland and increased pressure for a second independence referendum. In Wales, it has presaged an increase in what has come to be called "indy-curiosity". Both of these trends have been exacerbated further by the Coronavirus pandemic.

Nowhere has post-Brexit constitutional debate become more loaded or more urgent than in Northern Ireland. Despite having supported and welcomed Brexit, the DUP has nonetheless been its primary casualty, with profound implications for unionism more broadly. Critically, by supporting the hardest possible form of Brexit, the DUP has backed unionism into a political and constitutional corner which it may not be able to work its way out of. Unionism is more or less united in seeking to overturn the Protocol. If this fails, which seems likely, then new and material forms of separation between Great Britain and Northern Ireland are liable to endure. If it succeeds, then the fall-back is a hard border on the island of Ireland which will only hasten the conversation about constitutional change. The heights to which the party was elevated after the 2017 general election have made its fall all the more dramatic. Since then, it has haemorrhaged support to both its left and its right, retreated to a largely ineffectual politics of protest and twice undergone a destabilizing and rancorous change in leadership. The direction in which the DUP is currently travelling risks making it even more unattractive to liberal voters, and it remains to be seen whether a UUP under an avowedly more liberal leadership can work to keep them in the unionist fold.

In a sense, the quickening debate about Irish unity owes as much, if not more, to unionism's strategic miscalculations as it does to successful nationalist agitation. On the face of it, Brexit has been something of a game-changer for Irish nationalism, in that it has altered the nature and context of the constitutional question, and brokered a new and more pressing conversation about it. Sinn Féin – now realistically aspiring to govern in and across both jurisdictions on the island of Ireland in the short to medium term – has been most rhetorically robust in calling for an immediate post-Brexit "border poll". All other nationalist political parties on both sides of the border have engaged, to differing degrees, with this new constitutional narrative. This disguises, however, the more nuanced ways in which Irish nationalism has engaged with Brexit. Even for Sinn Féin, this has ultimately been more about mitigating its risks for the island of Ireland, and seeking to protect the status quo, rather than urgently pursuing immediate constitutional transformation.

Of all political parties in Northern Ireland, it is the centre ground Alliance Party which appears to have reaped the greatest political and electoral rewards of the Brexit fallout. The party's pro-Remain stance has resonated with a constituency that previously overwhelmingly voted for unionist parties. Its growing electoral appeal is consequential for the institutions of the Belfast/Good Friday Agreement and the conversation about Northern Ireland's constitutional future. The bigger the party gets, the more urgent becomes the necessity for (potentially destabilizing) reform of Northern Ireland's devolved institutions. As it stands, Northern Ireland's consociational governance framework cannot adequately accommodate the possibility of Northern Ireland's non-aligned "others" electorally outstripping either unionism or nationalism. Alliance's neutrality on the constitutional question is part of its electoral appeal, but ultimately untenable if the constitutional conversation continues to accelerate. Brexit has created a scenario whereby Alliance could find itself being a key stakeholder (even kingmaker) in a debate about Irish unity which it would simply rather not have. There is something of a paradox in that the decision about Northern Ireland's constitutional future will ultimately be determined by those parties and voters who are least liable to identify themselves and their political preferences primarily in terms of the unionist–nationalist, British–Irish ethnonational and constitutional binaries.

Historically key to managing instability, crisis and political conflict in Northern Ireland has been a strong British–Irish relationship based on consensus and high levels of trust. The very act of holding a referendum on the UK's EU membership was disruptive of this. The subsequent British mismanagement of the withdrawal negotiations, and the political challenges this represented for both the UK and Ireland, critically undermined British–Irish relations. There were marked differences in how the British and Irish governments approached the question of Brexit before, during and after the referendum. The Irish government identified a possible Brexit as a strategic and political risk as early as 2014, and prepared accordingly, whereas the British government entered into the 2016 referendum casually and with no contingency plan. During the referendum, the Irish government took a position that explicitly recognized the particular vulnerability of Northern Ireland, whereas the UK government-led Remain campaign largely ignored these specific risks. Leave campaigners (including those in the government) simply dismissed them. Following the referendum vote, the Irish government's position quickly consolidated around full protection of the open border on the island of Ireland, and ensuring that this was foregrounded in EU–UK negotiations. It was successful in ensuring that this was understood and accepted by the EU institutions and member states. Conversely, the British government entered the negotiations with no clearly defined strategy (beyond the pursuit of the hardest form of Brexit), with an approach inimical to the interests and preferences of devolved government in Scotland and Wales, and a particular blind-spot when it came to Northern Ireland and the Irish border.

Brexit placed Ireland and the UK on opposite sides of the negotiating table and saw profound divergence in their respective political positions. For the first time since the 1980s, the UK and Irish governments were at odds on how best to manage political and constitutional conflict in and about Northern Ireland. This led to a rapid deterioration in the East–West relationship and a critical breakdown in trust. The UK's limited regard for the island of Ireland and Irish concerns has been a defining feature of this relationship since 2016. The Irish state was required to respond strategically and flexibly to a crisis not of its own making, and in a context in which the UK had become an unreliable partner. The fallout from Brexit for Ireland also forced the constitutional question to the political forefront, but not on specifically Irish terms. There is little evident support among key figures in Irish politics for a critical constitutional juncture. The burgeoning constitutional conversation in Ireland is largely a consequence of decisions taken on the other side of the Irish Sea.

## Does Brexit mark a "critical *constitutional* juncture" for Northern Ireland?

Brexit represents a "critical juncture" for the UK. The vote in favour of Leave in June 2016 can be causally linked to both historical factors and contemporary conditions. The EU referendum decision ushered in a period of significant change which set the UK on a new constitutional trajectory: one which promises long-term effects and legacies. Brexit is thus "an intensive period of fluidity and crisis" which has precipitated "a revised institutional equilibrium" (Rosamond 2016: 866) where the UK has to adjust – economically, politically and institutionally – to no longer being an EU member state. The effect of this critical juncture has been to create a "critical *constitutional* moment" for the UK in general, and for its devolved regions in particular.

A key feature of a "critical moment" is that opportunities for institutional change and innovation are not just available, they are at their widest. In this context, Brexit "brought longstanding constitutional ambiguities, ambivalences and abeyances to the surface" (Wincott *et al.* 2020: 2). The unprecedented Covid-19 global pandemic further exacerbated concerns about the ability of the British state to accommodate the UK's devolved administrations (see Morphet 2021). Indeed, questions about the scope and limits of devolution have become numerous and noisy since Brexit. The marginalization and sidelining of the devolved administrations before and after the referendum vote increasingly became an issue of immediate concern in Edinburgh, Cardiff and Belfast. The dismay – acutely felt by the Scottish and Welsh administrations (the Northern Ireland Executive was suspended between 2017 and 2020) – convinced political parties and leaders that (some form of) change was necessary. Scottish Cabinet Secretary, Michael Russell, derided the Scottish experience of devolution during this time: "It seems to me an object lesson on how you cannot succeed within the current constitutional structure" (UK in a Changing Europe 2021d; and see UK in a Changing Europe 2021e for a similar Welsh perspective).

For Scotland, this meant growing calls for a second Scottish independence referendum; for Wales, it produced a push in favour of a revised devolution settlement. In Northern Ireland, the issues were even more complex and politically charged, and grievances with the system were informed by the traditional communal character of local politics. Overall, Brexit has not interacted well with the UK's territorial settlement and this is the wider context within which Northern Ireland's own "critical constitutional moment" is situated. More specifically, there are a series of contingencies and conditions in place which add further to the space within which far-reaching constitutional reforms, more incremental constitutional change or the maintenance of the status quo, might be contemplated and pursued.

The fact of the Brexit crisis, and the disruption and destabilization it entailed, however, is not a guarantee that this "critical moment" will become a "critical constitutional juncture". As Hay (1999: 317) reminds us, crisis can be "a moment of decisive intervention and not merely a moment of fragmentation, dislocation or destruction". This unsettled constitutional environment creates opportunities for agents of change who are incentivized by circumstances to leverage the situation and to more robustly pursue specific political and constitutional goals. But critically, there are a variety of options and alternatives available to key agents, and the outcome of this particular "critical moment" will be contingent on a confluence of factors and conditions (some known and others unknown). By focusing on the agency of parties, people and polities, we have sought to identify how Brexit's loosening of the constraints of structure has altered the context within which change may take place.

That altered context revealed a marked disconnect between the UK centre and Northern Ireland which was further exacerbated by the British government's messy approach to the EU–UK negotiations. This had a two-fold effect in Northern Ireland. It stoked unionist fears about the constitutional integrity of the UK and Northern Ireland's place in it, and simultaneously alarmed nationalists who were concerned about the possible return of a hard border on the island of Ireland. These circumstances of uncertainty, instability and fluidity meet the conditions necessary for a constitutional moment to morph into a constitutional juncture. In Northern Ireland, however, this period has not (yet) propelled a constitutional shift commensurate with the achievement of Irish unity and synonymous with a critical constitutional juncture. The principle outworking of this period has instead been the Protocol on Ireland/Northern Ireland, which – notwithstanding unionists' concerns about it – represents a form of structural and institutional change that falls far short of constitutional transformation. Although this is not a guarantee that progress towards constitutional change has been halted, nor should it be assumed that Irish unity is the inevitable longer-term outcome of this Brexit period. There are both push and pull forces at play which frame and determine the extent to which change can be pursued (or prevented). Those forces are endogenous to Northern Ireland and are political, electoral, and structural in character. There are also exogenous factors – linked to the British and Irish governments, and developments in Scotland (and Wales) – which are similarly consequential for Northern Ireland's future.

Politically, ongoing (and intractable) problems in operationalizing the Protocol may potentially strengthen nationalist (and also middle-ground) support for a more advanced constitutional alternative to the Protocol, if such a prospect is deemed to better secure Northern Ireland interests. Even absent majority support for constitutional change, pressure to reform the institutions of the Belfast/Good Friday Agreement looks set to develop in the context of the electoral rise of the Alliance Party.

Changed political party electoral fortunes in Northern Ireland after Brexit have increased and intensified discussion of the constitutional question. This evolving narrative is challenging for unionism in general, and for the DUP in particular. An altered electoral landscape, where unionism is no longer dominant, curtails the extent to which that political bloc can be kingpin in shaping Northern Ireland's constitutional future. A smaller unionist constituency is decidedly less able to stave off the constitutional threat represented by Irish unity.

In structural terms, support for constitutional change in Northern Ireland is contingent on the principle of consent. There can be no change to Northern Ireland's constitutional position within the UK unless a majority support such a prospect. Polling indicates that although support for Irish unity has increased in the aftermath of the referendum, there is still, currently, a majority in favour of the constitutional status quo. The Brexit crisis, therefore, has not (yet) fundamentally altered the arithmetic on which Northern Ireland's place in the UK depends. The critical mass needed to trigger a border poll does not (currently) exist and this essentially precludes the achievement of Irish unity. There is however, an element of discontent with current institutional arrangements: a plurality of voters support reforming the Belfast/Good Friday Agreement (see Hayward & Rosher 2020, 2021). Therefore, although there is no clear mandate for advanced constitutional change in Northern Ireland, there is support for lesser forms of institutional reform which do not meet the conditions for a critical juncture. Instead, they hint at a less ambitious process of incremental change. This preference, however, co-exists alongside a belief among voters that Brexit has increased the likelihood of Irish unity (see, e.g., Hayward & Rosher 2021; BBC News 2021b). This tells us that voters are beginning to contemplate the possibility of an altered constitutional future. It may also be a sign that the fallout from Brexit has not (yet) reached a crisis point which is capable of fully mobilizing voters in support of constitutional change.

Also relevant, and potentially mobilizing, is the fact that voters conceive a link between the achievement of Scottish independence and the greater likelihood of Irish unity (see LucidTalk 2021c). A more serious crisis tipping point, therefore, could well be events in Scotland which would propel and mobilize support for advanced constitutional change in Northern Ireland. In other words, a key trigger for a "critical constitutional juncture" may not have arrived yet, and depending on how other contingencies play out, that moment may or may not come.

The British and Irish governments are key political agents in Northern Ireland. They were instrumental in the achievement of the Belfast/Good Friday Agreement and in the context of Brexit, their actions since 2016 have been consequential. Neither government currently supports constitutional change on the back of Brexit. The British government has been bullish in its pursuit of a muscular form of unionism. For its part, the Irish government has long harboured grave concerns about the impact of Brexit on the island of Ireland. Although senior Irish government figures are clearly supportive of Irish unity in the long term, support for the constitutional status quo has been the hallmark of its approach to Northern Ireland. The durability of these positions, however, is not necessarily assured (and critically, they are subject to international treaty obligations in relation to facilitating a border poll should circumstances dictate).

There are some important caveats in how we understand the influence and agency of both governments in this Brexit era. Having been late to fully understand and appreciate the gravity of Brexit for Northern Ireland, the British government proceeded to demonstrate its willingness to compromise (or capitulate) when it came to a choice between getting Brexit done or supporting unionism. Elements within the Conservative Party proved capable of betraying unionism when deemed politically and ideologically necessary. The effect of such British government choices have consequences: they not only engender alarm among unionists, they also feed nationalist reservations about the integrity of the British government and contribute to a general air of insecurity and instability. Of course, a change of British government may impact on perceptions, and this could either stabilize or subvert the current constitutional status quo. The British government is also subject to external pressures, most notably from the US administration which has been quite unrestrained in its calls for the Protocol to be implemented in full. Either of these prospects – a change of British government or a conflict with the US over the implementation of the Protocol – has the potential to alter the circumstances of the "critical moment" and, depending on how such developments are framed and received, to potentially alleviate or stimulate pressures for constitutional change.

The Irish government is subject to different political influences and forces. The need to confront (and arrest) the electoral rise of Sinn Féin means that other political parties in Ireland are challenged to respond to the Republican agenda and this has meant a very difficult political balancing act. Moreover, the prospect of Sinn Féin leading government on both sides of the border in the near future is a very real one. Such a political/electoral "earthquake" may well be decisive in determining Northern Ireland's future constitutional destination because, given such a platform, the party will, in all likelihood, leverage the opportunity and pursue the Irish unity project with renewed intensity and vigour. Politics on the island of Ireland, however, has not yet reached such a moment of historic political and electoral realignment. Should that moment materialize, it may constitute an irresistible pressure point and propel Northern Ireland towards a new constitutional future. For now, however, both the Irish and British polities are insistent that the constitutional status quo applies, and therefore the necessary conditions to occasion a "critical constitutional juncture" await the outcome of future elections, political decisions and diplomatic manoeuvring.

Throughout the Brexit era, the decisions, actions and rhetoric of important actors have been causally decisive. What our analysis of political parties, people and polities reveals is a number of different possible future scenarios for Northern Ireland arising from Brexit's "critical moment". There are alternatives to a "critical constitutional juncture" which offer either a lesser element of change or a state of enduring stasis. Specifically, we note three potential alternatives to a "critical constitutional juncture" for Northern Ireland.

Firstly, the Brexit process may be resolved or addressed by what Hay (1999: 325) calls a "tipping point" where a relatively minor intervention subsequently proves to be decisive in terms of transforming the system (either by unintentionally enhancing its stability or by exacerbating its latent incongruities). In this context, "minor" issues – perhaps unrelated to Brexit – may prove decisive in allowing the question of constitutional change or its lesser equivalent, institutional reform, to be addressed and settled. Secondly, Hay (1999) identifies a "Gramscian" moment where difficulties and contradictions are widely perceived, but these have not (yet) produced an acute sense of crisis. In this scenario, Northern Ireland occupies a state of inbetweenness where the situation has not (yet) reached a point of crisis capable of prompting decisive change. Difficulties and contradictions are understood but there is no attempt to pursue or impose decisive interventions. Thirdly – and possibly the most plausible scenario – Northern Ireland muddles through the Brexit period without settling on a definitive resolution. This latter scenario has been the hallmark of Northern Ireland's fate (to date) during the Brexit process and critically, it may be one which suits key political actors. As Wincott *et al.* (2020: 8) note: "ambiguites may allow a state to carry on – to endure at times when clarity or a decisive choice between constitutional interpretations would make it unsustainable". In general, the critical junctures (and path dependency) approach is quite sceptical about the prospects of successful constitutional change (see Broschek 2011). Instead, there is an expectation of the persistence of limited and ineffective solutions (Pierson 2004). The sustainability of this situation, however, is likely to only remain valid if and until a further crisis point is reached and the conditions necessary to prompt decisive change materialize. The prospect of allaying such a crisis may be reliant on factors like how the implementation of the Protocol is managed. Alternatively, the possibility of a new "crisis point" arriving – for example, via Scottish independence or the installation of a Sinn Féin-led government in Dublin – cannot be discounted.

## When post-conflict meets post-Brexit

For a society like Northern Ireland with a history of violent conflict, dealing with renewed crisis is especially challenging, disruptive and has high stakes. This Brexit "critical moment" is therefore all-the-more critical in and for Northern Ireland. Post-conflict societies and political systems invariably remain vulnerable as they navigate the post-conflict period. When this is complicated by an exogenous shock like Brexit, the challenges are all the more acute.

At the time of the 1998 critical constitutional juncture, unionists and nationalists were open to dialogue and compromise, and in broad agreement about some form of devolved settlement as the desired outcome of peace talks. This did not entail abandoning their respective key principles and aspirations, which were accommodated by the "constructive ambiguity" of the 1998 Agreement. In the context of the end of the Cold War and in an atmosphere marked by wider political and economic optimism, the British and Irish governments were critical facilitators in supporting the process of institutional change. Third parties (such as the EU, and more particularly the US) acted as impartial brokers. This negotiating architecture created the conditions which made agreement possible and legitimate.

In the post-Brexit era, these essential conditions are not present. The environment, the atmosphere and the situation are radically different and, as it stands, unconducive to moderation and compromise. In this context, "constructive ambiguity" and a settlement which loosely accommodates both unionist and nationalist preferences is no longer available. Such is the nature of Brexit (and the EU itself) that it requires legal clarity: a formula which precludes the kind of political opacity which facilitated Northern Ireland's earlier critical juncture.

In addition, and in contrast to 1998, the Irish and British governments are on fundamentally different pages with opposing geopolitical visions, strategic objectives and worldviews. This has fundamentally compromised their capacity to collaborate as co-facilitators, as was the case during the peace process. Rather than fulfilling the role of independent arbiter, the EU is now a principal and partisan stakeholder in contemporary processes of political change on the island of Ireland. And the position of the US is also different: no longer a mediating force, America has been highly critical of Britain reneging on its Protocol commitments. This is all happening in a context where the EU, the UK and Ireland are managing the ongoing consequences of multiple economic and political crises which have stretched state resources and bandwidths ever more thinly. Since 2020, this has included an unprecedented public health emergency.

Brexit has also weakened the apparatus of the British state. Its fallout has been political, economic and cultural. It has cost the careers of two prime ministers, damaged Britain's global image, challenged Westminster's legitimacy and will have long-lasting consequences for economic growth and prosperity. Collectively, this has limited the capacity of the state to manage and mediate Brexit as a source of political conflict and instability. The response at the constitutional centre has been to seek to reassert and reinscribe Westminster's writ in the "regions" through a more "muscularly" unionist approach to governance. This has arguably only served to give further succour to separatist nationalisms. Northern Ireland has been subject to all of these processes in especially damaging ways.

Although it has arguably emerged as more robust, certain weaknesses in the Irish state have also been exposed during the Brexit process. Ireland has been subject to – and forced to respond to – a crisis from without, in which it has had limited capacity to ultimately determine the course of events. Brexit is Ireland's "English Problem". While its position is undoubtedly strengthened by EU membership, what happens in and to Ireland as a result of Brexit is ultimately contingent on decisions taken in London and Brussels. The support and solidarity which Ireland has enjoyed as a part of the EU cannot be assumed to be unconditional, and the deterioration of British–Irish relations has undermined the extent to which the UK can be counted on as a reliable and trustworthy partner. This has potentially profound implications for managing any process of constitutional or institutional change on the island of Ireland. A close and effective working relationship between the British and Irish governments will be needed to manage any future border poll and subsequent transition to Irish unification (CUWGUR 2021). After Brexit, this cannot necessarily be counted on. Against this backdrop, key decisions will need to be taken in order to prepare for the possibility of constitutional change. The Shared Island initiative – the Irish government's official response to the growing demand for constitutional change – arguably demonstrates as much hesitancy as it does willingness to engage with key constitutional questions and take these decisions. In sum, and as it stands, Ireland is arguably underprepared for the kinds of constitutional transformation that have become possible at this "critical constitutional moment".

The precise eventual outcomes of this period are not predetermined. Instead, it is (and is liable to remain) marked by contingency, intensified by the influence of unknowns: both known and unknown. Brexit has, in essence, been like throwing institutional plates into the air. It remains to be seen how they will land, and which ones will be smashed (perhaps irreparably) in the process. For the time being, what remains is chronic uncertainty. In Northern Ireland this is a particular problem. The question of Northern Ireland's relationship with the EU is now inseparable from its territorial politics, and it will remain so in perpetuity. This has become a new vector for zero-sum conflict between unionism and nationalism. At precisely the time that Brexit has thus acted to compound and deepen existing ethnonational conflict in Northern Ireland, its political institutions have been radically undermined. Indeed, across all three strands of the Belfast/Good Friday Agreement, the very institutions designed to manage conflict between competing constitutional preferences in Northern Ireland have themselves become imbricated in constitutional conflict. This creates conditions for further political instability.

## The future is changed ...

Brexit changes Northern Ireland. The withdrawal deal and the Ireland/ Northern Ireland Protocol mean that there is no prospect of a return to the *status quo ante*. However, what this means institutionally and constitutionally for Northern Ireland remains unclear. If and when this "critical moment" eventually resolves into either constitutional realignment or a new less radical constitutional "settlement", this will be nearly impossible to reverse. And this makes the stakes all the higher, particularly for unionists, whose resistance to constitutional change (especially in the form of Irish unity) is near absolute, based as it is on a heightened attachment to British identity and sovereignty.

Different possible futures are being pursued in a fluid and shifting structural context by different agents. The precise shape and depth of any eventual constitutional reordering will depend on the relative strength of these actors, their future strategic decisions and, likely, mistakes. Throughout this book, we have examined how decisions and (mis)calculations made by different actors at earlier stages of the Brexit process have impacted on their capacity and ability to influence the course of the constitutional future.

The British government is, to coin a phrase, "navigating without maps" (McHarg 2018), with an approach to constitutional issues that is clumsy and haphazard, and profoundly alienating of those who do not share its rhetorically "muscular" unionism. And critically, we contend that political agents on the island of Ireland are particularly reactive to British government actions and rhetoric in ways which are causally decisive. In general, the Irish government has been, and remains, more prepared for managing the fallout from Brexit, though this currently stops somewhat short of engaging in any sustained planning for constitutional change, in general, and Irish unity, in particular. Irish nationalism more broadly is in a strong position after Brexit, but is also marked by division over whether and to what extent Brexit represents a wedge issue to be exploited or a risk to be mitigated, and whether the time is currently ripe to push for constitutional transformation. Unionism emerges from its dalliances with Brexit bruised and (potentially fatally) weakened. Those who have arguably emerged in the strongest position from Brexit are Northern Ireland's "others" although they are reluctant to engage energetically with emerging debates. Their preferences, however, will ultimately be a key determining factor in shaping how, when and what sort of change will happen in Northern Ireland, although this is a role that those whose politics are not primarily defined by the constitutional question are reticent to fulfil.

We hope that a key lesson that emerges from this book is that processes of potentially profound political, economic and institutional change should not be entered into casually and without due attention paid to possible consequences and contingencies. Leadership and dialogue between different actors is key. There are some encouraging signs in this regard, with initiatives like the University of Liverpool's Civic Space, the UCL Constitution Unit Working Group on Unification Referendums on the Island of Ireland and the Royal Irish Academy and University of Notre Dame-led Analysing and Researching Ireland North and South (ARINS) project emerging to facilitate debate and discussion. Certainly the most lively and engaging, and probably the most constructive, dialogue about possible political and constitutional futures is arguably being driven from the grassroots by groups like Ireland's Future, Shared Ireland, Uniting UK and We Make NI, among others. However, given the damage that Brexit has wrought across the three strands of the Belfast/Good Friday Agreement, this currently lacks a critical degree of institutional and political support. The space for constructive dialogue is narrow, and liable to be narrowed further by a British government seeking to confront the post-Brexit destabilization (and possible disintegration) of the Union state with "muscularly" unionist posturing. For its part, the space created for sustained constitutional dialogue by the Irish government's "Shared Island" initiative is also constrained. The initiative has so-far been fairly low-key and has had only limited reach. However reluctant it may be to do so, there is an onus on the Irish government to think more expansively about facilitating dialogue on Northern Ireland's future. It cannot, however unfortunately, depend on its current British counterpart to be a reliable partner in doing so.

There is unprecedented interest in and discussion about Ireland's constitutional future and the question of Irish unity is now definitively on the political agenda in Ireland. It is clear too that many of the ingredients necessary for a "critical constitutional juncture" in Northern Ireland certainly exist. However, the sum of the dispositions, incentives and actions of key agents, as we have mapped them in this book, does not yet point to (immediate) advanced constitutional reform. In that context, Irish unification is far from a foregone conclusion and incremental institutional change may be a more likely (short-term) outcome. Unionist resistance, "others'" reticence to engage, and the shallowness of support for unity among sections of the Southern electorate (based on material factors) are all pulling in the opposite direction. There is also little steer coming from the Irish government, and resistance to entertaining the possibility of a border poll on the part of the UK government (who, after all, has the ultimate say here). The hard evidence to support an imminent critical constitutional juncture is simply lacking. However, political, economic, electoral and diplomatic contingencies matter, and how these are managed and mediated will be critically decisive in shaping Northern Ireland's constitutional evolution.

Critical constitutional moments can evolve into critical junctures where constitutional change results. These new political arrangements invariably resolve into new and more stable institutional settlements, based on new terms of inclusion; framed by newly defined relationships; and linked to new institutional compromises. This is what happened in 1998. In order for this to be the case post-Brexit when the potential for disruption, instability and conflict is ever-present, responsible leadership and good faith engagement by all political agents is once again required. The future of Northern Ireland (and of "these islands") depends on it.

# References

10 Downing Street 2016. PM press conference with Enda Kenny. 25 January. https:// www.gov.uk/government/speeches/pm-press-conference-with-enda-kenny- january-2016.

Alliance Party 2013. "Dickson criticises Cameron over EU referendum". APNI press release, 23 January. https://archive.allianceparty.org/dickson-criticises-cameron- over-eu-referendum/.

Alliance Party 2014. *Step Forward in Europe.* Belfast: Alliance Party. https://cain.ulster. ac.uk/issues/politics/docs/apni/apni_2014-05-06_eu-man_r.pdf.

Alliance Party 2016a. *Manifesto 2016: An Agenda to Increase the Speed of Change in Northern Ireland.* Belfast: Alliance Party. https://d3n8a8pro7vhmx.cloudfront. net/allianceparty/pages/3583/attachments/original/1537969097/2016-alliance- assembly-manifesto.pdf?1537969097.

Alliance Party 2016b. "Long says any Brexit negotiations must reflect desire of local remain voters". APNI press release, 27 June. https://archive.allianceparty.org/long- says-any-brexit-negotiations-must-reflect-desire-of-local-remain-voters/.

Alliance Party 2016c. "Nicholl: lack of leadership after Brexit vote is dangerous". APNI press release, 30 June. https://archive.allianceparty.org/nicholl-lack-of-leadership- after-brexit-vote-is-dangerous/.

Alliance Party 2016d. "Dickson hits out at First Minister over remain remarks". APNI press release, 30 June. https://archive.allianceparty.org/dickson-hits-out-at-first- minister-over-remain-remarks/.

Alliance Party 2017. *Change Direction: Westminster Manifesto 2017.* Belfast: Alliance Party. https://d3n8a8pro7vhmx.cloudfront.net/allianceparty/pages/3583/attachments/ original/1537969137/2017-general-election-manifesto.pdf?1537969137.

Barrett, A. *et al.* 2015. "Scoping the possible economic implications of Brexit on Ireland". Research Series 48, November. Dublin: ESRI. https://www.esri.ie/system/ files?file=media/file-uploads/2015-11/RS48.pdf.

Barrett, G. 2016. "What the UK could learn from Ireland's EU referendum campaigns". LSE Blog, 27 April. https://blogs.lse.ac.uk/europpblog/2016/04/27/what-the-uk- could-learn-from-irelands-eu-referendum-campaigns/.

Barry, A. 2020. "Exit poll shows support for Irish unity referendum, especially among 18–24 age group". TheJournal.ie, 9 February. https://www.thejournal.ie/ge2020- border-poll-4999083-Feb2020/.

Barry, J. 2018. "Unionists should spell out why they reject NI in customs union". *News Letter,* 14 March. https://www.newsletter.co.uk/news/unionists-should-spell-out- why-they-reject-ni-customs-union-324611.

BBC 2021. "Year '21, episode 4: the uncrowned king of Ulster". Podcast, 22 January. https://www.bbc.co.uk/programmes/p094vbbp.

BBC News 2016. "EU referendum: Northern Ireland votes to Remain". 24 June. https://www.bbc.com/news/uk-northern-ireland-36614443.

BBC News 2019a. "General election 2019: Boris Johnson 'does not understand' deal trade checks". 8 November. https://www.bbc.co.uk/news/uk-northern-ireland-50352678.

BBC News 2019b. "Brexit: Nigel Dodds 'would rather stay in EU than risk union'". 29 March. https://www.bbc.co.uk/news/uk-northern-ireland-47747945.

BBC News 2020. "Northern Ireland Secretary admits new bill will 'break international law'". 8 September. https://www.bbc.co.uk/news/uk-politics-54073836.

BBC News 2021a. "Arlene Foster: Brexit is a 'gateway of opportunity'". 3 January. https://www.bbc.co.uk/news/av/uk-northern-ireland-55521667.

BBC News 2021b. "NI 100: majority believes NI will leave UK within 25 years". 20 April. https://www.bbc.com/news/uk-northern-ireland-56777985.

Bean, K. 2007. *The New Politics of Sinn Féin*. Liverpool: Liverpool University Press.

*Belfast Telegraph* 2016a. "Sinn Féin 'campaigning vigorously' for Remain vote in referendum". 3 June. https://www.belfasttelegraph.co.uk/news/republic-of-ireland/sinn-fein-campaigning-vigorously-for-remain-vote-in-referendum-34770636.html.

*Belfast Telegraph* 2016b. "Sinn Féin calls for border poll on united Ireland after Brexit win in EU referendum". 24 June. https://www.belfasttelegraph.co.uk/business/brexit/sinn-fein-calls-for-border-poll-on-united-Ireland-after-brexit-win-in-eu-referendum-34829501.html.

Bell, C. & K. Cavanaugh 1999. "Constructive ambiguity or internal self-determination: self-determination, group accommodation, and the Belfast Agreement". *Fordham International Law Journal* 22(4): 1345–71.

Bell, D. 1990. *Acts of Union: Youth Culture and Sectarianism in Northern Ireland*. Basingstoke: Palgrave Macmillan.

Bell, J. 2020. "Finance Minister Murphy casts doubt over DUP confidence and supply cash payout". *Belfast Telegraph*, 15 January. https://www.belfasttelegraph.co.uk/news/northern-ireland/finance-minister-murphy-casts-doubt-over-dup-confidence-and-supply-cash-payout-38864376.html.

Bergin, J. 2016. "How Brexit could affect Irish agriculture". *AIB Business*, 9 April. https://business.aib.ie/blog/2016/04/how-brexit-could-affect-irish-agriculture.

Bernhard, M. 2015. "Chronic instability and the limits of path dependence". *Perspectives on Politics* 13(4): 976–91.

Birrell, D. & D. Heenan 2017. "The continuing volatility of devolution in Northern Ireland: the shadow of direct rule". *Political Quarterly* 88(3): 473–9.

Birrell, D. & D. Heenan 2020. "The confidence and supply agreement between the Conservative Party and the Democratic Unionist Party: implications for the Barnett formula and intergovernmental relations in the UK". *Parliamentary Affairs* 73(3): 586–602.

Blok, A. 1998. "The narcissism of minor differences". *European Journal of Social Theory* 1(1): 33–56.

Boffey, D. & J. Rankin 2018a. "Barnier criticizes May's UK-wide Brexit backstop plan". *The Guardian*, 8 June. https://www.theguardian.com/politics/2018/jun/08/michel-barnier-rejects-may-uk-wide-brexit-backstop-plan.

Boffey, D. & J. Rankin 2018b. "Michel Barnier kills off Theresa May's Brexit customs proposals". *The Guardian*, 26 July. https://www.theguardian.com/politics/2018/jul/26/michel-barnier-tears-up-theresa-mays-brexit-customs-proposals.

Boffey, D., J. Rankin & A. Asthana 2017. "May's weakness exposed as DUP derails Brexit progress". *The Guardian*, 5 December. https://www.theguardian.com/politics/2017/dec/04/juncker-and-may-fail-to-reach-brexit-deal-amid-dup-doubts-over-irish-border.

Bogdanor, V. 2019. *Beyond Brexit: Towards a British Constitution*. London: I. B. Tauris.

Breen, S. 2020a. "Just 29% in Northern Ireland would vote for unity, major study reveals". *Belfast Telegraph*, 18 February. https://www.belfasttelegraph.co.uk/news/northern-ireland/just-29-in-northern-ireland-would-vote-for-unity-major-study-reveals-38966196.html.

Breen, S. 2020b. "Poll: NHS could be crucial in border poll with support for united Ireland and the Union running neck-and-neck". *Belfast Telegraph*, 25 October. https://www.belfasttelegraph.co.uk/news/northern-ireland/poll-nhs-could-be-crucial-in-border-poll-with-support-for-united-ireland-and-the-union-running-neck-and-neck-39666639.html.

Breen, S. 2020c. "2020 a year Sinn Féin would probably like to forget". *Belfast Telegraph*, 28 December. https://www.belfasttelegraph.co.uk/opinion/columnists/suzanne-breen/2020-a-year-sinn-fein-would-probably-like-to-forget-39904748.html.

Breen, S. 2021a. "Bobby Storey funeral: PPS decision shows some are above the law". *Belfast Telegraph*, 30 March. https://www.belfasttelegraph.co.uk/opinion/columnists/suzanne-breen/bobby-storey-funeral-pps-decision-shows-some-are-above-the-law-40257054.html.

Breen, S. 2021b. "DUP's support takes a dive in wake of Irish sea border row". *Belfast Telegraph*, 1 February. https://www.belfasttelegraph.co.uk/news/northern-ireland/dups-support-takes-a-dive-in-wake-of-irish-sea-border-row-40033751.html.

Breen, S. 2021c. "*Belfast Telegraph* opinion poll: Northern Ireland's changing political landscape as support for parties revealed". *Belfast Telegraph*, 22 May. https://www.belfasttelegraph.co.uk/news/northern-ireland/belfast-telegraph-opinion-poll-northern-irelands-changing-political-landscape-as-support-for-parties-revealed-40453232.html.

Broschek, J. 2011. "Conceptualizing and theorizing constitutional change in federal systems: insights from historical institutionalism". *Regional & Federal Studies* 21(4/5): 539–59.

Brown, K. & E. Viggiani 2010. "Performing Provisionalism: Republican commemorative practice in post-Agreement Northern Ireland". In L. Fitzpatrick (ed.), *Performing Violence in Contemporary Ireland*, 225–48. Dublin: Carysfort Press.

Bryson, J. 2021. *Brexit Betrayed: Writings From the Referendum to the Betrayal Act*. Donaghadee: Unionist Voice Publications.

Bulmer, S. & M. Burch 1998. "Organizing for Europe: Whitehall, the British state and European Union". *Public Administration* 76(4): 601–28.

Burgess, T. & G. Mulvenna (eds) 2015. *The Contested Identities of Ulster Protestants*. Basingstoke: Palgrave Macmillan.

Cabinet Office 2017. Confidence and Supply Agreement between the Conservative and Unionist Party and the Democratic Unionist Party on Support for the Government in Parliament. https://assets.publishing.service.gov.uk/government/uploads/system/

uploads/attachment_data/file/621794/Confidence_and_Supply_Agreement_ between_the_Conservative_Party_and_the_DUP.pdf.

Campbell, J. 2021a. "Cross-border trade in Ireland has 'increased dramatically' in 2021". BBC News, 15 April. https://www.bbc.co.uk/news/uk-northern-ireland-56760634.

Campbell, J. 2021b. "Surge in Irish cross-border trade continued in March". BBC News, 19 May. https://www.bbc.co.uk/news/uk-northern-ireland-57169151.

Campbell, S. 2015. *Gerry Fitt and the SDLP: "In a Minority of One"*. Manchester: Manchester University Press.

Capoccia, G. 2016. "Critical junctures". In O. Fioretos, T. Falleti & A. Sheingate (eds), *The Oxford Handbook of Historical Institutionalism*, 89–106. Oxford: Oxford University Press.

Capoccia, G. & R. Kelemen 2007. "The study of critical junctures: theory, narrative, and counterfactuals in historical institutionalism". *World Politics* 59(3): 341–69.

Carswell, S. 2021. "North-South trade post-Brexit: 'I'm avoiding England, it doesn't work for me any more'". *Irish Times*, 26 June. https://www.irishtimes.com/business/ north-south-trade-post-brexit-i-m-avoiding-england-it-doesn-t-work-for-me- any-more-1.4603451.

Clark, S. 2019. "Naomi Long makes history in the North by becoming the Alliance Party's first MEP". Hot Press, 29 May. https://www.hotpress.com/music/naomi-long- makes-history-north-becoming-alliance-partys-first-mep-22773901.

Clements, B. 2010. "Exploring and explaining public attitudes towards the European integration process in Northern Ireland". *Irish Political Studies* 25(3): 393–416.

Coakley, J. 2008. "Has the Northern Ireland problem been solved?". *Journal of Democracy* 19(3): 98–112.

Coakley, J. 2018. "The British–Irish relationship in the twenty-first century". *Ethnopolitics* 17(3): 306–24.

Coakley, J. 2020. "Choosing between unions? Unionist opinion and the challenge of Brexit". *Irish Political Studies* 35(3): 356–77.

Coakley, J. & J. Garry 2016. "Brexit: understanding why people voted as they did in the choice of a lifetime". *News Letter*, 15 October. https://www.newsletter.co.uk/news/ brexit-understanding-why-people-voted-they-did-choice-lifetime-1190201.

Coakley, J. & J. Garry 2017. "Exclusive poll: unionist supporters content with East– West post #Brexit border controls...". Slugger O'Toole, 26 November. https:// sluggerotoole.com/2017/11/26/exclusive-poll-unionist-supporters-content-with- east-west-post-brexit-border-controls/.

Coakley, J. & J. Todd 2020. *Negotiating a Settlement in Northern Ireland, 1969–2019*. Oxford: Oxford University Press.

Cochrane, F. 2020. *Breaking Peace: Brexit and Northern Ireland*. Manchester: Manchester University Press.

Collier, R. & D. Collier 1991. *Shaping the Political Arena: Critical Junctures, the Labor Movement, and Regime Dynamics in Latin America*. Princeton, NJ: Princeton University Press.

Collins, S. & C. Meehan 2020. *Saving the State: Fine Gael from Collins to Varadkar*. Dublin: Gill Books.

Connelly, T. 2017a. Tweet, 4 December. https://twitter.com/tconnellyRTE/status/ 937642355322212353.

Connelly, T. 2017b. "Brexit and the Irish border: how the deal was salvaged". RTÉ News, 9 December. https://www.rte.ie/news/analysis-and-comment/2017/1209/926089-brexit-negotiations/.

Connelly, T. 2018. *Brexit and Ireland: The Dangers, the Opportunities and the Inside Story of the Irish Response*. Dublin: Penguin.

Connelly, T. 2019. "Theresa May: how strategic mistakes and the Irish question brought her down". RTÉ News, 25 May. https://www.rte.ie/news/analysis-and-comment/2019/0525/1051593-theresa-may-brexit/.

Connelly, T. 2020. "Brexit: a tangle of high-wire deadlines and ultimatums". RTÉ News, 26 September. https://www.rte.ie/news/2020/0925/1167545-tony-connelly-brexit/.

Connelly, T. 2021a. "EU negotiating with a partner it cannot trust – Coveney". RTÉ News, 4 March. https://www.rte.ie/news/brexit/2021/0304/1200853-northern-ireland-protocol/.

Connelly, T. 2021b. "Dead end: Arlene Foster, the Northern Ireland Protocol and Europe". RTÉ News, 1 May. https://www.rte.ie/news/analysis-and-comment/2021/0501/1213180-tony-connelly-brexit/.

Connolly, E. & J. Doyle 2019a. "Brexit and the changing international and domestic perspectives of sovereignty over Northern Ireland". *Irish Studies in International Affairs* 30: 217–33.

Connolly, E. & J. Doyle 2019b. "Brexit and the Irish Border". *European Journal of Legal Studies* 11(Special 2): 153–86.

Constitution Unit Working Group on Unification Referendums on the Island of Ireland (CUWGUR) 2021. *Final Report*. London: The Constitution Unit, UCL. https://www.ucl.ac.uk/constitution-unit/sites/constitution-unit/files/working_group_final_report.pdf.

Costello, R. 2021. "Rally around the EU flag: Irish party positions on the EU in the wake of Brexit". *Journal of Contemporary European Studies* 29(4): 502–18.

Coulter, C. 2015. "Not quite as British as Finchley: the failed attempt to bring British Conservatism to Northern Ireland". *Irish Studies Review* 25(4): 407–23.

Creighton, S. 2020. "What is a shared island?" Slugger O'Toole, 23 October. https://sluggerotoole.com/2020/10/23/what-is-a-shared-island/.

Creighton, S. 2021a. "When are the DUP going to ditch the Tories?". Slugger O'Toole, 14 January. https://sluggerotoole.com/2021/01/14/when-are-the-dup-going-to-ditch-the-tories/.

Creighton, S. 2021b. "A shared Northern Ireland: how people in the North are reimagining life in the UK". The Currency, 24 April. https://thecurrency.news/articles/44315/a-shared-northern-ireland-how-people-in-the-north-are-reimagining-life-in-the-uk/.

Creighton, S. 2021c. "The Union's at risk if the DUP swings further to the right". *Belfast Telegraph*, 29 April. https://www.belfasttelegraph.co.uk/opinion/news-analysis/the-unions-at-risk-if-the-dup-swings-further-to-the-right-40368762.html.

Crowley, J. *et al.* (eds) 2017. *Atlas of the Irish Revolution*. Cork: Cork University Press.

Curtis, J. 2014. *Human Rights as War by Other Means: Peace Politics in Northern Ireland*. Philadelphia, PA: University of Pennsylvania Press.

Daly, L. & M. Lawless 2020. "Examination of the sectoral overlap of COVID-19 and Brexit shocks". Working Paper No. 677. Dublin: ESRI. https://www.esri.ie/system/files/publications/WP677_0.pdf.

de Bréadún, D. 2015. *Power Play: The Rise of Modern Sinn Féin*. Sallins: Merrion Press.

Deerin, C. 2021. "Boris Johnson's 'muscular unionism' will only drive Scotland further towards independence". *New Statesman*, 10 June. https://www.newstatesman.com/politics/2021/06/boris-johnson-s-muscular-unionism-will-only-drive-scotland-further-towards.

de Mars, S. *et al.* 2018. *Bordering Two Unions: Northern Ireland and Brexit*. Bristol: Policy Press.

Department of Foreign Affairs (DFA) 1998. Belfast/Good Friday Agreement. https://www.dfa.ie/media/dfa/alldfawebsitemedia/ourrolesandpolicies/northernireland/good-friday-agreement.pdf.

Department of Foreign Affairs (DFA) 2020. *New Decade, New Approach*. https://www.dfa.ie/media/dfa/newsmedia/pressrelease/New-Decade-New-Approach.pdf.

Department of Foreign Affairs (DFA) 2021a. *Ireland-Scotland Joint Bilateral Review: Report and Recommendations 2021–25*. https://www.dfa.ie/media/dfa/ourrolepolicies/ourwork/Ireland-Scotland-Review-English.pdf.

Department of Foreign Affairs (DFA) 2021b. *Ireland–Wales Shared Statement and Joint Action Plan 2021–25*. https://www.dfa.ie/media/dfa/ourrolepolicies/ourwork/Ireland-Wales-Shared-Statement-Action-Plan-Final.pdf.

Devlin, M. 2020. "Time to open the debate on a united Ireland, urges Stormont politician Trevor Lunn". *Irish Independent*, 21 December. https://www.independent.ie/irish-news/politics/time-to-open-the-debate-on-a-united-ireland-urges-stormont-politician-trevor-lunn-39884584.html.

Dingley, J. 2005. "Constructive ambiguity and the peace process in Northern Ireland". *Low Intensity Conflict and Law Enforcement* 13(1): 1–23.

Dixon, P. 1997. "Paths to peace in Northern Ireland (I): civil society and consociational approaches". *Democratization* 4(2): 1–27.

Donaghy, P. 2020. "The mystery of the 'shy nationalists' – online and face-to-face polling on Irish unity continues to give different results". Slugger O'Toole, 19 February. https://sluggerotoole.com/2020/02/19/the-mystery-of-the-shy-nationalists-online-and-face-to-face-polling-on-irish-unity-continues-to-give-different-results/.

Donnellan, T. & K. Hanrahan 2016. *Brexit: Potential Implications for the Irish Agri-Food Sector Report*. Galway: Teagasc. https://www.teagasc.ie/media/website/publications/2012/BrexitPaperApril13final.pdf.

Dougan, M. *et al.* 2020. *UK Internal Market Bill, Devolution and the Union*. London: Centre on Constitutional Change. https://www.centreonconstitutionalchange.ac.uk/sites/default/files/2020-10/UK%20INTERNAL%20MARKET%20BILL%2C%20DEVOLUTION%20AND%20THE%20UNION%20%282%29_0.pdf.

Duggan, A. 2019. "Irish presidential election 2018". *Irish Political Studies* 34(2): 303–14.

Duffy, R. 2017. "Arlene Foster slams Dublin over reported text of Brexit border deal (but Scotland wants in)". TheJournal.ie, 4 December. https://www.thejournal.ie/dup-border-brexit-deal-3731537-Dec2017/.

Duffy, R. 2020. "Q&A: Here's where the parties stand on a united Ireland and holding a border poll". TheJournal.ie, 6 February. https://www.thejournal.ie/united-ireland-audit-4993911-Feb2020/.

DUP 2021. *DUP – Free us from the Protocol*. 2 February. Belfast: DUP.

Eastwood, C. 2020. Tweet, 13 February. https://twitter.com/columeastwood/status/1227888433500164096?ref_src=twsrc%5Etfw%7Ctwcamp%5Etweetembed

%7Ctwterm%5E1227888433500164096%7Ctwgr%5E%7Ctwcon%5Es1_&ref_url=https%3A%2F%2Fwww.bbc.com%2Fnews%2Fuk-51487695.

Edwards, A. 2010. "The Progressive Unionist Party of Northern Ireland: a left-wing voice in an ethnically divided society". *British Journal of Politics and International Relations* 12: 590–614.

Emerson, N. 2017. "The sea border that's there already". TheDetail.tv, 1 December. https://www.thedetail.tv/articles/the-sea-border-that-s-there-already.

Emerson, N. 2018. "We may need to hold a Border poll just to clear the air". *Irish Times*, 6 September. https://www.irishtimes.com/opinion/we-may-need-to-hold-a-border-poll-just-to-clear-the-air-1.3619254.

Emerson, N. 2019. "How much direct rule has crept in since Stormont collapsed?". TheDetail.tv, 8 March. https://www.thedetail.tv/articles/how-much-direct-rule-has-crept-in-since-stormont-collapsed.

Emerson, N. 2020. "Sinn Féin still trying to wish away economic realities of a united Ireland". *Irish Times*, 19 November. https://www.irishtimes.com/opinion/sinn-f%C3%A9in-is-still-trying-to-wish-away-economic-realities-of-a-united-ireland-1.4412734.

Emerson, N. 2021a. "Unionists have no choice but to make sea border work". *Irish Times*, 7 January. https://www.irishtimes.com/opinion/newton-emerson-unionists-have-no-choice-but-to-make-the-irish-sea-border-work-1.4451521.

Emerson, N. 2021b. "Donaldson must reconcile unionism to the protocol". *Irish Times*, 24 June. https://www.irishtimes.com/opinion/newton-emerson-donaldson-must-reconcile-unionism-to-the-protocol-1.4601438.

European Commission 2019. The EU-UK Withdrawal Agreement. https://ec.europa.eu/info/relations-united-kingdom/eu-uk-withdrawal-agreement_en.

European Commission 2020. The EU–UK Trade and Cooperation Agreement. https://ec.europa.eu/info/relations-united-kingdom/eu-uk-trade-and-cooperation-agreement_en.

European Council 2017. *Guidelines following the United Kingdom's notification under Article 50 TEU.* 29 April. https://www.consilium.europa.eu/media/21763/29-euco-art50-guidelinesen.pdf.

Evans, J. & J. Tonge 2003. "The future of the "radical centre" in Northern Ireland after the Good Friday Agreement". *Political Studies* 51(1): 26–50.

Evershed, J. 2018a. *Ghosts of the Somme: Commemoration and Culture War in Northern Ireland.* Notre Dame, IN: University of Notre Dame Press.

Evershed, J. 2018b. "Not with a bang but a whimper". Centre on Constitutional Change, 15 November. https://www.centreonconstitutionalchange.ac.uk/opinions/not-bang-whimper.

Evershed, J. 2020. "Scottish Conservatism and Northern Ireland: mapping an ambivalent relationship". In D. Torrance (ed.) *Ruth Davidson's Conservatives: The Scottish Tory Party 2011–19*, 154–68. Edinburgh: Edinburgh University Press.

Evershed, J. & M. Murphy 2021. "*An bhfuil ár lá tagtha?* Sinn Féin, special status and the politics of Brexit". *British Journal of Politics and International Relations.* https://doi.org/10.1177/13691481211026153.

The Executive Office 2016a. "Letter to the Prime Minister, The Rt Hon Theresa May MP". 10 August. https://www.executiveoffice-ni.gov.uk/publications/letter-prime-minister-rt-hon-theresa-may-mp.

The Executive Office 2016b. "Letter to the First Minister, Arlene Foster and the deputy First Minister, Martin McGuinness from the Prime Minister, The Rt Hon Theresa May MP". 14 October. https://www.executiveoffice-ni.gov.uk/publications/ letter-first-minister-arlene-foster-and-deputy-first-minister-martin-mcguinness-prime-minister-rt.

Farrell, M. 1980. *Northern Ireland: The Orange State*. London: Pluto Press.

Farren, S. 2010. *The SDLP: The Struggle for Agreement in Northern Ireland, 1970–2000*. Dublin: Four Courts Press.

Farry, S. & S. Neeson 1998. "Beyond the 'band-aid' approach: an Alliance Party perspective upon the Belfast Agreement". *Fordham Law Journal* 22(4): 1221–49.

Fianna Fáil 2016a. "Speech of Fianna Fáil Leader Micheál Martin on the UK EU Referendum". 27 June. https://www.fiannafail.ie/blog/speech-of-fianna-fail-leader-micheal-martin-on-the-uk-eu-referendum.

Fianna Fáil 2016b. "Speech of Fianna Fáil Leader Micheál Martin at MacGill Summer School". 17 July. https://www.fiannafail.ie/blog/speech-of-fianna-fail-leader-micheal-martin-at-macgill-summer-school.

Fine Gael 2021. Speech from Tánaiste Leo Varadkar at the opening of the 2021 Fine Gael Ard Fheis, 15 June. https://www.finegael.ie/speech-of-the-tanaiste-leo-varadkar-at-the-opening-of-the-2021-fine-gael-ard-fheis/.

Finucane, J. 2019. "Brexit: a Belfast perspective". 21 February. https://www.youtube.com/ watch?v=f9IMWxOFqGI.

Fitzgerald, J. & E. Morgenroth 2019. "The Northern Ireland economy: problems and prospects". TEP Working Paper No. 0619. https://www.tcd.ie/Economics/TEP/2019/ tep0619.pdf.

Flanagan, C. 2015. Minister Flanagan addresses Chatham House in London on "Brexit", 7 November. https://www.dfa.ie/news-and-media/press-releases/press-release-archive/2015/september/flanagan-addresses-chatham-house-on-brexit/.

Ford, D. 2016. "Forward. Faster". Speech to the Alliance Party of Northern Ireland annual conference, Belfast, 5 March. https://cain.ulster.ac.uk/issues/politics/docs/apni/df_2016-03-05.htm.

Foster, P., S. Payne & J. Brunsden 2020. "UK plan to undermine withdrawal treaty puts Brexit talks at risk". *Financial Times*, 6 September. https://www.ft.com/content/ 9906e0d4-0c29-4f5f-9cb0-130c75a2f7a7.

Gallaher, C. 2007. *After the Peace: Loyalist Paramilitaries in Post-Accord Northern Ireland*. Ithaca, NY: Cornell University Press.

Ganiel, G. 2009. "'Battling in Brussels': the DUP and the European Union". *Irish Political Studies* 24(4): 575–88.

Garry, J. 2016a. "The EU referendum vote in Northern Ireland: implications for our understanding of citizens' political views and behaviour". Knowledge Exchange Seminar Series. http://www.niassembly.gov.uk/globalassets/documents/raise/ knowledge_exchange/briefing_papers/series6/garry121016.pdf.

Garry, J. 2016b. *Consociation and Voting in Northern Ireland: Party Competition and Electoral Behaviour*. Philadelphia, PA: University of Pennsylvania Press.

Garry, J. et al. 2021. "The future of Northern Ireland: border anxieties and support for Irish reunification under varieties of UK exit". *Regional Studies* 55(9): 1517–27.

Geoghegan, P. 2020. *Democracy for Sale: Dark Money and Dirty Politics*. London: Head of Zeus.

Geoghegan, P. 2021. "Tory dominance is likely to hasten the break-up of the union". *Irish Times*, 10 May. https://www.irishtimes.com/opinion/tory-dominance-is-likely-to-hasten-break-up-of-the-union-1.4559816.

Gillespie, P. 2014. "The complexity of British–Irish interdependence". *Irish Political Studies* 29(1): 37–57.

Goodhart, D. 2017. *The Road to Somewhere: The Populist Revolt and the Future of Politics*. London: Hurst.

Gormley-Heenan, C. & D. Birrell 2015. *Multi-Level Governance and Northern Ireland*. Basingstoke: Palgrave Macmillan.

Gosling, P. 2020. *A New Ireland: A New Union, A New Society: A Ten Year Plan*. http://www.paulgosling.net/wp-content/uploads/2020/05/A-New-Ireland-A-New-Union-A-New-Society.pdf.

Government of Ireland 2014. *National Risk Assessment 2014*. Dublin: Government Publications.

Government of Ireland 2017. *Brexit: Ireland's Priorities*. Dublin: Government Publications.

Gudgin, G. & R. Bassett 2018. "Getting over the line: solutions to the Irish border. Why the UK (including Northern Ireland) can leave the Customs Union, avoid a hard border – and protect the Good Friday Agreement". London: Policy Exchange. https://policyexchange.org.uk/wp-content/uploads/2018/05/Getting-over-the-line.pdf.

Halliday, D. & N. Ferguson 2016. "When peace is not enough: the flag protests, the politics of identity and belonging in East Belfast". *Irish Political Studies* 31(4): 525–40.

Hanna, C. 2019a. Jean Monnet Lecture at University College Cork, March 2019. Medium. https://medium.com/@clairehanna_21747/good-afternoon-6f764cf096e8.

Hanna, C. 2019b. MacGill Summer School 2019. Medium. https://medium.com/@clairehanna_21747/macgill-summer-school-2019-28e5c7b1d7b4.

Harvey, C. 2016. "Northern Ireland's transition and the constitution of the UK". UK Constitutional Law Association, 12 December. https://ukconstitutionallaw.org/2016/12/12/colin-harvey-northern-irelands-transition-and-the-constitution-of-the-uk/.

Harvey, C. 2018. "Sharing the island: Brexit, 'no deal' and the constitutional future". BrexitLawNI Blog, 18 December. https://brexitlawni.org/blog/sharing-the-island-brexit-no-deal-and-the-constitutional-future/.

Harvey, C. & M. Bassett 2019. "The EU and Irish unity: planning and preparing for constitutional change in Ireland". Belfast: Queen's University Belfast. https://www.guengl.eu/issues/publications/the-eu-irish-unity/.

Haughey, S. 2020. "Back to Stormont: The *New Decade, New Approach* agreement and what it means for Northern Ireland". *Political Quarterly* 91(1): 134–40.

Haughey, S. & J. Pow 2020. "Remain reaffirmed: the 2019 European election in Northern Ireland". *Irish Political Studies* 35(1): 29–45.

Hay, C. 1999. "Crisis and the structural transformation of the state: interrogating the process of change". *British Journal of Politics and International Relations* 1(3): 317–44.

Hayward, K. 2006. "Reiterating national identities: the European Union conception of conflict resolution in Northern Ireland". *Cooperation and Conflict* 41(3): 261–84.

Hayward, K. 2018. "The pivotal position of the Irish border in the UK's withdrawal from the European Union". *Space and Polity* 22(2): 238–54.

Hayward, K. 2020a. "Why it is impossible for Brexit Britain to 'take back control' in Northern Ireland". *Territory, Politics, Governance* 8(2): 273–8.

Hayward, K. 2020b. "How does the UK Internal Market Bill relate to Northern Ireland?". LSE Brexit, 19 October. https://blogs.lse.ac.uk/brexit/2020/10/19/how-does-the-uk-internal-market-bill-relate-to-northern-ireland/.

Hayward, K. *et al.* 2021. "What do voters in Northern Ireland think about the Protocol on Ireland/Northern Ireland". https://www.qub.ac.uk/sites/media/Media,1058598,smxx.pdf.

Hayward, K. & C. McManus 2019. "Neither/nor: the rejection of unionist and nationalist identities in post-agreement Northern Ireland". *Capital and Class* 43(1): 139–55.

Hayward, K. & M. Murphy (eds) 2010. *The Europeanization of Political Parties in Northern Ireland, North and South.* London: Routledge.

Hayward, K. & M. Murphy 2012. "The (soft) power of commitment: the EU and conflict resolution in Northern Ireland". *Ethnopolitics* 11(4): 439–52.

Hayward, K. & M. Murphy 2018. "The EU's influence on the peace process and agreement in Northern Ireland in light of Brexit". *Ethnopolitics* 17(3): 276–91.

Hayward, K. & D. Phinnemore 2019. "Breached or protected? The 'principle' of consent in Northern Ireland and the UK government's Brexit proposals". LSE Brexit, 11 January. https://blogs.lse.ac.uk/europpblog/2019/01/11/breached-or-protected-the-principle-of-consent-in-northern-ireland-and-the-uk-governments-brexit-proposals/.

Hayward, K. & B. Rosher 2020. "Political attitudes at a time of flux". ARK Research Update No. 133. https://www.ark.ac.uk/ARK/sites/default/files/2020-06/update133.pdf.

Hayward, K. & B. Rosher 2021. "Political attitudes in Northern Ireland in a period of transition". ARK Research Update No. 142. https://www.ark.ac.uk/ARK/sites/default/files/2021-06/update142.pdf.

Heffer, G. 2020. "Brexit: UK to ditch Internal Market Bill clauses after reaching agreement in principle on Northern Ireland Protocol". Sky News, 8 December. https://news.sky.com/story/brexit-uk-to-ditch-internal-market-bill-clauses-after-reaching-agreement-in-principle-on-northern-ireland-protocol-12155176.

Henderson, A. & R. Wyn Jones 2021. *Englishness: The Political Force Transforming Britain.* Oxford: Oxford University Press.

Hennessey, T. *et al.* 2019. *The Ulster Unionist Party: Country Before Party?* Oxford: Oxford University Press.

Hiraeth 2021. "Wales moves forward". Podcast, 5 May. https://www.youtube.com/watch?v=WY37l1PHh3o.

HM Government 2019. UK Government Commitments to Northern Ireland and its Integral Place in the United Kingdom. 9 January. https://assets.publishing.service.gov.uk/government/uploads/system/uploads/attachment_data/file/769954/NI_unilateral_commitments_-_9_January_FINAL.pdf.

Holmes, M. 2021. "Irish political parties and the EU: Euro-nationalism, not Euro-scepticism". In M. Holmes & K. Simpson (eds), *Ireland and the European Union: Economic, Political and Social Crises*, 72–87. Manchester: Manchester University Press.

Horowitz, D. 1985. *Ethnic Groups in Conflict.* Berkeley, CA: University of California Press.

House of Commons Northern Ireland Affairs Committee. *First Report of Session 2016–17: Northern Ireland and the EU referendum.* HC 48. London: House of Commons. https://publications.parliament.uk/pa/cm201617/cmselect/cmniaf/48/48.pdf.

House of Commons Welsh Affairs Committee 2021. *Oral Evidence: One off-session with the First Minister of Wales*, HC 1255, 4 March. https://committees.parliament.uk/oralevidence/1824/html/.

House of Lords European Union Committee 2016a. *Sixth Report of Session 2016–17: Brexit: UK–Irish Relations*. HL Paper 76. London: House of Lords. https://publications.parliament.uk/pa/ld201617/ldselect/ldeucom/76/76.pdf.

House of Lords European Union Committee 2016b. *Nineth Report of Session 2015–16: The EU Referendum and EU Reform*. HL Paper 122. London: House of Lords. https://publications.parliament.uk/pa/ld201516/ldselect/ldeucom/122/122.pdf.

House of Lords European Union Committee (HL EC) 2017. *4th Report of Session 2017–19: Brexit: Devolution*. HL Paper 9. London: House of Lords.

Houses of the Oireachtas Joint Committee on European Union Affairs 2015. *UK/EU Future Relationship: Implications for Ireland*. Dublin: Houses of the Oireachtas. https://ec.europa.eu/dgs/secretariat_general/relations/relations_other/npo/docs/ireland/own_initiative/oi_uk_eu_relations_and_the_implications_for_ie/oi_uk_eu_relations_and_the_implications_for_ie_oireachtas_opinion_en.pdf.

Houses of the Oireachtas Joint Committee on the Implementation of the Good Friday Agreement 2017. *Brexit and the Future of Ireland: Uniting Ireland and its People in Peace and Prosperity*. Dublin: Houses of the Oireachtas. https://data.oireachtas.ie/ie/oireachtas/committee/dail/32/joint_committee_on_the_implementation_of_the_good_friday_agreement/reports/2017/2017-08-02_brexit-and-the-future-of-ireland-uniting-ireland-and-its-people-in-peace-and-prosperity_en.pdf.

Houses of the Oireachtas Joint Committee on the Implementation of the Good Friday Agreement 2020. *Evidence Session*. 12 November. https://www.oireachtas.ie/en/debates/debate/joint_committee_on_the_implementation_of_the_good_friday_agreement/2020-11-12/3/.

Hudson, C. & G. Spencer 2021. "Is the centenary of the Union the right time for a different sort of unionism?". *Belfast Telegraph*, 27 April. https://www.belfasttelegraph.co.uk/opinion/comment/is-the-centenary-of-the-union-the-right-time-for-a-different-sort-of-unionism-40363446.html.

Humphreys, R. 2018. *Beyond the Border: The Good Friday Agreement and Irish Unity after Brexit*. Newbridge: Merrion Press.

Hunt, J. & R. Minto 2017. "Between intergovernmental relations and paradiplomacy: Wales and the Brexit of the regions". *British Journal of Politics and International Relations* 19(4): 647–62.

Ingoldsby, S. 2020. "Results of a future border poll on a knife edge". TheDetail.tv, 24 February. https://thedetail.tv/articles/a-majority-favour-a-border-poll-on-the-island-of-ireland-in-the-next-10-years.

Institute for Government 2020. "Sewel Convention". 8 December. https://www.instituteforgovernment.org.uk/explainers/sewel-convention.

Ireland's Future 2019a. *Beyond Brexit: The Future of Ireland*. 26 January. https://irelandsfuture.com/publications/beyond-brexit/.

Ireland's Future 2019b. *Shaping Our Constitutional Future: Calling for a Citizen's Assembly*. 28 November. https://irelandsfuture.com/publications/shaping-our-constitutional-future/.

Irish Business and Employers Confederation (IBEC) 2016. "The impact of a possible Brexit on Irish business". https://borderpeople.info/site/wp-content/uploads/TheUKreferendumonEUmembership-TheimpactofapossibleBrexitonIrishbusiness.pdf.

Irish Congress of Trade Unions (ICTU) 2016. "The case against Brexit". https://www.ictu. ie/download/pdf/brexit_briefing_paper.pdf.

*Irish News* 2021. "Secretary of State Brandon Lewis declines to spell out border poll criteria". 13 January. https://www.irishnews.com/news/northernirelandnews/2021/ 01/12/news/secretary-of-state-brandon-lewis-declines-to-spell-out-border-poll-criteria-2185038/.

*Irish Times* 2018. "Now not the time for Border poll on unity, says McDonald". 30 July. https://www.irishtimes.com/news/politics/now-not-the-time-for-border-poll-on-unity-says-mcdonald-1.3581145.

*Irish Times* 2019. "DUP welcomes victory of 'committed Unionist' Boris Johnson". 23 July. https://www.irishtimes.com/news/world/uk/dup-welcomes-victory-of-committed-unionist-boris-johnson-1.3964905.

*Irish Times* 2020. Election 2020 Results Hub. https://www.irishtimes.com/election2020/results-hub.

Jeffrey, C. 2009. "Devolution in the United Kingdom: problems of a piecemeal approach to constitutional change". *Publius: The Journal of Federalism* 39(2): 289–313.

Jennings, W. & M. Lodge 2019. "Brexit, the tides and Canute: the fracturing politics of the British state". *Journal of European Public Policy* 26(5): 772–89.

Johnston, S. 2020. "The 2019 European parliamentary elections in Ireland". *Irish Political Studies* 35(1): 18–28.

Kane, A. 2019. "Why demonising the Alliance Party as Sinn Féin fellow travellers backfired on DUP". *Belfast Telegraph*, 16 December. https://www.belfasttelegraph. co.uk/opinion/news-analysis/alex-kane-why-demonising-the-alliance-party-as-sinn-fein-fellow-travellers-backfired-on-dup-38789601.html.

Kane, A. 2021. "The DUP has been betrayed by its own stupidity as much as by the Tories". *News Letter*, 19 April. https://www.newsletter.co.uk/news/opinion/columnists/alex-kane-the-dup-has-been-betrayed-by-its-own-stupidity-as-much-as-by-the-tories-3205160.

Keating, M. 2019. "The backstop is gone. Welcome to the backstop". Centre on Constitutional Change, 18 October. https://www.centreonconstitutionalchange.ac.uk/news-and-opinion/backstop-gone-welcome-backstop.

Kelly, B. 2019. "Dominic Raab's ignorant indifference to the Good Friday Agreement is an insult to Northern Irish people like me". *Independent*, 1 February. https:// www.independent.co.uk/voices/dominic-raab-good-friday-agreement-brexit-irish-border-a8758076.html.

Kelly, F. 2018. "Britain urged Ireland to reduce emphasis on NI in Brexit talks". *Irish Times*, 10 August. https://www.irishtimes.com/news/ireland/irish-news/britain-urged-ireland-to-reduce-emphasis-on-ni-peace-in-brexit-talks-1.3591310.

Kenny, M. & J. Sheldon 2020. "'A place apart' or 'integral to our precious Union'? Understanding the nature and implications of Conservative Party thinking about Northern Ireland, 2010–19". *Irish Political Studies* 36(2): 291–317.

Kenny, M. & J. Sheldon 2021. "When planets collide: the British Conservative Party and the discordant goals of delivering Brexit and preserving the domestic union, 2016–2019". *Political Studies* 69(4): 965–84.

KLC Consulting 2016. *Modelling Irish Unification*. New York: Harvard Club of New York. https://cain.ulster.ac.uk/issues/unification/hubner_2015-08.pdf.

Kroll, D. & D. Leuffen 2016. "Ties that bind, can also strangle: the Brexit threat and the hardships of reforming the EU". *Journal of European Public Policy* 23(9): 1311–20.

Laffan, B. 2018. "Brexit: re-opening Ireland's 'English Question'". *Political Quarterly* 89(4): 568–75.

Lagana, G. 2020. *The European Union and the Northern Ireland Peace Process*. Basingstoke: Palgrave Macmillan.

Leach, A. *et al.* 2021. "Stormont: where Northern Ireland politics splits and where it holds together". *The Guardian*, 22 June. https://www.theguardian.com/politics/ng-interactive/2021/jun/22/stormont-where-northern-irish-politics-splits-and-where-it-holds-together.

Leahy, P. 2016. "Brexit: Ireland unsure of Plan B in the event of departure". *Irish Times*, 11 May. https://www.irishtimes.com/news/politics/brexit-ireland-unsure-of-plan-b-in-the-event-of-departure-1.2642685.

Lijphart, A. 1996. "The framework document in Northern Ireland". *Government and Opposition* 31(3): 267–74.

The Literific 2021. *LitTalks: Naomi Long*. 20 March. https://touch.facebook.com/QUBLiterific/?__tn__=%2Cg.

Little, A. 2006. "Theorizing democracy and violence: the case of Northern Ireland". *Theoria* 53(111): 62–86.

Long, N. 2019. "A People's Vote needs to be tested in Parliament as a matter of urgency after the prime minister's proposed Brexit Withdrawal Agreement was rejected by MPs". Letter to the editor, *News Letter*, 13 March. https://www.newsletter.co.uk/news/opinion/naomi-long-peoples-vote-clearest-route-out-impasse-over-brexit-78931.

Long, N. 2021a. "Brexit, Northern Ireland and the Protocol". UCC Jean Monnet Lecture Series, 24 March. https://www.youtube.com/watch?v=sWOaN8_CdIo.

Long, N. 2021b. "The future of Northern Ireland". The Cambridge seminar on the future of the island of Ireland, 1 June. https://www.cfg.polis.cam.ac.uk/island-ireland.

Lord Ashcroft Polls 2019. "My Northern Ireland survey finds the Union on a knife-edge". 11 September. https://lordashcroftpolls.com/2019/09/my-northern-ireland-survey-finds-the-union-on-a-knife-edge/.

Lowry, B. 2016. "Despite what supporters of Brexit say, it might just blow the UK apart". *News Letter*, 18 June. https://www.newsletter.co.uk/news/politics/ben-lowry-despite-what-supporters-brexit-say-it-might-just-blow-uk-apart-1229001.

Lowry, B. 2019. "Loyalist protest meeting in Portadown against Boris Johnson's 'Betrayal Act' was packed and angry". *News Letter*, 25 November. https://www.newsletter.co.uk/news/ben-lowry-loyalist-protest-meeting-portadown-against-boris-johnsons-betrayal-act-was-packed-and-angry-1320544.

LucidTalk 2018. LT NI quarterly "tracker" poll: winter 2018. https://docs.wixstatic.com/ugd/024943_b89b42d32364461298ba5fe7867d82e1.pdf.

LucidTalk 2021a. LT NI quarterly "tracker" poll: winter 2021. https://www.lucidtalk.co.uk/single-post/lt-ni-quarterly-tracker-poll-winter-2021.

LucidTalk 2021b. LT NI quarterly "tracker" poll: spring 2021. https://www.lucidtalk.co.uk/single-post/lt-ni-quarterly-tracker-poll-spring-2021.

LucidTalk 2021c. LT BBC NI Spotlight poll-project – Northern Ireland (NI) and Republic of Ireland (ROI). https://www.lucidtalk.co.uk/single-post/lt-bbc-ni-spotlight-poll-project-northern-ireland-ni-and-republic-of-ireland-roi.

Madden, A. 2019. "Poll: most Tory members would sacrifice Northern Ireland for Brexit". *Belfast Telegraph*, 18 June. https://www.belfasttelegraph.co.uk/news/brexit/poll-most-tory-members-would-sacrifice-northern-ireland-for-brexit-38229896.html.

Mahoney, J. 2002. *The Legacies of Liberalism: Path Dependence and Political Regimes in Central America*. Baltimore, MD: Johns Hopkins University Press.

Maillot, A. 2009. "Sinn Féin's approach to the EU: still more 'critical' than 'engaged'?" *Irish Political Studies* 24(4): 559–74.

Mallon, S., with A. Pollak 2019. *A Shared Home Place*. Dublin: Lilliput Press.

Manley, J. 2017. "Simon Coveney seeking united Ireland 'in his political lifetime'". *Irish News*, 24 November. https://www.irishnews.com/news/2017/11/24/news/simon-coveney-seeking-united-ireland-in-his-political-lifetime--1195785/.

Manley, J. 2020a. "Colum Eastwood says border poll should be called when it's winnable". *Irish News*, 21 July. https://www.irishnews.com/news/northernirelandnews/2020/07/21/news/colum-eastwood-says-border-poll-should-be-called-when-it-s-winnable-2011135/.

Manley, J. 2020b. "Steve Aiken rules out engagement with Shared Island Unit while accusing Boris Johnson of 'attempting to curry favour with Dublin'". *Irish News*, 6 November. https://www.irishnews.com/news/northernirelandnews/2020/11/06/news/steve-aiken-rules-out-engagement-with-shared-island-unit-while-accusing-boris-johnson-of-attempting-to-curry-favour-with-du-2121522/.

Manley, J. 2020c. "Boris Johnson letter welcomes Micheál Martin's Shared Island Unit". *Irish News*, 5 November. https://www.irishnews.com/news/northernireland news/2020/11/05/news/boris-johnson-letter-welcomes-michea-l-martin-s-shared-island-unit-2120391/.

Manley, J. 2020d. "Naomi Long ready to engage with any conversation about Irish unity". *Irish News*, 6 March. https://www.irishnews.com/news/northernirelandnews/2020/03/06/news/naomi-long-is-ready-to-engage-with-any-conversation-about-irish-unity-1860279/.

Mansergh, M. 2002. "The new context of British–Irish relations". In B. Tonra & E. Ward (eds), *Ireland in International Affairs: Interests, Institutions and Identities*, 93–103. Dublin: Institute of Public Administration.

Mason, R. *et al.* 2016 "EU referendum to take place on 23 June, David Cameron confirms". *The Guardian*, 20 February. https://www.theguardian.com/politics/2016/feb/20/cameron-set-to-name-eu-referendum-date-after-cabinet-meeting.

McAuley, J. 2010. *Ulster's Last Stand? Reconstructing Unionism after the Peace Process*. Dublin: Irish Academic Press.

McAuley, J. 2015. *Very British Rebels: The Culture and Politics of Ulster Loyalism*. London: Bloomsbury.

McBride, S. 2016. "No other nationalist parties back SF's demand for a border poll". *News Letter*, 25 June. https://www.newsletter.co.uk/news/no-other-nationalist-parties-back-sfs-demand-border-poll-1226946.

McBride, S. 2019a. *Burned: The Inside Story of the "Cash-for-Ash" Scandal and Northern Ireland's Secretive New Elite*. Newbridge: Merrion Press.

McBride, S. 2019b. "A small band of DUP voters always opposed Brexit, fearing for the Union". *News Letter*, 26 January. https://www.newsletter.co.uk/news/sam-mcbride-small-band-dup-members-always-opposed-brexit-fearing-union-132321.

McBride, S. 2020a. "Sinn Féin's triumph could set back its grand goal of Irish unity – despite rudderless unionism". *News Letter*, 15 February. https://www.newsletter.co.uk/news/politics/sam-mcbride-sinn-feins-triumph-could-set-back-its-grand-goal-irish-unity-despite-rudderless-unionism-1741086.

McBride, S. 2020b. "2020 has seen Sinn Féin reach its zenith, but also revealed its key weaknesses". *News Letter*, 19 December. https://www.newsletter.co.uk/news/politics/sam-mcbride-2020-has-seen-sinn-fein-reach-its-zenith-also-revealed-its-key-weaknesses-3073683.

McBride, S. 2021a. "No border to see here, insists Secretary of State Brandon Lewis – six days into Irish Sea border reality". *News Letter*, 6 January. https://www.newsletter.co.uk/news/politics/no-border-see-here-insists-secretary-state-brandon-lewis-six-days-irish-sea-border-reality-3087823.

McBride, S. 2021b. "A week into the Irish Sea border, it is already clear that Northern Ireland will be profoundly reshaped by Brexit". *News Letter*, 9 January. https://www.newsletter.co.uk/news/politics/sam-mcbride-week-irish-sea-border-it-already-clear-northern-ireland-will-be-profoundly-reshaped-brexit-3090600.

McCall, C. 2021. *Border Ireland: From Partition to Brexit*. Abingdon: Routledge.

McCann, D. 2019. "Fianna Fáil and SDLP announce joint partnership". Slugger O'Toole, 24 January. https://sluggerotoole.com/2019/01/24/fianna-fail-and-sdlp-announce-joint-partnership/.

McCann, G. & P. Hainsworth 2017. "Brexit and Northern Ireland: the 2016 referendum on the United Kingdom's membership of the European Union". *Irish Political Studies* 32(2): 327–42.

McClements, F. 2019. "A new Ireland? 1,000 leading people call on Varadkar to lead change". *Irish Times*, 4 November. https://www.irishtimes.com/news/ireland/irish-news/a-new-ireland-1-000-leading-people-call-on-varadkar-to-lead-change-1.4071063.

McCormack, J. 2020a. "Brexit: NI Assembly votes to withhold Brexit bill consent". BBC News, 20 January. https://www.bbc.co.uk/news/uk-northern-ireland-51174448.

McCormack, J. 2020b. "Brexit: Northern Ireland food supply warnings 'taken seriously'". BBC News, 10 November. https://www.bbc.co.uk/news/uk-northern-ireland-548 92142.

McDaid, S. 2018. "A post-Brexit hard border has attractions for both DUP and Sinn Féin". *Irish Times*, 5 April. https://www.irishtimes.com/culture/books/a-post-brexit-hard-border-has-attractions-for-both-dup-and-sinn-f%C3%A9in-1.3451429.

McDonald, H. 2017. "Northern Irish unionist parties alienating young Protestants, study says". *The Guardian*, 4 August. https://www.theguardian.com/uk-news/2017/aug/04/northern-irish-unionist-parties-alienating-young-protestants-study.

McEwen, N. 2020. "Negotiating Brexit: power dynamics in British intergovernmental relations". *Regional Studies*, online first, doi: 10.1080/00343404.2020.1735000.

McEwen, N. et al. 2018. *Reforming Intergovernmental Relations in the United Kingdom*. Cambridge: Bennett Institute for Public Policy. https://www.bennettinstitute.cam.ac.uk/media/uploads/files/Reforming_Intergovernmental_Relations_in_the_United_Kingdom_nov18.pdf.

McGarry, J. & B. O'Leary 2004. *The Northern Ireland Conflict: Consociational Engagements*. Oxford: Oxford University Press.

McGarry, J. & B. O'Leary 2019. "Matters of consent: the Withdrawal Agreement does not violate the Good Friday Agreement". LSE Brexit, 28 October. https://blogs.lse.ac.uk/politicsandpolicy/brexit-good-friday-agreement/.

McGee, H. 2020. "Gloves come off as Fine Gael and Sinn Féin take bitter row to social media". *Irish Times*, 14 November. https://www.irishtimes.com/news/politics/gloves-come-off-as-fine-gael-and-sinn-f%C3%A9in-take-bitter-row-to-social-media-1.4408874.

McGee, H. & D. Scally 2012. "UK role at core of EU fundamental for Ireland, says Kenny". *Irish Times*, 10 January. https://www.irishtimes.com/news/uk-role-at-core-of-eu-fundamental-for-ireland-says-kenny-1.441943.

McGlinchey, M. 2019. *Unfinished Business: The Politics of "Dissident" Irish Republicanism*. Manchester: Manchester University Press.

McGlynn, M., D. McConnell & PA 2021. "EU 'not triggering' Article 16, NI protocol will be 'unaffected'". *Irish Examiner*, 29 January. https://www.irishexaminer.com/news/arid-40217120.html.

McGonagle, S. 2018. "Anti-Brexit rally to take place in Belfast tomorrow". *Irish News*, 19 October. https://www.irishnews.com/news/2018/10/19/news/anti-brexit-rally-to-take-place-in-belfast-tomorrow-1462803/.

McGonagle, S. 2021. "Matthew O'Toole: Brexit could lead to 'two parts of Ireland moving further apart'". *Irish News*, 4 February. https://www.irishnews.com/news/brexit/2021/02/04/news/matthew-o-toole-brexit-could-lead-to-two-parts-of-ireland-moving-further-apart--2209146/.

McGowan, L. & J. O'Connor 2004. "Exploring Eurovisions: awareness and knowledge of the European Union in Northern Ireland". *Irish Political Studies* 19(2): 21–42.

McGrath, D. 2020. "Principle or pragmatism: ambiguity surrounds the Shared Island Unit, months after launch". TheJournal.ie, 12 October. https://www.thejournal.ie/shared-island-unity-sinn-fein-fianna-fail-5227662-Oct2020/.

McGraw, S. & E. O'Malley (eds) 2018. *One Party Dominance: Fianna Fáil and Irish Politics 1926–2016*. Abingdon: Routledge.

McHarg, A. 2018. "Navigating without maps: constitutional silence and the management of the Brexit process". *International Journal of Constitutional Law* 16(3): 952–68.

McHarg, A. *et al.* (eds) 2016. *The Scottish Independence Referendum: Constitutional and Political Implications*. Oxford: Oxford University Press.

McKay, S. 2000. *Northern Protestants: An Unsettled People*. Belfast: Blackstaff Press.

McKay, S. 2021a. *Northern Protestants: On Shifting Ground*. Belfast: Blackstaff Press.

McKay, S. 2021b. "Unionist leaders in Northern Ireland must banish the ghosts of grievance and rage". *The Guardian*, 15 April. https://www.theguardian.com/commentisfree/2021/apr/15/unionist-leaders-northern-ireland-grievance-rage-dup-loyalists.

McKay, S. 2021c. "The DUP has a new leader, but language is still Northern Ireland's sticking point". *The Guardian*, 24 June. https://www.theguardian.com/commentisfree/2021/jun/24/dup-new-leader-language-northern-ireland-irish-jeffrey-donaldson.

McKinnion, D. 2015. "Devolution, state restructuring and policy divergence in the UK". *Geographical Journal* 181(1): 47–56.

McLoughlin, P. 2009. "The SDLP and the Europeanization of the Northern Ireland problem". *Irish Political Studies* 24(4): 603–19.

McLoughlin, P. 2010. *John Hume and the Revision of Irish Nationalism*. Manchester: Manchester University Press.

McQuinn, K. *et al.* 2020. *Quarterly Economic Commentary: Autumn 2020*. Dublin: ESRI. https://www.esri.ie/sites/default/files/media/file-uploads/2020-10/SLIDES_ Quarterly%20Economic%20Commentary%20Autumn%202020_McQUINN.pdf.

McWilliams, D. 2018. *Renaissance Nation: How the Pope's Children Rewrote the Rules for Ireland*. Dublin: Gill Books.

Meehan, E. 2000. "'Britain's Irish Question: Britain's European Question?' British–Irish relations in the context of European Union and the Belfast Agreement". *Review of International Studies* 26(1): 83–97.

Merrion Street 2012. "British Irish relations: The next decade", Joint Statement by the Prime Minister, David Cameron and the Taoiseach, Enda Kenny, 12 March. https://merrionstreet.ie/en/category-index/international/united-kingdom/ british-irish-relations-the-next-decade.html.

Merrion Street 2016. "Statement by An Taoiseach, Enda Kenny TD, on the UK Vote to Leave the European Union", 24 June. https://merrionstreet.ie/en/news-room/ speeches/statement_by_an_taoiseach_enda_kenny_td_on_the_uk_vote_to_leave_ the_european_union.html.

Merrion Street 2020. "Online address by An Taoiseach on Shared Island", 22 October. https://merrionstreet.ie/en/news-room/speeches/online_address_by_an_ taoiseach_on_shared_island.html.

Mitchell, C. 2018. "Future Ireland: where can the North thrive?". Slugger O'Toole, 4 September. https://sluggerotoole.com/2018/09/04/future-ireland-where-can-the- north-thrive/.

Mitchell, D. 2009. "Cooking the fudge: constructive ambiguity and the implementation of the Northern Ireland Agreement, 1998–2007". *Irish Political Studies* 24(3): 321–36.

Mitchell, D. 2018. "Non-nationalist politics in a bi-national consociation: the case of the Alliance Party of Northern Ireland". *Nationalism and Ethnic Politics* 24(3): 336–47.

Mitchell, P. 1991. "Conflict regulation and party competition in Northern Ireland". *European Journal of Political Research* 20: 67–92.

Mitchell, P. 1995. "Party competition in an ethnic dual party system". *Ethnic and Racial Studies* 18(4): 773–96.

Mitchell, P. 1999. "The party system and party competition". In P. Mitchell & R. Wilford (eds), *Politics in Northern Ireland*, 91–116. Boulder, CO: Westview.

Mitchell, P., G. Evans & B. O'Leary 2009. "Extremist outbidding in ethnic party systems is not inevitable: tribune parties in Northern Ireland". *Political Studies* 57(2): 397–421.

Montgomery, R. 2021. "Protocol problems for both parts of Ireland: North and South". *Fortnight* 481, April. https://fortnightmagazine.org/articles/protocol-problems-for- both-parts-of-ireland-north-and-south/.

Moore, A. 2020. "Shared Island Initiative, Day 3: half of North say 'not unionist nor nationalist'". *Irish Examiner*, 29 December. https://www.irishexaminer.com/news/ spotlight/arid-40198167.html.

Moriarty, G. 2017. "SDLP calls for border poll on united Ireland after Brexit negotiations". *Irish Times*, 30 May. https://www.irishtimes.com/news/politics/sdlp- calls-for-border-poll-on-united-ireland-after-brexit-negotiations-1.3101566.

Moriarty, G. 2020a. "Northern Ireland: polls can provide more confusion than clarity". *Irish Times*, 5 September. https://www.irishtimes.com/news/ireland/irish-news/ northern-ireland-polls-can-provide-more-confusion-than-clarity-1.4344768.

Moriarty, G. 2020b. "No current case for united Ireland Border poll – Alliance party". *Irish Times*, 7 March. https://www.irishtimes.com/news/ireland/irish-news/no-current-case-for-united-ireland-border-poll-alliance-party-1.4196502.

Morphet, J. 2021. *The Impact of Covid-19 on Devolution: Recentralising the British State Beyond Brexit?* Bristol: Bristol University Press.

Morris, A. 2021. "Loyalist paramilitary groups withdraw support for Good Friday Agreement". *Irish News*, 4 March. https://www.irishnews.com/paywall/tsb/irishnews/irishnews/irishnews//news/northernirelandnews/2021/03/04/news/loyalist-paramilitary-groups-withdraw-support-for-good-friday-agreement-2243573/content.html.

Morris, C. 2018. "Reality check: red lines on the Irish Border". BBC News, 4 October. https://www.bbc.com/news/uk-politics-45737229.

Morrow, D. 2017. "Reconciliation and after in Northern Ireland: the search for political order in an ethnically divided society". *Nationalism and Ethnic Politics* 23(2): 98–117.

Mullen, T. 2014. "The Scottish independence referendum 2014". *Journal of Law and Society* 41(4): 627–40.

Murphy, M. 2009. "Pragmatic politics: the Ulster Unionist Party and the European Union". *Irish Political Studies* 24(4): 589–602.

Murphy, M. 2014. *Northern Ireland and the European Union: The Dynamics of a Changing Relationship*. Manchester: Manchester University Press.

Murphy, M. 2016a. "Northern Ireland and the EU referendum: the outcome, options and opportunities". *Journal of Cross-Border Studies in Ireland* 11: 18–31.

Murphy, M. 2016b. "The EU referendum in Northern Ireland: closing borders, re-opening border debates". *Journal of Contemporary European Research* 12(4): 844–53.

Murphy, M. 2018a. *Europe and Northern Ireland's Future: Negotiating Brexit's Unique Case*. Newcastle upon Tyne: Agenda Publishing.

Murphy, M. 2018b. "Brexit and the Irish case". In P. Diamond, P. Nedergaard & B. Rosamond (eds), *The Routledge Handbook of the Politics of Brexit*, 27–39. Abingdon: Routledge.

Murphy, M. 2019a. "The Brexit crisis, Ireland and British–Irish relations: Europeanisation and/or de-Europeanisation?". *Irish Political Studies* 34(4): 530–50.

Murphy, M. 2019b. "What are the Irish government's Brexit priorities? A united Ireland is not one of them". Centre on Constitutional Change, 17 January. https://www.centreonconstitutionalchange.ac.uk/opinions/what-are-irish-governments-brexit-priorities-united-ireland-not-one-them.

Murphy, M. 2020. "What Sinn Féin's election success means for Irish relations with the EU – and Brexit". *Irish Examiner*, 13 February. https://www.irishexaminer.com/business/arid-30981571.html.

Murphy, M. 2021a. "Brexit and the election: the issue that wasn't". In M. Gallagher, M. Marsh & T. Reify (eds), *How Ireland Voted 2020: The End of an Era*, 93–112. Basingstoke: Palgrave Macmillan.

Murphy, M. 2021b. "Northern Ireland and Brexit: where sovereignty and stability collide?" *Journal of Contemporary European Studies*, online first, doi: 10.1080/14782804.2021.1891027.

Murphy, M. & J. Evershed 2020a. "The DUP and the European Union: from contestation to conformance and back again …". *Irish Political Studies* 35(3): 378–98.

Murphy, M. & J. Evershed 2020b. "Between the devil and the DUP: the Democratic Unionist Party and the politics of Brexit". *British Politics* 15(4): 456–77.

Murphy, M. & J. Evershed 2021. "Contesting sovereignty and borders: Northern Ireland, devolution and the Union". *Territory, Politics, Governance*, online first, doi: 10.1080/21622671.2021.1892518.

Murray, C. 2021. "Stop worrying and love the Ireland/Northern Ireland Protocol". LSE Brexit, 4 March. https://blogs.lse.ac.uk/brexit/2021/03/04/stop-worrying-and-love-the-ireland-northern-ireland-protocol/.

Murray, C. & M. Armstrong 2021. "A mobile phone in one hand and Erskine May in the other: the European Research Group's parliamentary revolution". *Parliamentary Affairs*, online first, doi: 10.1093/pa/gsab004.

Murray, C. & A. O'Donoghue 2019. "Life after Brexit: operationalising the Belfast/ Good Friday Agreement's principle of consent". *Dublin University Law Journal* 42(1): 147–89.

Murtagh, C. 2015. "Reaching across: institutional barriers to cross-ethnic parties in post-conflict societies and the case of Northern Ireland". *Nations and Nationalism* 21(3): 544–65.

Murtagh, C. 2020. "The plight of civic parties in divided societies". *International Political Science Review* 41(1): 73–88.

Nadeau, R., P. Martin & A. Blais 1999. "Attitude towards risk-taking and individual choice in the Quebec referendum on sovereignty". *British Journal of Political Science* 29(3): 523–39.

Nagle, J. 2018. "Between conflict and peace: an analysis of the complex consequences of the Good Friday Agreement". *Parliamentary Affairs* 71(2): 395–416.

New Ireland Forum 1984. *Report*. Dublin: The Stationery Office. https://cain.ulster. ac.uk/issues/politics/nifr.htm.

*News Letter* 2016. "Full statement: Foster explains why DUP want to leave EU". 22 February. https://www.newsletter.co.uk/news/full-statement-foster-explains-why-dup-want-leave-eu-1265505.

*News Letter* 2020. "Reg Empey: Sammy Wilson and the DUP share much of the blame for the full-scale Irish Sea border which is emerging in Larne and other ports". 27 November. https://www.newsletter.co.uk/news/opinion/columnists/reg-empey-sammy-wilson-and-dup-share-much-blame-full-scale-irish-sea-border-which-emerging-larne-and-other-ni-ports-3049631.

Ní Aodha, G. 2018. "Tory MP suggests using possible 'no-deal' food shortages to force Ireland to drop the backstop". TheJournal.ie, 7 December. https://www.thejournal.ie/brexit-threat-food-shortages-ireland-4381228-Dec2018/.

Nolan, P. *et al.* 2014. *The Flag Dispute: Anatomy of a Protest*. Belfast: Queen's University Belfast. https://pureadmin.qub.ac.uk/ws/portalfiles/portal/13748797/The_Flag_ Dispute_report_PRINTED.pdf.

Ó Beacháin, D. 2018. *From Partition to Brexit: The Irish Government and Northern Ireland*. Manchester: Manchester University Press.

O'Brennan, J. 2019. "Requiem for a shared interdependent past: Brexit and the deterioration in UK–Irish relations". *Capital and Class* 43(1): 157–71.

O'Callaghan, J. 2021. "The political, economic and legal consequences of Irish reunification". https://jimocallaghan.com/wp-content/uploads/2021/03/Jim_Speech_Irish_ reunification_.pdf.

O'Carroll, L. 2021. "Northern Ireland suspends Brexit checks amid safety fears for port staff". *The Guardian*, 2 February. https://www.theguardian.com/uk-news/2021/feb/ 01/northern-ireland-port-staff-removed-urgently-due-to-safety-concerns.

Ó Cionnaith, F. 2020. "Just 1% of voters concerned about Brexit, poll suggests". RTÉ News, 9 February. https://www.rte.ie/news/election-2020/2020/0209/1114111-election-exit-poll/.

O'Dochartaigh, N. 2021. "Beyond the dominant party system: the transformation of party politics in Northern Ireland". Irish Political Studies, early access.

O'Leary, B. 1999. "The nature of the British–Irish Agreement". New Left Review 233: 66–96.

O'Leary, B. 2018. "The twilight of the United Kingdom & Tiocfaidh ár lá: twenty years after the Good Friday Agreement". Ethnopolitics 17(3): 223–42.

O'Leary, B. 2019a. A Treatise on Northern Ireland, Volume I: Colonialism. Oxford: Oxford University Press.

O'Leary, B. 2019b. A Treatise on Northern Ireland, Volume II: Control. Oxford: Oxford University Press.

O'Leary, B. 2019c. A Treatise on Northern Ireland, Volume III: Consociation and Confederation. Oxford: Oxford University Press.

O'Leary, N. 2021. "No alternative to Northern Ireland Protocol, EU says". Irish Times, 5 May. https://www.irishtimes.com/news/world/europe/no-alternative-to-northern-ireland-protocol-eu-says-1.4574611.

O'Mahony, J. 2015. "Visions of EU reform: the Irish perspective". Written evidence to the House of Lords EU Select Committee's Visions of EU Reform Inquiry 2016-2016, 30 November. http://data.parliament.uk/writtenevidence/committeeevidence.svc/evidencedocument/european-union-committee/visions-of-eu-reform/written/25243.pdf.

O'Reilly, S. 2017. "Apes, psychos, alcos: how British cartoonists depict the Irish". Irish Times, 11 July. https://www.irishtimes.com/culture/art-and-design/apes-psychos-alcos-how-british-cartoonists-depict-the-irish-1.3149409.

O'Toole, F. 2016. "The English have placed a bomb under the Irish peace process". The Guardian, 4 June. https://www.theguardian.com/commentisfree/2016/jun/24/northern-irish-peace-sacrificed-english-nationalism.

O'Toole, F. 2017. "In humiliating May, DUP killed the thing it loves". Irish Times, 9 December. https://www.irishtimes.com/opinion/fintan-o-toole-in-humiliating-may-dup-killed-the-thing-it-loves-1.3318091.

O'Toole, M. 2017. "Ireland an afterthought during Brexit campaign when I was Cameron adviser". Irish Times, 4 October. https://www.irishtimes.com/opinion/ireland-an-afterthought-during-brexit-campaign-when-i-was-cameron-adviser-1.3242732.

Phinnemore, D. & K. Hayward 2017. "UK Withdrawal ('Brexit') and the Good Friday Agreement". AFCO Committee, Policy Department for Citizens' Rights and Constitutional Affairs, European Parliament. https://www.europarl.europa.eu/RegData/etudes/STUD/2017/596826/IPOL_STU(2017)596826_EN.pdf.

Phinnemore, D. & K. Hayward 2021. "Crisis of confidence: government has a lot to do to win back our trust". Belfast Telegraph, 21 April. https://www.belfasttelegraph.co.uk/news/northern-ireland/crisis-of-confidence-government-has-a-lot-to-do-to-win-back-our-trust-40337296.html.

Phinnemore, D. & L. Whitten 2021. "Northern Ireland and Brexit: a unique challenge in unique circumstances". In Holmes & Simpson (eds), Ireland and the European Union, 278–303. Manchester: Manchester University Press.

Pierson, P. 2000. "Increasing returns, path dependence and the study of politics". *American Political Science Review* 94(2): 251–67.

Pierson, P. 2004. *Politics in Time: History, Institutions, and Social Analysis*. Princeton, NJ: Princeton University Press.

Press Association 2021. "Arlene Foster calls Simon Coveney 'tone deaf to unionist concerns' as talks start over NI Protocol". TheJournal.ie, 4 February. https://www.thejournal.ie/marcos-sefcovic-london-brexit-trade-issues-5344509-Feb2021/.

Preston, A. 2020. "Border poll not on Dublin's agenda for at least five years, Taoiseach reassures unionists". *Belfast Telegraph*, 23 October. https://www.belfasttelegraph.co.uk/news/northern-ireland/border-poll-is-not-on-dublins-agenda-for-at-least-five-years-taoiseach-assures-unionists-39657259.html.

Progressive Unionist Party (PUP) 2020. "Statement from PUP leader Billy Hutchinson". 7 December. https://twishort.com/L0Vnc.

Quinlivan, A. 2020. "The 2019 local elections in the Republic of Ireland". *Irish Political Studies* 35(1): 46–60.

Quinn, A. 2019. "Watch Boris Johnson tell the DUP in 2018 he would never put border in the Irish Sea – today he put a border in the Irish Sea". *News Letter*, 17 October. https://www.newsletter.co.uk/news/politics/watch-boris-johnson-tell-dup-2018-he-would-never-put-border-irish-sea-today-he-put-border-irish-sea-816300.

Quinn, A. 2021. "Arlene Foster describes EU decision to invoke Article 16 as 'incredible act of hostility'". *Newsletter*, 9 January. https://www.newsletter.co.uk/news/politics/arlene-foster-describes-eu-decision-to-invoke-article-16-as-incredible-act-of-hostility-3118100.

RedC 2019. "Exit poll for the European elections, local election and divorce referendum". 24 May. https://redcresearch.ie/wp-content/uploads/2019/05/378419-RTE-Exit-Poll-European-Elections-Local-Elections-and-Divorce-Referendum-le-Gaeilge-FINAL.pdf.

Rees-Mogg, J. 2018. "If the Irish Government obliges us to choose between the Republic and the Union, then we will choose the Union". *The Telegraph*, 14 May. https://www.telegraph.co.uk/politics/2018/05/14/irish-government-obliges-us-choose-republic-union-will-choose/.

Rees, N. & J. O'Brennan 2019. "The dual crisis in Irish foreign policy: the economic crash and Brexit in a volatile European landscape". *Irish Political Studies* 34(4): 595–614.

Reid, C. 2008. "Protestant challenges to the 'Protestant State': Ulster Unionism and Independent Unionism in Northern Ireland, 1921–1939". *Twentieth Century British History* 19(4): 419–45.

Reinisch, D. 2019. "The influence of loyalist paramilitaries on the UK election". RTÉ Brainstorm, 9 December. https://www.rte.ie/brainstorm/2019/1208/1097913-the-influence-of-loyalist-paramilitaries-on-the-uk-election/.

Rice, C. 2020. "A road to nowhere? The UK's approach to implementing the NI Protocol". UK in a Changing Europe, 23 May. https://ukandeu.ac.uk/a-road-to-nowhere-the-uks-approach-to-implementing-the-ni-protocol/.

Richardson, J. & B. Rittberger 2020. "Brexit: simply an omnishambles or a major policy fiasco?" *Journal of European Public Policy* 27(5): 649–65.

Richmond, N. 2021. *Towards a New Ireland*. https://www.finegael.ie/app/uploads/2021/04/Towards-a-new-ireland-Neale-Richmond-2021.pdf.

Roos, C. & N. Zaun 2016. "The global economic crisis as a critical juncture? The crisis's impact on migration movements and policies in Europe and the U.S.". *Journal of Ethnic and Migration Studies* 42(10): 1579–89.

Rosamond, B. 2016. "Brexit and the problem of European disintegration". *Journal of Contemporary European Research* 12(4): 864–71.

RTÉ News. 2016. "Britain remaining in EU a critical issue for Ireland – Kenny". 5 January. https://www.rte.ie/news/2016/0125/762668-enda-kenny-eu-reform/.

RTÉ News 2017. "Taoiseach expresses concern over May's proposed EU deal". 11 June. https://www.rte.ie/news/uk-election-2017/2017/0611/881797-dup-conservative-party/.

RTÉ 2021. "Brexit republic: Montgomery's Brexit memories". Podcast, 23 April. https://www.rte.ie/news/brexit/2021/0423/1211734-podcast-brexit-republic-montgomerys-brexit-memories/.

Ruane, J. & J. Todd 2007. "Path dependence in settlement processes: explaining settlement in Northern Ireland". *Political Studies* 55(2): 442–58.

Rutter, J. & A. Menon 2020. "Who killed soft Brexit?" *Prospect*, 9 November. https://www.prospectmagazine.co.uk/magazine/who-killed-soft-brexit-eu-european-union-no-deal.

Sandford, M. & C. Gormley-Heenan 2020. "'Taking back control', the UK's constitutional narrative and Schrodinger's devolution". *Parliamentary Affairs* 73(1): 108–26.

Sheahan, F. 2021. "Majority favour a united Ireland, but just 22pc would pay for it". *Irish Independent*, 1 May. https://www.independent.ie/irish-news/centenaries/centenarypoll/majority-favour-a-united-ireland-but-just-22pc-would-pay-for-it-40375875.html.

Sheehy, P. 2021. "Mistake to signal triggering of Article 16 – Taoiseach". *RTÉ News*, 30 January. https://www.rte.ie/news/coronavirus/2021/0130/1194003-coronavirus-vaccines/.

Shipman, T. 2016. *All Out War: The Full Story of How Brexit Sunk Britain's Political Class*. London: William Collins.

Shipman, T. & J. Allardyce 2021. "Union in crisis as voters want referendum on Scottish independence and united Ireland". *The Times*, 23 January. https://www.thetimes.co.uk/article/union-in-crisis-as-poll-reveals-voters-want-referendum-on-scottish-independence-and-united-ireland-wwzpdlg7b.

Shirlow, P. 2021. "Without pragmatism, the protocol will poison Northern Irish politics". *The Guardian*, 26 April. https://www.theguardian.com/commentisfree/2021/apr/26/protocol-northern-irish-politics-jobs-investment.

Shirlow, P. & M. McGovern (eds) 1997. *Who Are the People? Unionism, Protestantism and Loyalism in Northern Ireland*. London: Pluto Press.

Singham, S. *et al.* 2017. "How the UK and EU can resolve the Irish border issue after Brexit". London: Legatum Institute. http://www.li.com/activities/publications/mutual-interest-how-the-uk-and-eu-can-resolvethe-irish-border-issue-after-brexit.

Sinn Féin 1994. *Towards a Lasting Peace in Ireland*. https://www.sinnfein.ie/files/2009/TowardsLastingPeace.pdf.

Sinn Féin 2016a. "Democratic imperative for border poll – Adams". Press release, 24 June. https://www.sinnfein.ie/contents/40500.

Sinn Féin 2016b. *The Case for the North to Achieve Special Designated Status Within the EU*. https://www.sinnfein.ie/files/2016/The_Case_For_The_North_To_Achieve_Special_Designated_Status_Within_The_EU.pdf.

Sinn Féin 2017a. "May's speech means a hard Brexit for Ireland – Adams". Press release, 17 January. https://www.sinnfein.ie/contents/43076.

Sinn Féin 2017b. *Securing Designated Special Status for the North within the EU*. https://www.sinnfein.ie/files/2017/BrexitMiniDocs_April2017_Final.pdf.

Sinn Féin 2020a. *Giving Workers and Families a Break: A Manifesto for Change*. https://www.sinnfein.ie/files/2020/Giving_Workers_and_Families_a_Break_-_A_Manifesto_for_Change.pdf.

Sinn Féin 2020b. *Economic Benefits of a United Ireland*. https://www.sinnfein.ie/files/2020/Economic_Benefits_of_a_United_Ireland.pdf.

Smith, J. 2016. "David Cameron's EU renegotiation and referendum pledge: a case of déjà vu?" *British Politics* 11(3): 324–46.

Smith, P. 2021. "New research shows that for 'neithers', the problem with the Union is unionists". *News Letter*, 25 January. https://www.newsletter.co.uk/news/politics/philip-smith-new-research-shows-neithers-problem-union-unionists-3111473.

Smith, R. 2019. "Alliance Party leader Naomi Long: 'We're not unionist or nationalist. I have a different identity, a different driver in politics'". *Belfast Live*, 10 June. https://www.belfastlive.co.uk/news/belfast-news/alliance-party-leader-naomi-long-16400764.

Soifer, H. 2012. "The causal logic of critical junctures". *Comparative Political Studies* 45(12): 1572–97.

Staunton, D. 2017. "Theresa May's Brexit speech wins praise and harsh criticism". *Irish Times*, 17 January. https://www.irishtimes.com/news/world/uk/theresa-may-s-brexit-speech-wins-praise-and-harsh-criticism-1.2940676.

Staunton, D. & P. Leahy 2017. "Brexit summit: EU accepts united Ireland declaration". *Irish Times*, 29 April. https://www.irishtimes.com/news/world/europe/brexit-summit-eu-accepts-united-ireland-declaration-1.3066569.

Steinmo, S. 2008. "Historical institutionalism". In D. Della Porta & M. Keating (eds), *Approaches and Methodologies in the Social Sciences: A Pluralist Perspective*, 118–38. Cambridge: Cambridge University Press.

Stewart, H., J. Rankin & L. O'Carroll 2019. "Johnson accused of misleading public over Brexit deal after NI remarks". *The Guardian*, 8 November. https://www.theguardian.com/politics/2019/nov/08/boris-johnson-goods-from-northern-ireland-to-gb-wont-be-checked-brexit.

Syal, R. & P. Walker 2017. "John Major: Tory–DUP deal risks jeopardising Northern Ireland peace". *The Guardian*, 13 June. https://www.theguardian.com/politics/2017/jun/13/john-major-tory-dup-deal-could-jeopardise-northern-ireland-peace.

Tannam, E. 2001. "Explaining the Good Friday Agreement: a learning process". *Government & Opposition* 36(4): 493–518.

Tannam, E. 2011. "Explaining British–Irish cooperation". *Review of International Studies* 37(3): 1191–214.

Tannam, E. 2018. "The Good Friday Agreement, Brexit and British–Irish inter-governmental cooperation". *Ethnopolitics* 17(3): 243–62.

Tannam, E. 2020. "Shared island? There's hope for British–Irish intergovernmental relations". LSE Brexit, 2 July. https://blogs.lse.ac.uk/brexit/2020/07/02/shared-island-theres-hope-for-british-irish-intergovernmental-relations/.

Taylor, R. 2009. *Consociational Theory: McGarry and O'Leary and the Northern Ireland Conflict*. Abingdon: Routledge.

Tilley, J., J. Garry & N. Matthews 2019. "The evolution of party policy and cleavage voting under power-sharing in Northern Ireland". *Government & Opposition* 56(2): 226–44.

Thompson, P. 2020. "The Irish general election isn't focused on Britain – so why is the media acting like it is?" *Prospect*, 7 February. https://www.prospectmagazine.co.uk/politics/irish-election-sinn-fein-varadkar-brexit-uk-eu.

Todd, J. 2015a. "Partitioned identities? Everyday distinctions in Northern Ireland and the Irish State". *Nations and Nationalism* 21(1): 21–42.

Todd, J. 2015b. "The vulnerability of the Northern Ireland settlement: British–Irish relations, political crisis and Brexit". *Études Irlandaises* 40(2): 61–73.

Tonge, J. 2017. "Supplying confidence or trouble? The deal between the Democratic Unionist Party and the Conservative Party". *Political Quarterly* 88(3): 412–16.

Tonge, J. 2019. "After Brexit, what's left for Northern Ireland's unionists?" *Foreign Affairs*, 21 December. https://foreignpolicy.com/2019/12/21/northern-ireland-unionism-irish-unity/.

Tonge, J. 2020a. "General election 2019: Northern Ireland". *Political Insight* 11(1): 13–15.

Tonge, J. 2020b. "Beyond unionism versus nationalism: the rise of the Alliance Party of Northern Ireland". *Political Quarterly* 91(2): 461–66.

Tonge, J. *et al.* 2014. *The Democratic Unionist Party: From Protest to Power*. Oxford: Oxford University Press.

Tonge, J. & J. Evans 2010. "Northern Ireland: unionism loses more leaders". *Parliamentary Affairs* 64(4): 742–59.

Tonge, J. & J. Evans 2020. "Northern Ireland: from the centre to the margins". *Parliamentary Affairs* 73(1): 172–88.

Traditional Unionist Voice (TUV) 2021. "TUV plan to disrupt protocol". 27 January. https://tuv.org.uk/tuv-plan-to-disrupt-the-protocol/.

UK in a Changing Europe 2021a. "Philip Hammond". Brexit Witness Archive. https://ukandeu.ac.uk/interview-pdf/?personid=42190.

UK in a Changing Europe 2021b. "David Lidington". Brexit Witness Archive. https://ukandeu.ac.uk/interview-pdf/?personid=41922.

UK in a Changing Europe 2021c. "Ivan Rogers". Brexit Witness Archive. https://ukandeu.ac.uk/brexit-witness-archive/ivan-rogers/.

UK in a Changing Europe 2021d. "Michael Russell". Brexit Witness Archive. https://ukandeu.ac.uk/brexit-witness-archive/michael-russell/.

UK in a Changing Europe 2021e. "Carwyn Jones". Brexit Witness Archive. https://ukandeu.ac.uk/brexit-witness-archive/carwyn-jones/.

Varadkar, L. 2019. Speech by Taoiseach Leo Varadkar, Alliance Party pre-Conference dinner, 1 March. https://www.gov.ie/ga/oraid/0a192e-speech-by-an-taoiseach-leo-varadkar-alliance-party-pre-conference-di/.

VICE News 2016. Gerry Adams says Brexit could lead to Northern Ireland leaving the UK. 25 July. https://www.youtube.com/watch?v=g-6gq2jlEJI.

Viggiani, E. 2014. *Talking Stones: The Politics of Memorialization in Post-Conflict Northern Ireland*. Oxford: Berghahn.

Walker, G. 2016. *The Labour Party in Scotland: Religion, The Union and the Irish Dimension*. Basingstoke: Palgrave Macmillan.

Walker, P. & L. O'Carroll 2019. "MPs vote to extend abortion and same-sex marriage rights to Northern Ireland". *The Guardian*, 9 July. https://www.theguardian.com/uk-news/2019/jul/09/mps-vote-to-extend-same-sex-marriage-to-northern-ireland.

Walker, P. & L. O'Carroll 2020. "Irish PM calls sacked minister Julian Smith 'one of Britain's finest'". *The Guardian*, 3 February. https://www.theguardian.com/uk-news/

2020/feb/13/irish-pm-says-sacked-northern-ireland-secretary-julian-smith-one-of-britains-finest.

Walker, W. 2014. "International reactions to the Scottish referendum". *International Affairs* 90(4): 743–59.

Weale, A. 2018. "Brexit and the improvised constitution". In B. Martill & U. Staiger (eds), *Brexit and Beyond: Rethinking the Futures of Europe*, 28–36. London: UCL Press.

Weeks, L. 2017. *Independents in Irish Party Democracy*. Manchester: Manchester University Press.

Wellings, B. & E. Vines 2016. "Populism and sovereignty: the EU Act and the in–out referendum, 2010–2015". *Parliamentary Affairs* 69(2): 309–26.

Welsh Labour 2021. *Moving Wales Forward: Welsh Labour Manifesto 2021.* https://movingforward.wales/documents/WEB-14542_21-Welsh-Labour-Manifesto_A5.pdf.

Whelan, N. 2011. *Fianna Fáil: A Biography of the Party*. Dublin: Gill & Macmillan.

Whiting, M. 2018. *Sinn Féin and the IRA: From Revolution to Moderation*. Edinburgh: Edinburgh University Press.

Whitten, L. 2020a. "Breaking walls and norms: a report on the UK general election in Northern Ireland, 2019". *Irish Political Studies* 35(2): 313–30.

Whitten, L. 2020b. "#LE19 – a turning of the tide? Report of local elections in Northern Ireland, 2019". *Irish Political Studies* 35(1): 61–79.

Wilson, S. 2020. "Sammy Wilson: the United Kingdom will not be free from European Union until the Northern Ireland protocol is replaced". *News Letter*, 16 July. https://www.newsletter.co.uk/news/opinion/columnists/sammy-wilson-united-kingdom-will-not-be-free-european-union-until-northern-ireland-protocol-replaced-2915002.

Wilson Foster, J. 2018. "United Ireland campaign is based on a delusion". *Irish Times*, 19 March. https://www.irishtimes.com/opinion/united-ireland-campaign-is-based-on-a-delusion-1.3431695.

Wincott, D. 2018. "Brexit and the state of the United Kingdom". In Diamond, Nedergaard & Rosamond (eds), *The Routledge Handbook of the Politics of Brexit*, 15–26. Abingdon: Routledge.

Wincott, D., G. Davies & A. Wager 2020. "Crisis, what crisis? Conceptualizing crisis, UK pluri-constitutionalism and Brexit politics". *Regional Studies*, online first, doi: 10.1080/00343404.2020.1805423.

Wright, F. 1989. "Northern Ireland and the British-Irish relationship". *Studies: An Irish Quarterly Review* 78(310): 151–62.

Young, D. 2020. "NI Protocol must be honoured, pro-Remain parties demand". *Belfast Telegraph*, 7 September. https://www.belfasttelegraph.co.uk/news/northern-ireland/ni-protocol-must-be-honoured-pro-remain-parties-demand-39510003.html.

# Index

Note: Page numbers in **bold** refer to tables